A QUEER NEW YORK

# A Queer New York

*Geographies of Lesbians, Dykes, and Queers*

Jen Jack Gieseking

NEW YORK UNIVERSITY PRESS

New York

NEW YORK UNIVERSITY PRESS
New York
www.nyupress.org

Sections of chapter 5 were originally published as Jen Jack Gieseking, "Mapping Lesbian and Queer Lines of Desire: Constellations of Queer Urban Space," *Society and Space* (2020). DOI: 10.1177/0263775820926513.

References to Internet websites (URLs) were accurate at the time of writing. Neither the author nor New York University Press is responsible for URLs that may have expired or changed since the manuscript was prepared.

Library of Congress Cataloging-in-Publication Data
Names: Gieseking, Jen Jack, author.
Title: A queer New York : geographies of lesbians, dykes, and queers / Jen Jack Gieseking.
Description: New York : New York University Press, [2020] | Includes bibliographical references and index.
Identifiers: LCCN 2020016949 (print) | LCCN 2020016950 (ebook) |
ISBN 9781479848409 (cloth) | ISBN 9781479835737 (paperback) |
ISBN 9781479891672 (ebook) | ISBN 9781479803002 (ebook)
Subjects: LCSH: Gays. | Sexual minorities. | Gender-nonconforming people. |
Intersex people. | Gender identity.
Classification: LCC HQ76.25 .G55 2020 (print) | LCC HQ76.25 (ebook) |
DDC 306.76/6—dc23
LC record available at https://lccn.loc.gov/2020016949
LC ebook record available at https://lccn.loc.gov/2020016950

New York University Press books are printed on acid-free paper, and their binding materials are chosen for strength and durability. We strive to use environmentally responsible suppliers and materials to the greatest extent possible in publishing our books.

Manufactured in the United States of America

10 9 8 7 6 5 4 3 2

*I dedicate this book to lesbians, bisexuals, trans people, gender non-conforming people, gays, Two-Spirits, queens, homos, genderqueers, dykes, fags, femmes, butches, enbies, bois, aggressives/AGs, studs, andros, aces, intersex people, and queers;*

> *the people they love;*
> *and the people who love them—*
> *everywhere and always.*

We are, I am, you are by cowardice or courage the one who
find our way back to this scene carrying a knife, a camera
a book of myths in which our names do not appear.
—Adrienne Rich, from "Diving into the Wreck" (1973)


But these stories don't mean anything /
When you've got no one to tell them to. /
It's true. I was made for you.
—Brandi Carlisle, "The Story" (2007)

# CONTENTS

# LIST OF FIGURES

# PREFACE

## *The Blue Star Tattoos of New York City*

Blue star tattoos. She took off her watch and I saw my first. An inked symbol on the wrist of a bisexual woman from the West Coast. It was 1998 and we were both students at my New England women's college. The next sighting was a set of stars, spotted as I got up to stretch on a flight to Tokyo and met two cuddling dykes from LA in 2001. The couple had matching blue stars on their forearms. Two years later, in 2003, I was more than tipsy late one night in a gay bar on New York City's Lower East Side dancing with trans Southerners when I spotted another, and there would be more in the years to come. Even as lesbian and queer spaces began to disappear, on arms with sleeves rolled up, blue stars shined in flashing lights, sweaty crowds, busy streets, and a sea of queer bodies.

In the summer of 2008, I began to lead group interviews with lesbians and queers about their spaces in New York City, and two of my research participants had visible blue star tattoos. These stars shone differently to me in my research. I asked both women what inspired their tattoos and both said they had heard them described as "a lesbian thing to do." Wide-eyed at its historical connection, I immediately described Elizabeth Kennedy and Madeline Davis's important history of a mid-twentieth-century Buffalo, New York, lesbian community, *Boots of Leather, Slippers of Gold*. Neither of them had heard of how Kennedy and Davis recorded the rich and complex lives of Buffalo lesbians, including how a group of them got blue star tattoos on their wrists that they could keep hidden behind their watchbands and embraced as a symbol of "community identity."[1] Suddenly, I realized that invisible lesbian-queer lives and spaces materialized, concretized, and could be traced through lesbian-queer bodies across the urban landscape and beyond, generation after generation.

In the decade since I conducted this research, the media's obsession with the closing of lesbian bars and "disappearing" lesbian, gay, bisexual, transgender, and queer (lgbtq) neighborhoods has reflected a perception that queer lives are cosmopolitan and assimilated.[2] These narratives of loss are fueled by a geographical imaginary of idealized clusters of lgbtq businesses and residences. Yet long-term, owned territorial spaces associated with lgbtq people—e.g., neighborhoods, bars, and cities—do not actually support how lesbians and queers produce (make, share, define, imagine, live) everyday urban spaces. Lesbians and queers must and do find other ways to produce space in order to resist heteropatriarchy.

Few have asked how women or transgender and gender non-conforming people (tgncp), who possess less economic and political power than many men and cisgender people, could ever thrive in one of the world's largest and fastest-changing cities. If not in a long-term *neighborhood*, where were and are lesbians and queers? For a group so often ignored, stereotyped, or sexualized, how do lesbians and queers create the city as it relates to capital? In other words, what is the role of lesbians and queers in the production of the city? And to what ends do lesbians and queers produce spaces on behalf of social justice, a project they so often prize?

The promise of securing long-term, fixed spaces in tourist-welcoming lgbtq bars and neighborhoods—in order to be legitimated through citizenship and rights—has not materialized for most lesbians and queers, as well as Black, Latinx, and Indigenous people, people from the Global South, working-class and poor people, refugees and immigrants, and/or disabled people. My participants and the archives I researched were both full of tales of closed bars and bookstores, itinerant parties, and apartments, cafés, and hangouts made further distant, declining, or even demolished due to gentrification. The blue star tattoos of lesbians and queers thus visualize the core argument of this book: the myth of lgbtq neighborhood liberation must be interrupted by seeing lesbian-queer spaces anew.

Like lesbian and queer knowledge that is limited, partial, and re-created in overlapping but distinct ways over generations, my research reveals that lesbians and queers seek out long-term territories in the form of property-owned neighborhoods. Lesbian-queer star-like places (in their range of import and brightness) relay the importance and comparative rarity of place-making in queer worlds, just as lesbian-queer lines and networks relay the constrained but constant mobilities as well as the interdependent relationality between these stars.

Largely lacking the financial or political capital to secure long-term spaces, lesbians' and queers' places are more scattered and visible only when you know where and when to look, in ways similar to stars and other celestial objects. Lesbians and queers rely on these places to make and make sense of their identities, relationships, and communities. Yet most of these places are temporary in ultra-expensive and ever-gentrifying New York City, which gives the sense of a fleeting landscape of stars imploding, even as their light still reaches us long after they are gone. Instead, these places are carried in and on these women's and tgncp's memories and bodies, in the paths they continue to take between these stars. Those assigned female at birth often remember how they must navigate public space as they draw lines between their places and experiences, and leave streams of memory in their wake.

I call these patterns of queering space *constellations*. Both a navigational practice and conceptual diagramming, participants draw lines between stars to make sense of their lives. As they attend the same bars, the LGBT Center, and the Dyke March, as well as the wide range of places that are unique to them—often based on their race, class, age, gender, and generation—lesbians and queers each create their own constellations even as they overlap with others', culturally and politically binding them in their production of the city. Constellations afford another way of seeing and acting in response to gender and sexual injustice. Constellations are the central thematic of this book, the lens through which I read and make sense of lesbian and queer lives, bodies, and spaces in New York City.

## WHY A QUEER NEW YORK

My research originated as a result of a series of contradictions I encountered in both academic and popular literature that I read through my experience as a queer, lesbian, butch, trans dyke living in New York City. I saw that coming out under varying political, economic, and social situations structured lgbtq people's understanding of themselves and the world. I felt strongly that the framing of a simple binary of pre-/post-Stonewall generations needed to be upended in order for lgbtq people to recognize our multiple interdependent and complicated histories—all the more so during the ultra-hyped fiftieth anniversary of Stonewall, which took place as I finished this book. The significance of generational shifts is highly evident in queer life when you compare coming out in 1983, early on during the AIDS epidemic (when I was in first grade, being taught that all homosexuals were pedophiles), versus 2008, when there had been a sustained discourse of lgbtq rights and heightened media attention to lesbians, like the five original seasons of *The L Word* (and when I had been out for over a decade and could watch this internationally syndicated TV show with friends and other queers at the local lesbian bar). When I wrote this book in the 2010s, lgbtq history had broadened but was still often limited to a retelling of the Stonewall riots, now along with the rise of ACT UP in the face of the AIDS epidemic and homophobia. And yet another version of *The L Word* has appeared.

While society came to be accepting of some lgbtq people by the late 2000s—more precisely, of white settler, middle-class, monogamous, parenting, cisgender lgbtq people—their geographies seemed to dim as lesbian-queer spaces and places often contracted or closed. My participants, none of whom were wealthy, faced the wild inflation of New York City living costs and the financialization of the housing market, which cleaved the meaning of home from the value of an investment property. The foreclosure/financial crisis became visible during our 2008–2009 conversations, but New York City property values would never diminish like those in most of the rest of the country. It began to become clear to me that the long-term fixation on the lgbtq, lesbian, and/or queer neighborhood was tied to the white heteropatriarchal promise of territory and project of ownership, as well as processes of gentrification. I decided to focus this book on the lesbian-queer role in producing New York City by creating space *otherwise* in constellations as a political response to the limitations and constraints in the urban political economic conditions revealed by my research. In other words, I wanted to understand how capital moved (or failed to move) through lesbian-queer spaces structured as much by radical politics as structural oppressions, and how lesbian-queer spaces reproduced and/or interrupted oppressions.

My project is based on and contributes to empirical research in lgbtq studies, while also drawing from the insights of queer and feminist theory. Most lgbtq studies in the social sciences rely on ethnographies (interviews mixed with field notes and participant observations) and/or archival research. Interviews seemed like a great fit; the idea of sitting and watching lesbian and queer spaces seemed off-putting. I imagined myself perched on a barstool at Ginger's Bar or Cubbyhole staring creepily over my beer, keeping stealth watch at places like the Park Slope Food Co-op while stocking cheese, peering over my laptop at the Tea Lounge café while only pretending to write, or attending yet another softball game, rugby match or craft club. In other words, I'd live my twenties all over again, but as an observer, which I found both unsettling and unproductive when it involved watching a group so sexualized and gazed upon to begin with. I was also determined not to reproduce the protest and potluck rhetoric that often defines lesbian-queer history—as much as I adore and support both protests and potlucks. My presumption of what is or isn't a lesbian and/or queer space would inevitably be antithetical to my desire to understand the everyday productions of lesbian-queer life in the city.

Further, I was determined to bring geography, which has long been grounded in feminist theory and methods, further into the discussion with queer theory and queer theorists, and vice versa. Queer theory commonly draws on performance, art, film, and literature, as well as psychoanalytic theory, and often focuses on queer temporalities at the cost of attending to queer space. I decided to apply queer and feminist theory to my social scientific research of participants' lives and spaces because both are often key to lesbian and queer self-understanding.

I came to theorize the production of lesbian-queer spaces as *constellations* to reflect my participants' own words and geographical imagination of queer New York. While theories of neighborhoods, community, and networks also lend themselves to how my participants described their experiences, it is unacceptable for lesbians and queers to rely on terms produced by the cis-white heteropatriarchy to define their lives. In other words, I selected the term "constellations" not only because of its apt evocation of astronomical constellations, but also because of its connection to astrology, which is often a part of lesbian-queer discourse, speaking to their ways of making worlds all at once mythical, imaginary, and physical. While the attachment to astrology risks sentimentality or nostalgia, it is also "the recognition that our [queer] worlds, imagined or otherwise, are fucked in totalizing and crushing ways" so that a "love for astrology carries for queers this unconvincing illusion, this mark of woundedness, of *wanting* to be convinced, together with others who have been rendered symptomatically suspicious."[3] Indeed, the stars, lines, and networks of constellations indicate how queers arrive at and keep going to create worlds while remaining "symptomatically suspicious" of heteropatriarchy.

Throughout my life, rights were created, extended, and evaporated; portrayals of lgbtq people in the arts generally became more positive or, at least, came into existence; positive media depictions could increasingly be found; and lgbtq people took positions of power while powerful people came out as lgbtq, and this was heralded as "progress." The public representation of my stories and the stories of those around me remained myopic and meted out sparingly, while I often read that lesbians were "invisible." As I aged—as a white, six-foot masculine-presenting person of sizeable girth with a more sizable personality—the prospect of being "invisible" or fully accepted was laughable to me and to many other masculine and androgynous women and tgncp. At the same time, feminine women and tgncp experienced constant sexualization and commodification, all the while having their concerns and stories silenced. Dominant narratives of lgbtq spaces often highlight activisms, leaving out everyday experience. Regardless of their focus, prevailing stories failed to account for generational change, and usually if not always ignored the lives of Black, Latinx, Asian, Indigenous, Two-Spirit, disabled, Muslim, poor, working-class, homeless, and/or imprisoned queers.

If the history of the lesbian-queer spaces is an invisible one, it is equally essential to remark on those Indigenous peoples made "invisible" by violent, dominant narratives of colonial history. New York City occupies the unceded and treaty lands of the Lenape, Canarsie, Matinecock, and Rockaway peoples. I acknowledge the unceded and treaty lands of Lenape, Haudenosauneega Confederacy, Canarsie, Matinecock, Rockaway, Pocumtuc, Nipmuck, Tunxis, Sicoags, Wangunks, Shawnee, Cherokee, and Osage peoples, where I resided without permission and wrote most of this book, as well as the land of the Piscataway people, where I grew up. As a white, Catholic-Lutheran-cum-Quaker settler with working-class and middle-class Norwegian, German, and Polish heritage, I recognize that my history and my own family history is complicit in the genocide of Indigenous peoples across these lands. I am thankful to live and work in these territories and thank and honor the Indigenous, Native American, and First Nations people who have been living on these lands from time immemorial. While land acknowledgments and antiracism statements are increasingly codified, I also make these statements precisely because my work around gender and sexuality engages with Black, Latinx, Asian American, and Indigenous feminist and queer scholarship to challenge territorial models of liberation based on property ownership.

My choice of multigenerational group interviews, mental mapping exercises, artifact-sharing exercises, and archival research helped me answer my questions, but it still placed me and my queer body in the midst of my research. (How funny, I thought I could overcome that, said the feminist trans butch.) More than a few participants across these generations remarked they were unsure what to expect of the project, but my visible queerness, cultural lesbianness, and my antiracist, anticlassist, and feminist language, demeanor, and approach left them feeling encouraged to share their stories. As much as I was a white settler antiracist over a decade ago, looking back through my interview transcripts, I was struck by how much I downplayed and ignored my own white, middle-class, and female masculine privilege. In so doing, I also downplayed and ignored the white privilege of some of my white participants in their stereotyping, disrespectful behavior, and suspicion. I account for this racism here to further the work of antiracist lesbian-queer historical geographies.

Participants were also informed of my own "politics of location," as essayist Adrienne Rich called it, in regard to my gender and sexual identity, which equally emerged through anecdotes and answers to inquiries.[4] I did my best to share the painful and pleasant parts of my story (trauma, self-loathing, an often-supportive family, and so on) from a childhood spent in Baltimore Catholic schools. I expect, too, that my Mohawk, U-hauling jokes, citation of Indigo Girls lyrics, and ties gave it away. As I researched and wrote A Queer New York, I came out as transgender, an identity I felt fully but had no words to share with close friends let alone with my participants. I go by Jack now; I went by Jen while conducting these interviews. I'm much more myself, and I'm still quite the person my participants met a decade ago—although with better ties and much better politics. This shift in my own identity has made me respond even more compassionately to the stories of my participants, and to my own story as well.

As a denizen of New York, I too took the F and Q trains and all other subway lines back and forth between the neighborhoods in this book, visited bars and parties and house parties to see my own queer friends, attended plays and concerts popular with lesbians, stood at vigils with straight and queer colleagues, walked in marches and protests, and made out on the Pier at sunset. I sometimes refer to my own experiences throughout the book in order to place me in this work. My own constellation—which now includes the spaces and paths I have shared with everyone mentioned above—is included in the stories in *A Queer New York*.

I am a nerdy, funny, able-bodied (although I wrote through many injuries, pain, and surgeries), white settler tenure-track professor, who was raised working middle-class but now sits firmly in the middle class as I still pay off student loans. I also remain an amateur woodworking, Brooks Brothers/L.L.Bean/local tailor/Levi's type of geographer who still identifies as a lesbian, queer, butch, and, now, trans dyke (top surgery, haven't tried testosterone, changed my name, did not change documentation) who drives a used Subaru, adores his girlfriend and her-now-our cat (after years of being on-and-off again single and then a U-hauler) (which is surely okay if it's your thing—I explain in this book that it's white heteropatriarchal capitalism's fault that we do that anyway), and finally got a dog now that this book is done. After fourteen years in New York City, I, ironically, resided in the lesbian-queer hubs of Northampton, Massachusetts, and Portland, Maine, while writing this book. I came to find a home in Lexington, Kentucky, at its conclusion, a space that has amplified how coastal urbanisms and settler colonialisms all too often structure default queer imaginaries.

## WHEN I WROTE *A QUEER NEW YORK*

In 2008 and 2009, surprising elements of everyday lesbian-queer life had changed and even more surprising elements remained the same. When *The L Word* went off the air in 2009, *The Rachel Maddow Show* had only launched the year before—someone who looks butch! on a major TV network! every night!—and yet same-sex couples could not yet marry in the State of New York. President Obama had just been elected under his banner of "Hope"—hope especially for working-class and poor people, people of color, women and tgncp, and lgbtq people. The subprime mortgage crisis was beginning to make international news, while the everyday sprawl of gentrification processes never paused. U-hauling, flannel, and the idealization of the dyke bar remained (and still remain) commonplace. This was the moment in which my research began.

I attempted to complete this book very quickly after finishing my dissertation in 2013, but it took me years to grapple both with the deep emotional and theoretical content of the arguments you are reading now. Only in retrospect did I realize that being able to look back on my period of study (1983–2008)—over the decade in which I wrote this book—would be so profoundly helpful in making sense of my project. The comparatively liberal period of 2008 to 2016 enabled me to dig deep into the ways lesbians and queers participated in capitalism, patriarchy, and heteronormativity, whether willing or unwilling. Writing during this period also gave me the room to hold lgbtq people accountable for their role in gentrification while also celebrating the ways in which they have survived, thrived, and contributed to resisting the precarity enforced by heteropatriarchy. Regardless of queer politics, the arrival of mainstream lesbian and gay political wins like same-sex marriage and the right to serve openly in the military afforded many lgbtq people, especially the white, middle- and upper-class among them and around me, a strong sense of self and an opportunity for relaxation after some of the worst years of homophobia in American history.[5] In particular, I became determined to place lesbian-queer politics, economies, and practices as central to the historical geography of New York City, all too often defined by real estate developers and pro-property policymakers, or what urban planner Samuel Stein calls the "real estate state."[6]

My project set out to fill the absence in lesbian-queer geographies of New York City. Yet it was only during my research that I also realized that while lesbian, gay, bisexual, trans, and queer memoirs, essays, journalism, and a handful of lgbtq historical monographs and one sociological monograph exist on New York City. Thus, this book is the first lesbian-queer historical geography of New York City. I titled this book *A Queer New York* as an homage to historian George Chauncey's important *Gay New York*, which greatly inspired my own research.[7] Sitting alongside academic monographs on lgbtq New York City by Chauncey, Christina Hanhardt, Hugh Ryan, and Mignon R. Moore, and books of essays by writer-activists like Sarah Schulman and Amber Hollibaugh, the "A" in the title is meant to signify the many stories of lesbian-queer New York City that are yet to be written. The arguments and ideas in my book are only a part of that effort, and it is impossible to record every queer place and experience—although the stories of the forty-seven women and tgncp and the archival data I examined do collectively reveal more than we knew before.[8]

In 2019, I finished writing this book under a vile regime of white settler nationalism, antieducation, xenophobia, and pro-wealth that quelled much of the expectation that change for the "better" would continue without radical intervention.[9] But it did not bring an end to queerness. I, like most other queers, recognize that the Trump administration will continue to work to decimate the rights, kinship ties, health, and sense of well-being that lgbtq and other marginalized people may have accumulated. I also know that pinkwashing—claiming to accept and include white, middle-class, cisgender lesbians and gays as a marketing or nationalism strategy—will continue to be used as a façade to conceal the perpetuation of injustice against people of color, Muslims, queers, tgncp, Two-Spirits, immigrants, refugees, sex workers, drug users, Indigenous people, Native Americans, First Nations people, and/or poor and working-class, homeless, and disabled people, and so on. The outlook is both bleak and cruel—and also hopeful in light of the resistance that always grows, often in new structures, and with a reoriented focus. I am not naïve when I write these words. Yet my research findings show that, in a time of violence, we must look not only to the stars but to ourselves and our ancestors for new paths forward, and we must respect one another and take action together.

I met activist and writer Madeline Davis, who co-authored *Boots of Leather* (the lez shorthand title) with Elizabeth Kennedy, in 2010 when I was beginning to write this book. I told her my blue star tattoo story and her whole body shook with laughter as she pulled her watch back and showed me her blue star tattoo. "My friends and I got drunk one night and I convinced them to do this. Then I put the story in the book," Davis said with a smile.[10] I told her that many, many lesbians and queers—i.e., women and tgncp alike—had these tattoos. Some of these blue star–tattooed lesbians, dykes, and queers have read Kennedy and Davis, some have not, but many feel their tattoos (or piercing or protest shirts or innuendo buttons or rainbow paraphernalia) afford meaning and connection. These stars trace an embodied and spatiotemporally interdependent history—for a people with so little history—that runs over half a century from one evening among friends in 1950s Buffalo, to the years Kennedy and Davis spent researching, writing, and publishing *Boots of Leather* in 1992, to the passing on of this story through that text and by word of mouth among lesbians and queers over generations, to the decade I spent researching and writing this historical geography of lesbian-queer New York City. All along, these tattoos (and other cultural markers, places, and embodiments) have been reproduced through word of mouth, placed on and in lesbian-queer bodies and places as a "lesbian thing to do."

While what a "lesbian thing to do" is wrought with the fragmented, fleeting, and networked qualities of lesbian-queer geographies, there is more that brings this group together than keeps it apart. During a group interview of participants who came out in the 1980s, Jackie turned to Gloria and asked her, "So what was it that brought you to New York? Did you have friends here?" Wanda smiled and added, "Tell us the truth! [*turns to Gloria, leans in close*] What was her name?" All of the participants laughed and I did too. Against all odds, I hope *A Queer New York* reminds us that desire, connection, and justice will and must always emerge in our constellations.

1

# Navigating *A Queer New York*

Birtha came out as a lesbian in 1984 and, by the time we spoke in 2008, identified as queer. She pointed to the top dot on her hand-drawn mental map of her lesbian and queer spaces that she had brought to our group interview, and offered the following overview:

> I went to a club in Chicago called the Lady Bug. . . . It was incredibly frightening. When I look back I think, "Oh, what was the big deal?" But for some reason it was just almost overwhelming for me to go in there. I remember, it took me awhile, but I decided to go speak to somebody. I couldn't think of what to say so I asked this woman if I could borrow a pen. And she lent me a pen and I pretended to use it and then I gave it back to her and she said, "No need to give it back. You may keep the pen." [*pauses*] And that was the end of the conversation. [*group laughter*] . . .
>
> And after that I moved to New Haven . . . and there was a bar there and I have no idea the name of that. So that's that [*points to second dot down*] . . . they had a cigarette machine so I would contemplate for weeks whether or not to go in and buy my cigarettes there. . . . I was never so brave as to meet someone.
>
> So then I migrated to New York and that would be this general region in here. [*points to many dots in the middle of the page*] . . . I went to, most frequently . . . this place called Cubbyhole . . . that used to be located on Hudson Street [in Greenwich Village].[1] And I went there a lot. I was living in Brooklyn but I was making a limited amount of money. So I could only . . . really afford to come into the city once a month because I would take a cab home. . . .
>
> I still walk by certain locations and I say [*points to a dot halfway down the map*] that's the first woman I slept with, [*points to another dot next to it*] that's the woman who went to law school, or that kind of thing.

Figure 1.1. Birtha '84's mental map (white, middle-class)

Birtha's map looked like nothing more than a collection of points on a sheet of paper, without any labels or text, but her story reveals these places are packed with a lifetime of meaning and experience (figure 1.1). All of the women and transgender and gender non-confirming people (tgncp) I interviewed drew and/or described a sense of space centered around nodes across the city, with gaps across space and time spanning the twenty-five years of my study from 1983 to 2008. Birtha's stories about the dots on her map record a series of specific places, people, and experiences that *are her*: what it means for her, specifically, to be white, middle-class, and lesbian (in the 1980s)/queer (in the 1990s and 2000s); how to interact with and operate within a world of lgbtq people; how to navigate and, when possible, ignore, heteropatriarchy; and where love, sex, relationship, and community could or could not be found, all the while painting a geographical imagination of where to look next.

Birtha's map and story visualize the central yet paradoxical premise of this book: the inability of lgbtq people, especially lesbians and queers, to claim fixed, long-term urban spaces like neighborhoods and bars even while they imagine them as central to queer life. This is not their failure alone—or often even their possibility—but rather the result of systematic white cis-heteropatriarchal oppression of the US settler capitalist state, which dominates by privileging liberal property ownership. Some affordances to some women and some lgbtq people have improved over my increasingly neoliberal period of study, but much injustice remains.

With an eye toward even larger patterns of urbanization over generations, I argue that lesbians and queers produce urban space in what I call *constellations*, a production of space that queers fixed, property-owned, territorial models of traditional lgbtq space as the only or best path toward radical liberation. Constellations are how women and tgncp constitute space in spite of and alongside cis-heteropatriarchal precarity. By tracing the contingent production of virtual, physical, and imagined places and the lines and networks between them, I show the formation of constellations as an alternative, queer feminist practice and geographical imagination of the production of urban space. The concept speaks to the mythical (imagined), calendrical (temporal), and navigational (wayfinding) qualities of lesbian-queer life under neoliberal cis-heteropatriarchal precarity.[2]

Many of my participants defined many of their spaces in relation to, and judged many of their spaces in reaction to, what they believe gay and queer man have as a production of the patriarchal state: tightly knit, long-lasting, and well-appointed neighborhoods, as exemplified by an idealized Greenwich Village of the past. Instead, the political and economic constraints women and tgncp face require them to innovate and produce space otherwise: like stars that come and go in the sky, contemporary urban lesbians and queers often create and rely on fragmented places and fleeting experiences. Their stars are fragmented in comparison to the ideal of the tightly clustered businesses and residences imagined but rarely realized in the lgbtq neighborhood; their stars are more fleeting than the stars of the sky, as they appear and collapse much more quickly due to rising rents and political shifts. Lesbians and queers draw lines between these stars, making sense of their lives between the spaces, people, and experiences available to them, and connecting them by their embodied paths. These often-overlapping lines (subways, bus routes, walks or rolls between the pizza place and the bookstore, life arcs) culturally and politically bind lesbians and queers in their sociospatial production of constellations. While individuals configure their own night sky on Earth, constellations become recognizable only in relation to each other.

Women and tgncp always share stars and lines across their individual constellations, and constellations are shaped by race, gender, class, and generation. Our point of view on these stars is based on knowing where one stands or sits, how one identifies, and knowing where and when to look. In order to understand the lesbian-queer urban production of space, I crafted a qualitative, mixed-method, multigenerational approach of gathering women's and tgncp's stories in their own words, namely through interviews, mental maps, and archival research.

Lesbian-queer constellations allow a way of reading patterns across these women's and tgncp's stories, maps, records, and other data of queering space that attend to their places, networks, and lines of desire. Constellations are often obscured by the *myth of neighborhood liberation*, which promises lgbtq people acceptance through creating and/or claiming their own long-term, urban, pseudo-ethnic enclaves and other fixed, enduring spaces, all of which necessitates property ownership to retain their legitimate claim to the American Dream. With lines drawn in their paths between the star-like places across the city, constellations serve as orientation devices for making sense of, recording, and navigating queer life.

Accordingly, *A Queer New York* is a historical geography of contemporary lesbian and queer politics, culture, and economies in New York City, as told through my participants' distinct yet overlapping and always interdependent constellations. I relay these women's and tgncp's roles in the production of urban space as it relates to capital in the form of constellations. The fragmented and fleeting aspects of these constellations are urban lesbians' and queers' ways of being, and in this sense I read them as a means of resisting cis-heteropatriarchal structures and those structures' ties to white supremacist, ableist, colonial, capitalist society.

My period of study—from 1983 to 2008—encompasses many of the extreme changes that have affected contemporary lgbtq lives, from the

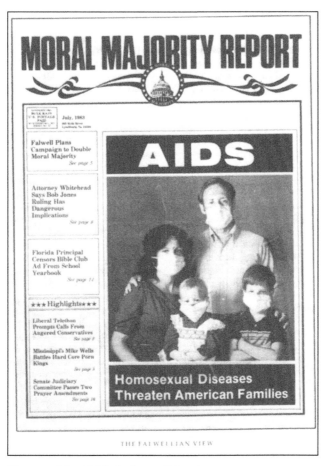

Figure 1.2. *Moral Majority Report*, July 1983

cultural touchstone of the AIDS epidemic to the pop phenomenon *The L Word* (see figures 1.2 and 1.3). With an eye toward larger patterns of urbanization, I ask: how can "invisible" lesbians' and queers' productions of space allow us to rethink and enact projects of spatial justice? How do the perpetually unrealized affordable, all-welcoming physical lgbtq and lesbian neighborhoods expand and/or contract the experiences of lesbian-queer life? What is the lesbian-queer role in the economic, cultural, and political production of the city in the forms of places and spaces, culture, and economies—both in and beyond standard narratives of "gay gentrification"?

Figure 1.3. "*The L Word*: Going Down in History" advertisement from the magazine *GO NYC: A Cultural Roadmap for the City Girl* (2008) © Showtime 2008

Stars are queer guides that accumulate mass and brightness through experiences, ideas, nostalgia, and desire in places, on bodies, and/or in memories. Lines are the embodied, imagined, and remembered paths my participants take and make between stars that deviate from straight culture and present as "deviant." The stars or nodes, like the lines and paths, of lesbian-queer life are visible sometimes, change over time, and tend to be found by those who know where and when to look. Constellations are a practice of producing lesbian-queer urban space in ways that move toward gender and sexual justice. Constellations are also a diagram of that production, depicting how lesbians and queer imagine and enact space around, alongside, and/or against cis-heteropatriarchal capitalism.

Figure 1.4 is a map that shows the neighborhoods most often mentioned by participants, within the context of other key areas in the city. In fact, my participants were contradictory as they asserted, in interview after interview, generation after generation: neighborhoods are *the* lesbian-queer spaces—and yet then described how they were unable to afford, sustain, or be sustained by them. Across these neighborhoods, stars are fragmented, meaning that lesbian-queer spaces are and always have been more dispersed than the lgbtq geographical imagination of neighborhood- or territory-making implies. Like stars in the cosmos, these spaces are born and many die, often in explosions (of promise, gossip, and intrigue, as much as through arson, breakups, and rent hikes).

Through the illumination of constellations, I counter and call for a rethinking of recent mainstream and academic writing on lgbtq and lesbian neighborhoods that merely describes them as declining due to the "assimilation" of lgbtq culture and politics in the United States, the "straightening" of "passé" lgbtq neighborhoods, and the eternal "disappearance" of the lesbian bar.[3] I ask not why these places are on the decline, rather, I want to understand what the conditions are that afforded their production in the face of white cis-heteropatriarchal capitalism in the first place. While major cities like Chicago, San Francisco, and New York City have been rife with processes of gentrification at the neighborhood scale, the lesbian-queer role in these processes requires attention.

My own critique of this simplified narrative of lgbtq neighborhoods' "degaying" or "heterosexualization" grows from and alongside queer, feminist, and urban scholarship in geography, and in conversation with history, anthropology, sociology, psychology, and feminist and queer theory across disciplines. After generations of queer resistance and community-making that often depended or, at times, fixated on territorial long-term spaces like neighborhoods and bars, I submit this turn to constellations as an alternative model of producing space that leaves room for radical difference and relational flux. As essayist Maggie Nelson describes queer life, constellations are "a deflation, but not a dismissal . . . [and] also a new possibility."[4]

Even as I began my project, it was clear to me that what the public refers to as "lgbtq spaces"—often reduced to the ever-popular

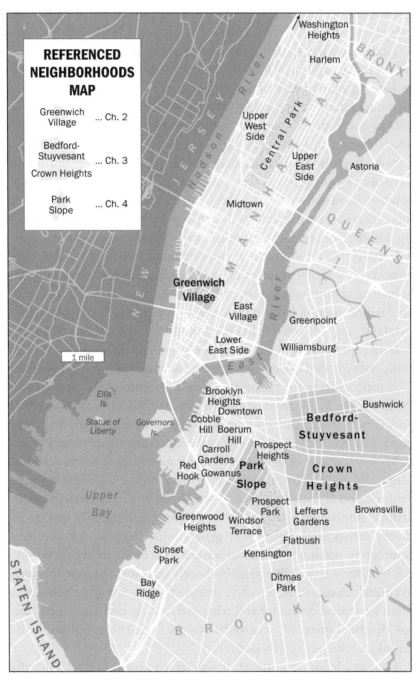

Figure 1.4. Map of New York City neighborhoods most often mentioned by participants

neighborhood, bar, and/or city—deeply failed to express lesbian-queer experience, as did territorial thinking more broadly. It was not my goal to add yet another theoretical concept regarding the production of space. Yet it became my project to show how lesbian-queer experiences necessitate and offer a new spatial and temporal theoretical vocabulary. I was at a loss how to explain lesbian-queer geographies without turning to another term, place, or world that was created by, for, and about heterosexual society, and usually by cisgender, white men at that. I share the idea of constellations to offer lesbians and queers something from their own experience (wrote the Leo sun, Aries ascendant, Cancer moon), especially their, sometimes, passionate or, often, passing knowledge of the myths of astrology. In turn, I seek to share lesbians' and queers' experience with geographic thought and theory in their own words, maps, and experiences.

## A Frame for the Stories of A Queer New York

A Queer New York is a historical geographic rendering of urban lesbian-queer spaces and places of the recent past. My training as an environmental psychologist and queer feminist, urban, digital, cultural geographer helped me to make sense of everyday queer life in the New York City landscape. I am particularly interested in constellations as part of the social production of space, or how spaces are constantly produced by the way that they are consciously designed and built, bought, rented, squatted, and/or sold, and used for a range of meanings, behaviors, and experiences.[5] I rely heavily on the concept of the *geographical imagination*, which affords means of thinking about how the ways we imagine space and place shape practices, behaviors, and social structures. The geographical imagination affords the user ways to pry open and even redefine the assumptions of power, stereotypes, and expectations associated with space, place, and people.[6] In rendering the lesbian-queer production of urban space in constellations, I work in an interdisciplinary fashion as I primarily draw from and direct my contributions to my home fields of geography, American studies, lgbtq studies, gender and women's studies, and environmental psychology.

The core contribution of A Queer New York is a queer feminist critique of propertied territoriality-as-liberation, and lesbian-queer resistance, reworking, and resilience in the face of this injustice. Constellations are a new way of recognizing and piecing together lesbian-queer productions of urban space, an alternative geographical imagination for reading the city that does not succumb to liberation-through-property ownership. Constellations developed from and speak to the embodied, situated values of feminist theory, alongside the antibinary, antinormative, fluid principles of queer theory that highlight desire and sexuality.

Within the urban context, historian Christina Hanhardt writes that one cannot "fully understand changing spatial development patterns apart from LGBT politics."[7] However, queer geographer David Seitz observes that critical urban theory "has most often treated sexuality as an attribute, rather than a diffuse discourse of subject-producing power intimately connected with race, class and gender."[8] The failure to perform an intersectional analysis that accounts for urban gender *and* sexuality *and* race—among other identities—can much more strongly inform an analysis of urban capital and urban geographies.[9] Prioritizing the feminist adage that the "personal is political," queer geographic studies have long contended that space is a constructed and contested medium of identity formation that plays out within individual, social, and structural power relations. Queer spaces are not merely transgressions of heteronormative and homophobic space; rather they are imbricated with the racialization, classing, and gendering of space. I more deeply address theories of queer space and time in my final chapter.

As I conducted my research, I became increasingly interested in how lesbians and queers produce urban space as it relates to capital. My analysis is especially indebted to thinking from feminist Marxist, critical race, and urban political economic scholarship that shows how economic exploitation, anti-Blackness, and cultural domination go hand in hand. Urban political economy critically examines capitalist systems of ownership, rentership, and meaning of place on behalf of all people's right to the city.[10] A queer feminist approach destabilizes assumptions, privileges, and normative models of "secure" heteronormative, patriarchal, and racist structural oppressions while recognizing the flux and fluidity of everyday life and the existence of a multitude of nonnormative perspectives.

Feminist Marxist geography contends that we must always attend to studies of social reproduction, which accounts for unpaid or drastically underpaid labor that is all too easily demarcated as "women's work" in the gendered division of labor—such as providing food, education, housing, and health care.[11] Much of "women's work" is also the politics of care, emotion, and affect, which I trace as well. A trans Marxist perspective adds that trans labor is almost always underpaid or unpaid, as well as understudied. In other words, my focus on lesbian-queer lives and spaces requires attention to capitalism, which depends upon this group but refuses to afford its members the respect of fair pay.

New York was known as home to so many independent women in the early twentieth century—all regarded as having loose morals—that any single, working woman in any city might be referred to as a "woman of New York."[12] Lesbians' and queers' role in shaping the city remains largely unrecorded. Yet, to many, another study on New York City seems unnecessary given the metronormativity that assumes lgbtq identity is inextricable from urban life.[13] Cultural theorist Karen Tongson writes in frustration of "the developmental logics of queer relocation starting in amorphous elsewheres and triumphantly ending somewhere—in the designated 'place for us' that is New York, New York."[14] I (clearly) love New York while I agree with anti-urbanists that the queer rural is often ignored, mocked, and belittled as backward, and the queer urban and cosmopolitanism is revered.[15] The mythos of queer New York, and queerer Brooklyn with it, is also then often a source of rejection and isolation of rural queers, mocking of suburban queers, and violence and indifference toward non-urban queers generally. At the same time, my research is one of the first lesbian-queer-specific historical geographic studies of New York City, showing how research on lesbian, queer, and lgbtq geographies is still needed in New York City and so many other cities, suburbs, and rural places. By revealing the complexity and possibility of lesbian-queer life in New York City, I intervene in the "get thee to the big city" narratives that fairly enrage Tongson and so many others (including myself), and make room to tell very different, antiproperty, and anticosmopolitan tales of lesbian-queer lives.[16]

While I am interested in the production of the city, I frame much of this book through the experience of participants' bodies producing their spaces, because my questions about spaces were almost always answered in stories about their bodies in space. By spaces, I mean the physical, virtual, material, imagined, and discursive star-like places central to lesbian-queer lives, from homes to books, dyke bars to bookstores, and first-date locales to queer-friendly bodegas and co-ops. It is the body that occupies space, and the geographic scales of the body and home are most associated with women and tgncp (compared to the city, state, or even global scales).[17] Feminist geographer Tamar Rothenberg writes of lesbians in 1990s Park Slope, Brooklyn: "What matters to the [lesbians] who live in a community is their experience of the place, how they feel walking down the street, the services available to them."[18] This account of the social-biological queer body anticipates my view of my participants' bodies as the defining force in the production, definition, and sustenance of queer spaces and constellations more broadly.

I consider bodies as mutually performed and visceral, in action and in space, a framework I developed through the work of two key feminist and queer thinkers—philosophers Judith Butler and Elizabeth Grosz. Butler's performativity theory (mentioned by my participants more than once) argues for a process-oriented, nonfoundational, ceaseless performance of one's being, which is inscribed in *and* on the body as well as on and in the cultures, economies, and societies surrounding it.[19] Feminist geographer Lise Nelson criticizes Butler for fixing and exhausting identities in specific spacetimes in her examples, while pointing out that performativity which breaks open gender norms can also open up space.[20] With an eye toward the urban, Grosz argues that bodies and cities mutually define one another through societies, economies, and politics that support recognition, as well as the pressure for and possibility of agency and access.[21] Aspects of identity like gender, sexuality, and race socially produce through space, as space co-produces gender, sexuality, and race.[22]

Theories of the everyday illuminate a wide range of place-making practices and places in urban women's and tgncp's lives, whose history has been made invisible, ignored, destroyed, and degraded in most cultures throughout history. Everyday practices possess the means to refute and subvert the received social order.[23] Oppressions are interdependent structural forms of injustice, including homophobia, transphobia, sexism, racism, and, of course, heteronormativity. Yet justice is a tricky concept as the oppressor and oppressed can be one and the same person or group, just as the measures of justice for some are surely not liberation for all.[24] Activist Barbara Smith reminds us that some forms of acceptance for some people certainly do not afford liberation:

> It doesn't mean that the material conditions of lesbians and gays have markedly changed, or that we're any closer to real freedom . . . at the very same time, people are getting fired from their jobs, being kicked out of their apartments, don't have benefits, can't extend health benefits to their partners, are losing their children, and, most importantly, are being physically assaulted and murdered on a daily basis.[25]

Efforts toward liberation need not be acts of total resistance to effect change. Feminist geographer Cindi Katz writes that responses to injustice and oppression must be broader than resistance alone, whereby resistance embraces "oppositional consciousness," an enacted capacity to repudiate and organize against injustice and oppression.[26] She argues that social change also can be brought about by projects of reworking and resilience to structural injustice. Throughout this book, I use the concept of *liberation*, a term used by the women's and lgbtq movements to mean the act of overcoming injustice and finding freedom from oppression.

## Everything I Do, I Do It For

My audience for this book is threefold: researchers, organizers, and lesbians, dykes, queers, and tgncp. First, paralleling feminist geographer J. K. Gibson-Graham's examination of forms of political economy alongside of and alternative to capitalism, I reveal constellations as an alternative production of space that are born from and inspire alternative productions of urban political economy. In other words, constellations as I present them here are one queer feminist example of how people resist succumbing to precarious politics and economics of neoliberal capitalism.[27] Building from critical geographical thought, I recognize that territory and place matter. I relate constellations to a range of other theoretical concepts (networks, mobilities, lines) that have been used to describe the lgbtq production of space, because, as I found in my project of studying lesbians and queers over generations in place, they have relied on all of these models for their survival. Constellations matter because they can extend these ideas and fuel new geographical imaginations on behalf of social and spatial justice. I am especially eager to place geographic thought and theory in conversation with queer feminist theory.

Second, there are too few geographical monographs on lgbtq spaces and lives. The work of feminist and queer geographers remains vastly underutilized in other fields. While historical and social science research is often labelled lgbtq studies, queer theory has largely been a project of the humanities, with most exceptions in the social sciences from the field of anthropology. My book labors at the intersection of these projects to put them in conversation, and to offer a sustained geographic analysis at their intersection in constellations.

Finally and most importantly, *A Queer New York* is written by, for, and about lesbians and queers, women and tgncp. Many of the terms we draw upon to theorize lgbtq space were originally conceived by and/or attributed to white, heterosexual, cisgender men. In this, the first lesbian-queer historical geography of New York City, I believe it is imperative to submit the idea of constellations to give lesbians and queers their own term inspired by their own world-making. This is part of the long project of recovering and working toward gender and sexual justice. I worked to make this book feel familiar yet reorienting to those who have lived, visited, dreamed of, hated, and made the city, and, in so doing, drew the lines between their own stars. Constellations afford lesbians, dykes, queers, and others a political perspective for understanding themselves and their past, and, most importantly, another way of moving toward social and spatial justice.

## The Gendered Geographical Imagination of the Sexualized City

Much can be gleaned by reexamining lesbian-queer geographies through a queer feminist approach to the financial and political dimensions of city life. A study comparing 2000 and 2010 census data about same-sex households (the only such decennial census data available on lesbians and gays and based on the presumption of binary gender) showed that the percentage of gay men who lived in predominantly same-sex census tracts fell from 47 percent to 43 percent.[28] The percentage of women also decreased, from 30 percent to 26 percent. While the respective 4 percent decreases are noteworthy, scholars have not taken up the *profound difference* in the share of lesbians who live in predominantly same-sex tracts compared to gay men—17 percent lower. This gap indicates lesbians and queer women have fewer lesbian enclaves, and fewer lesbians in principally gay male enclaves. It is time to address both this absence in the literature and the striking decline in the number of lesbian-queer spaces all at once.

Lgbtq scholars, activists, the mainstream media, and my participants alike often present a limited, territorial geographical imagination of "lgbtq spaces" as neighborhoods, bars, and the city itself. Yet feminist critiques of these same types of spaces mark them as untenable and/or unwelcoming for women and tgncp: studies of urban transgender lives show similar patterns of urban fear and anxiety; and processes of gentrification have disproportionate effects upon women and tgncp.[29] What's key here is that these narratives of the lgbtq city and women's and tgncp's city are also contradictory. As a result, for decades lgbtq people have participated in the *myth of neighborhood liberation*. When my participants were quick to describe lgbtq spaces as neighborhoods, they then described how they failed to meet their needs, often by blaming themselves. Most striking, my participants would then proceed to name a multitude of other places in their constellations, thereby reasserting a way of producing space that was not based foremost on territorial neighborhoods.

A "neighborhood," broadly, is often defined by residential uses, walkable or rollable in scale, and has a physical territory that is often conflated with the social communities that live within it. Lgbtq neighborhoods are now often described using the colloquial "gayborhood" in the United States, or "village" or "district" outside of the United States. The mainstream story of lgbtq history goes that US gays and lesbians found themselves in urban "gay ghettos" in the 1960s and 1970s. Using a cultural appropriation of the term "ghettos"—a place that many poor Black and brown people are forced to live in—these territories were reprieves from isolation, storybook lands of opportunity, and bedrocks for political organizing.[30] With the world and, especially, city economies like that of New York gutted by the 1973 financial crisis, austerity measures defined a new neoliberal order. Those few "settled" or "reclaimed" urban neighborhoods came to represent late-twentieth-century cities at their best in so far as they mimicked the American Dream of white, heteronormative, patriarchal small-town life played out in (purportedly) meritocratic home ownership. At the same time, by asserting an ethnic enclave–like account in which lesbians and gays pulled themselves up by their bootstraps and heel straps, gays and lesbians legitimated themselves by legitimating gayborhoods. Writing on recent trends in lgbtq neighborhoods, queer geographers Catherine J. Nash and Andrew Gorman-Murray write that "the shift towards a 'human rights approach' supported the conceptualization of gays and lesbians as some form of 'ethnic minority,' an argument buttressed by the visibility of a defined territorial base."[31]

These narratives also tell us that lgbtq people supposedly and especially create many businesses and hangouts as they lay claim to long-term, expensive neighborhoods—regardless of gender, race, or class. However, given the emphasis on the roles of bars and parties in lesbian-queer lives, it is revealing that there were over fifty-one of these places for men on a 2008 Pride map of the southern half of Manhattan, and only three bars for women.[32] Only two lesbian bars remained there as of 2019, with a third in Brooklyn and a fourth—the only bar, Bum Bum Bar, serving primarily working-class, Latinx women and tgncp—closing that same year in Queens, New York City's most ethnically and racially diverse borough. In the decade since I conducted this research, the closing of most lesbian bars across the country has evoked both a sense of mourning and a debate over present-day queer feminist politics and their related geographies. While these recent shifts in lesbian-queer spatialities require attention, my focus on the 1983 to 2008 time period takes us back to an era when a dyke bar was a given in most major US cities.[33]

Some gay men's and lgbtq neighborhoods still persist, and some of these areas are upheld as indicators of a city's economic superiority—even as they are surely not welcoming of all gay and queer men (of color) (of certain classes). Marked by the unique confluence of culture, economy, and physical spaces, sociologist Manuel Castells contended as early as 1983 that the difference between a "marginalized" ghetto and the "deliberately constructed" and "liberated" neighborhood was a way for "gay people to create their own city."[34] Even though scholarship in geography, sociology, and cultural studies shows that lgbtq people increasingly socialize and live in a wider range of cities, suburbs, and rural areas, the myth of neighborhood liberation outlined in the early 1980s by Castells is still pervasive in the popular lgbtq geographical imagination.[35]

Scholars have demonstrated that (purportedly) lgbtq or gay neighborhoods are read as "legitimate" when partaking in practices of gentrification and homonormativity, whereby gay identity is almost exclusively white and middle- or upper-class, gay politics are aligned with dominant forms of power, and marginalized, racialized, and non-heteronormative knowledge is refused.[36] As sociologist and queer of color theorist Jin Haritaworn writes, responding to Castells and those who follow his approach, the claim of gay neighborhood as "its own territory . . . [presents] a non-intersectional landscape where 'gays' (white) exist along racialized populations (straight) who . . . are excessive to the newly forming gay community."[37] Similarly, the indifference to women and people of color, and profound absence of tgncp in popular portrayals of purportedly "lesbian and gay neighborhoods" is agonizing.

What performance studies scholar Charles I. Nero wrote about the 1980s and 1990s remains the same today: there is a "paradox that gayness is multicultural yet gay neighborhoods are overwhelmingly white and male."[38] Stuck in their determination to claim a place of their own somewhere between the rank-and-file suburbs and towers of finance, (some white, middle-class, and cis-male) lgbtq people began to create a visible community all the while acting as agents of liberal urbanization through racial and economic segregation. Legal scholar Dean Spade argues that queerness must move beyond a fixation on "US property law," which has been organized by "chattel slavery, land theft, and genocide."[39] Instead of grappling with this legacy, urban lgbtq people are pinkwashed by the state and city, upholding their gentrification as a sign of gay and lesbian assimilation into "normal" life.

As I finish this book, I now recognize the intensity and significance of the effort to read the lesbian and gay movement through the territorial gayborhood model. For example, Castells claimed gay men's "territorial aspirations" as their galvanizing inspiration.[40] Further, he wrote, "We can hardly speak of lesbian territory . . . as we can with gay men, and there is little influence by lesbians on the space of the city." While many scholars have responded to these claims about lesbian and queer urban space over the years, my hope is that *A Queer New York* reveals how central lesbians and queers are to the production of the city.

Castells also wrote that lesbians tended to be more placeless and more politically radical, less moneyed and less powerful, and attached "more importance to relationships" and "networks . . . of solidarity and affection."[41] Decades later, queer geographer Julie Podmore noted that many geographical studies of lgbtq spaces "demonstrated that while gay men have often produced highly visible territorial enclaves in inner-city areas, lesbian forms of territoriality at the urban scale have been relatively 'invisible.'"[42] And social networks are clearly important to lesbians and queers who lacked claims to space. *The L Word's* Alice kept a massive, up-to-date diagram of the sex and relationship networks between Los Angeles lesbians that featured prominently on the show, which she launched into a radio show/podcast named "Our Chart." (Notably, corporate attempts to monetize larger lesbian social networks on a lesbian blog of the same name failed within two years—even though the new *L Word* exists in a world where Alice's show has become repurposed into a TV talk show sensation.) The spatialization of social networks was said to geographically form in lesbian spatial "concentrations" rather than full, traditional territories or neighborhoods (residential, commercial, or a mix thereof), because women did not and could not majority own, visibly occupy, and/or control these areas over the long term.[43]

This determination to mend the deficit of landed political and economic power by claiming neighborhood, all the while remaining under cis-heteropatriarchal racial capitalism, is reminiscent of what literary scholar Lauren Berlant calls a queer practice of "cruel optimism": trying to produce a "neighborhood" perpetuates the very inequality of white cis-heteropatriachy that these women and tgncp seek to interrupt.[44] Thus, in reframing the American Dream through a lesbian-queer lens, I interrogate the white settler notion that oppressed groups can be liberated by claiming, owning, maintaining, and "revitalizing" a collection of properties in the city to demonstrate that they are deserving of rights. Instead, I address the role of lesbians and queers as both gentrifiers and resisters to white cis-heteropatriarchal norms in producing constellations.

## Assimilation Debates: Gentrification, Post-gay Identities, and Digital Lives

Debates around gentrification have long been central to conversations about lesbian and gay neighborhoods.[45] In the 1970s and 1980s, New

Figure 1.5. "Can Gays Save New York City?" cover, *Christopher Street*, September 1977

York City was characterized by street crime and fiscal crisis. In 1977, a local gay magazine, *Christopher Street*, showed two larger-than-life, white, mustachioed men—presumably gay and wealthy—encircling a miniature Downtown Manhattan with the title "Can Gays Save New York City?" (see figure 1.5). The accompanying article argued for gay and lesbian acceptance not through the merit of their being but the thickness of their wallets and their devotion to city upkeep: "How many neighborhoods in Manhattan would be slums by now had gay singles and couples not moved in and helped maintain and upgrade them? A thriving Manhattan-based gay community has become necessary to New York City's survival."[46] In the urge to declare the gay and lesbian role in the maintenance *of* rather than rejection *from* the city, this argument confuses (white) gays' and lesbians' gentrification of financially broken, (Black) urban neighborhoods as the path to their liberation. My arguments in this book offer an intervention in the lgbtq gentrification debates: I reveal queer belonging in the city as both essential to white settler, cis-heteropatriarchal capitalist expansion even as queers often experience that belonging as geographically itinerant, temporally iterant, and emotionally partial.

Gentrification is best understood as a series of processes in which a wide variety of actors, institutions, and practices on the ground, and in top-down policies and financial decisions, control the amount, price, and quality of housing available. Living in mid-nineteenth-century Manhattan and Brooklyn, Walt Whitman even then described the "'pull-it-down-and-build-it-over-again spirit' as the main characteristic of modern America."[47] While gentrification is an ever-developing concept, in the broadest sense the influx of economic capital forces the (sometimes incredibly violent) displacement of long-term residents, especially people of color and working-class and poor people. Gentrification is a set of processes propelled by state polices of housing financialization, infrastructural investment, deregulation, and privatization; mortgage securities; media portrayals; real estate development; and financial actors such as banks, landlords, hedge funds, and, finally, homeowners and renters.[48] When I conducted research and still today, processes of gentrification have been fed by skyrocketing residential and commercial property values, the racist intensification of policing and growth of the prison industrial complex, privatization of schools, investor-biased policies, and the exorbitant financial and social cost of post-9/11 securitization and hypersurveillance. Processes of gentrification limit if not exclude the possibility of making New York City a home for most people, namely people of color, women and tgncp, and young people and the elderly.[49] In figure 1.6, census maps of median housing values from 1980 to 2010 in south Manhattan and northwest Brooklyn illustrate the crushing waves of gentrification that placed and then displaced many of my participants as they shaped the rental market. The complications of gentrification became more apparent to the public since the dual foreclosure/financial crisis of 2008–2009, a saga just beginning to be evident during the time of my interviews.

Mainstream media and some scholarship praise gentrification as redeeming disinvested communities.[50] Yet such needed investment displaces long-time residents and increases costs for all. Tactics like the financialization of housing (turning housing into a commodity, distinct from its meaning as a home), as well as pinkwashing (financial and political promotions that are "gay friendly") and homonationalism (nationalist ideologies that support lgbtq rights in order to justify violence against other groups), were manufactured by real estate agents, landlords, financial portfolio managers, planners, and local and state political actors.[51] In fact, urban planner Samuel Stein argues that the processes of gentrification have been largely manufactured since the 1970s as a way to revitalize urban areas they had targeted for disinvestment in creating suburbanization.[52]

Sexuality, class, and race eclipsed a gender analysis in research into housing trends long ago, and, as such, urban theory and public policy can obscure the inequalities also suffered by women and tgncp.[53] In fact, in as far back as 1996, urban geographer Neil Smith wrote of a "link between women and gentrification. More difficult to discern, however, is precisely what role women do play."[54] Most of my participants (my white, middle-class self included) fit urban geographer Damaris Rose's figure of "marginal gentrifiers," who do not "have the same class position as each other," but are not "'structurally' polarized from the displaced."[55] Regardless and in fact because of the racial and class privilege of such a position, I come down hard on the lesbian-queer role in gentrification, so often portrayed as a corrective for homophobia and heteronormativity by the mainstream press. Through my multigenerational lens of analysis, my book aims to point to visible (to one another, at times) lesbian-queer geographies amid processes of gentrification that, ironically, have further made queers and lesbians invisible.

In the long view from 1983 to 2008, my research reveals that lesbians and queers cannot secure the community or recognition they seek through capitalist means and instead become both the gentrifiers and the gentrified. Early waves of lesbian and queer gentrifiers (among others) who possess less wealth are eventually displaced by later waves of gentrification. In other words, many women and tgncp of color are gentrified out of neighborhoods of color and not welcome in lgbtq and lesbian neighborhoods, and many middle-class women and tgncp are priced out

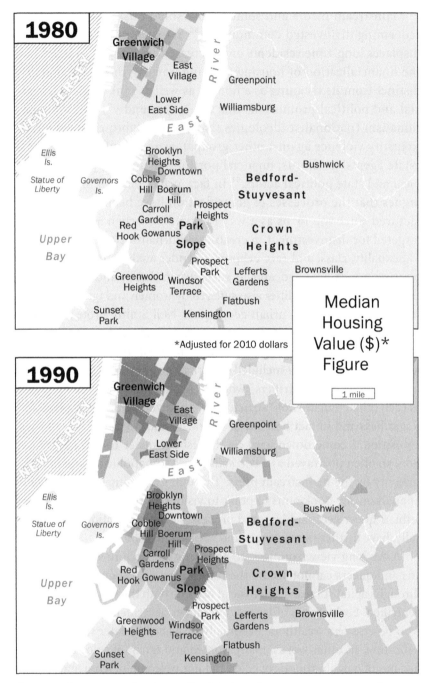

Figure 1.6. Census maps showing median housing values, 1980, 1990, 2000, and 2010

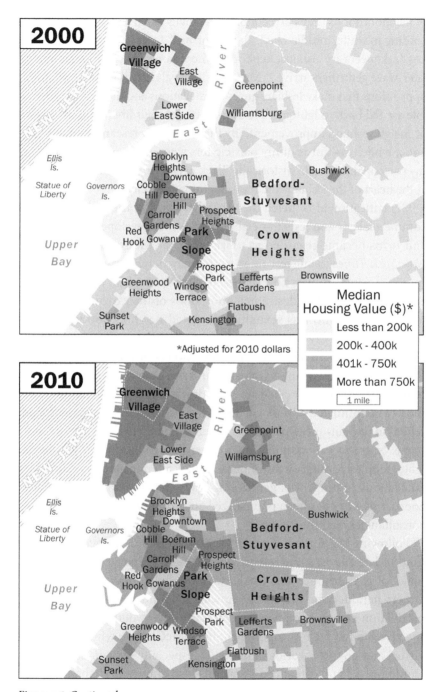

Figure 1.6. *Continued*

of neighborhoods they had economically invigorated and "improved" according to white, middle-class, liberal norms.[56] Later generations of lesbians and queers are also just kept out of these same areas as more affluent, later-wave gentrifiers arrive.[57] My analysis reveals how the same structural oppressions that make lesbian-queer constellations and their history invisible are fed back to lgbtq people as evidence of their liberation as a form of "neighborhood improvement." By the time of my research in 2008 and 2009, while two-thirds of my participants were white, over half of all of my participants lived in historically Black neighborhoods. This paradox is at the heart of the lesbian-queer production of the city.

Gentrification also fueled the ways that many of the residential and commercial gay and lesbian neighborhoods that developed in the 1960s and 1970s became regarded as tourist hubs by the 2000s, leading the *New York Times* to suggest in 2007 that gay neighborhoods might be "passé."[58] Some scholars now suggest that lgbtq people in this "post-gay" era no longer need or desire neighborhoods of their own, and choose to "assimilate" into less sexually segregated neighborhoods.[59] To be professedly post-gay is to no longer necessarily see one's sexuality as a primary identity. This post-gay phenomenon is primarily the privilege of the white and wealthy who can choose to assimilate as such. Most of my participants expressed no such power and/or expectations, and those who intimated at post-gay identities still frequented, desired, and relied on lesbian-queer places as central elements to their urban landscape. Narratives of assimilation and gentrification as positives for all lgbtq people are outgrowths of decades of academic literature about an amorphous contingent of gentrifying "gays and artists." Since the early 2000s, this story has been popularized and commodified by politicians, consultancies, and the media.[60]

Following the spread of social media and mobile device use in the mid- to late 2000s, some researchers in the 2010s posited that the "demise" of gayborhoods was linked to such digital devices and apps.[61] Others heralded the increased knowledge found online and network production among lgbtq people, especially queer youth. I take the perspective offered by anthropologist Shaka McGlotten, who argues that virtual and physical worlds of lgbtq life, especially sexual relations, are "confounded" and can afford a state of "virtual intimacy" that reworks conceptualizations of kinship, desire, and experience.[62]

In 2008 and 2009, like my participants, I was not looking foremost at digital productions of lesbian-queer places even though technology surely shaped and spread word of lesbian-queer spaces over generations. Here, my work also contributes to digital studies: my 2000s-generation participants' stories show it is not just the increased use of social media and mobile devices that has propelled the decline of lgbtq spaces, but other phenomena as well: the post-gay assimilation narrative, limited access to lgbtq history, policies and incentives that make the city welcome to landlords and not renters, and processes of gentrification that now include "heterosexual individuals and couples . . . moving into [lgbtq] neighbourhoods to take advantage of the cosmopolitan lifestyle."[63] Participants remarked how recently emerging sites, apps, and the devices to access them also shaped their lives and were even spaces of their own, including chat rooms, Tumblr hashtags (since 2007), Facebook groups and events (since 2006), websites like AfterEllen and OkCupid (since 2002 and 2004), Wikipedia pages (since 2002), and iPhones (since 2007). (Notably, Grindr had just launched, and Tinder, Instagram, and Autostraddle did not yet exist.)

## Queering the Gender Pay Gap: Urban Political Economy of Dyke Politics

While gay men are often (narrowly) depicted through the lens of partying and public sex, lesbians are more often (narrowly) associated with what I call a rhetoric of potlucks and protests.[64] What historian John D'Emilio rightly asserted in 1983 about such constricted retellings of lgbtq life still holds true: "These myths [of gay and lesbian history] have limited our political perspectives."[65] The actuality of everyday lesbian-queer life is, obviously, more complicated.

Underlying lesbian-queer productions of space and place are the antiracist and anticapitalist politics that fuel queer feminist ideas of community, or what I refer to as *dyke politics*. Dyke politics not only blend production and social reproduction through this group's paid, underpaid, and unpaid labor but also manifests in its commitment to the production of community, culture, knowledge, and shared identities in place. From the 1980s to the 2000s, the dyke politics of my participants could be traced to radical civil rights, feminist, Marxist, and Third

World movements of the 1960s and 1970s that inspired a "democratic conception of activism" in the early lesbian and gay movement, which called for "resistance to the regulation of sex and [an] aspiration to a queerer world," often in cities.[66] Participants also drew upon sentiments of community and collectivity, antiracism and anticapitalism central to 1970s lesbian feminism, while refusing its reliance on whiteness, binary gender, and anti-man frameworks.

"Dyke" is a reclaimed pejorative term, much like the word "queer." Drawing on feminist science studies scholar Angela Willey, I use "dyke" because it "offers a lens through which to see history and embodiment, community and desire, the *literary* and the *corporeal* in the same frame."[67] Also fueling dyke politics are what Willey theorizes as a "dyke ethics" that is part of a shift "toward an embodied politics wherein the inextricability of desire from context is taken for granted."[68] These politics take the form of do-it-yourself events, sliding-scale fees or free spaces, nonprofit jobs, and a focus on community building and activism on behalf of rights, acceptance, opportunities, and recognition, often through volunteer and unpaid labor, as well as informal economies.[69] Women worldwide tend to volunteer more than men and studies find that women dedicate more time *per day* to unpaid work; most of my participants mentioned volunteering despite limited incomes.[70]

Lesbian interventions central to and shaped by feminist politics were a response to the multitude of injustices facing their everyday lives, including lack of access to knowledge, adoption, health care, and legal supports, and the normalization of domestic violence, poverty, rape culture, general misogyny, and on and on. Construed "as a good for all," neoliberalism involves laws and policies that expand private markets and space and shrink public services, as well as shape "individual gendered subjectivities."[71] Historian Laura Briggs writes that the ever-growing redistribution of wealth since the 1980s created a gender gap as well between the rich and poor, revealing the feminization of poverty.[72] Lgbtq people continue to report employment discrimination.[73] Urban lesbians and queers steadily responded to neoliberalism's spread with dyke politics of feminism, antiracism, and/or anticapitalism.

The accumulated wealth necessary to buy a residence in New York City or in most cities requires high incomes, dual incomes, and/or shared familial wealth, all of which are bound to and support white su-premacy. Lgbtq economist M. V. Lee Badget wrote in 2003, "The glossy picture framed by the myths of affluence, protective invisibility, conspic-uous consumption, and DINK [double-income, no-kid couple] heaven persists."[74] She went on to add that DINKs were a deliberate construct of "marketers and gay rights opponents and supported by the public focus on affluent gay and lesbian celebrities."

Looking back, the tactics of dyke politics were some of the ways les-bians and queers navigated a deficit of political and economic control by making sense of their fragmented and fleeting spaces as constella-tions. New York City is not affordable to most people, and my partici-pants often mentioned their inability to take cabs, purchase apartments, or even afford rents in popular neighborhoods, let alone nights out on the town. Yet what is unique to women and tgnpc's economic situation? Studying the lesbian-queer production of space requires attention to the racialized gender pay income gap. Women generally possess less wealth and property than their male counterparts, with a female-male pay ratio of $.77 to $1.00 at the time of my 2008–2009 study. Women have had a measly $.03 raise since—a number often cited without accounting for the more profound injustices facing Black, Latinx, and Native American and Indigenous women—and data on tgncp show that they have lower incomes than cisgender people and/or are often harassed, fired, and/or unable to find work.[75]

Surely not all lgbtq people are coupled, but the gender pay data analyzed through the lens of the couple provides powerful insights into how cis-heteronormative racial capitalism shapes everyday queer life. As figure 1.7 shows, the extrapolated pay-ratio gap for US couples is profound, with a median pay-ratio gap of $11,027 between hetero-sexual and lesbian-queer or gay-queer male couples.[76] The pay-ratio gap is a striking $22,054 between gay-queer male and lesbian-queer couples.[77] The racialized dimensions of lesbian couples' incomes are even more shatteringly apparent when they are compared to the ex-trapolated income of white, cisgender, heterosexual couples: Asian American lesbian couples earn $2,548 less, white couples $8,788 less, African American couples $20,332 less, Hispanic/Latinx couples $28,444 less, and Native American/Indigenous couples $32,349 less. However, the gender pay ratio gap in 2010 New York City was $.81 to

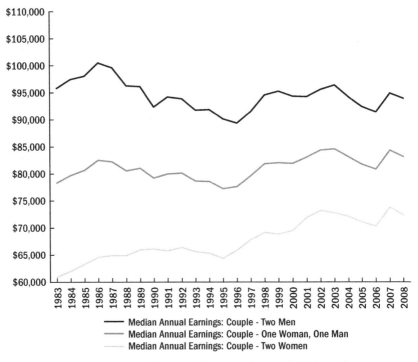

Figure 1.7. Extrapolated US median annual earnings for couples (adjusted to 2010 dollars), from 1983 to 2008. Source data: Hegewisch and Williams, IWPR

$1.00, suggesting that the pay gap may be slightly less there, though it was still persistent throughout my period of study.[78]

While these numbers allow me only to gesture at averages, they also reveal how the inability of many lesbians and queers to accumulate wealth is central to many of the inequalities they face. When wealth is compounded over time, lesbians, queer women, and tgncp are, on average, tremendously disadvantaged in regard to savings, investments, debt (student, credit, etc.), leisure spending, and, most importantly for this study, the ability to buy property. Further, women are more likely than men to have custody of children, and lesbians are more likely to have children than gay men, so that the increased financial costs pile up, ranging from room and board and tending to children to choosing neighborhoods based on school access. Lesbians tend to rent longer and buy homes later in life, tgncp have difficulty finding housing, and lgbtq people consistently face housing, employment, workplace, and data identity discrimination.[79] All signs and findings indicate that tgncp—who suffer harassment, stress, violence, and unfair hiring and policing practices in the workplace and throughout their everyday lives—continue to earn drastically less than their cisgender counterparts. The chances of tgncp taking part in sustainable spatialized communities through property ownership have always been near nil—lgbtq neighborhoods are always restricted by race and class even as dyke politics idealize them.

When discussing the now expensive, longtime lesbian neighborhood of Park Slope in a multigenerational interview, Gloria, who came out in 1983, shared, "When I first started going there it was a cheap place to live and not as nice . . . in the early eighties. . . . [W]hen I moved to New York in 1990 I got a place there. I was there for a year and a half and it was *very gay* then. Now I think it's less gay. All of the lesbians got priced out." In another interview, Linda, who came out in 1996, said, "Well, we're being priced out of Park Slope. . . . it's hard to find, um, lesbians now, I think we're very spread out." As historian Finn Enke writes, lesbian life is often defined by a "lack of capital and spatial hardship."[80] That lesbians' and queers' spaces come and go, and are bound together by the paths of their bodies in constellations makes all the more sense when reading their experience through the lens of urban political economy.

In other words, the geographical imagination of queer life through a straight, white, cisgender lens of finance does not account for all lgbtq people. Hanhardt's research reveals how white gays and lesbians have used claims to citizenship and rights in producing "neighborhoods" that depended both upon claims to "safety" and property ownership—which in turn grew from and added to the pathologization, policing, mass imprisonment, and harassment of and violence toward people of color and youth.[81] I extend Hanhardt's project by looking at how gender has also played a role in white claims to lgbtq and lesbian neighborhoods.

But many of my participants still desired lgbtq and lesbian neighborhoods to find what they described as "community" there. Feminist theorist Miranda Joseph wrote on the slippery, vague, and romanticized notion of "community": "community functions in complicity with 'society,' enabling capitalism and the liberal state."[82] Adding a geographical reading to Joseph's insights, I show how lesbians and queers were both gentrifiers and gentrified in embracing the myth of gay and lesbian neighborhood liberation and—like so many other scholars before me—demonstrate the white privilege it relies upon. In contrast, (white and well-off) homonormative narratives of lesbian and queer lives made "better" and "legitimate" through cosmopolitanism, marriage, property ownership, and economic security are reiterated in media sound bites. My ambivalent relationship with territory accumulation through property ownership and consumption—and my participants' ambivalence as well—inform my anticapitalist approach in this text. My findings demonstrate that racial capitalism will continue only to commodify the struggles and spaces of lesbians and queers rather than afford liberation.

### Unraveling Lesbian and Trans Identities: During and after Women Were Supposedly (White) "Women"

In her research on Montréal lesbian spaces, Podmore describes the "disappearance" of lesbian political visibility and social spaces since the 1990s, a trend that came to New York City in the 2000s. She asserts that lesbian deterritoralization and economic invisibility can be traced to the declining number of lesbian-owned properties and businesses targeting a lesbian clientele, the increasing disidentification with essentialized identities like "lesbian," and the fact that lesbian commercial spaces are sometimes not as common or commercially successful as gay men's commercial spaces.[83] Women and tgncp experienced not only a de-essentialization of lesbian identity but also what Podmore calls a "transformation and multiplication of lesbian identities" due to the increase in media attention to and everyday "visibility of lesbians in society generally due to transformative political changes."[84] My research also shows that the unraveling and, for some, redefining of what is "lesbian" relates to whiteness. The feminist movement was made up of predominantly white women even as it centered antiracist politics, and it also stabilized notions of "women" in the increasing rise and recognition of transgender identities.

Lgbtq and labor historian Allan Bérubé has written about "the many whitening practices that structure everyday life and politics in what is often called the 'gay community' and the 'gay movement.'"[85] Indeed, white privilege and supremacy permeated the conversations I had with my participants; one interaction demonstrates how whiteness often dominates lesbian and queer experience without consequences. In an interview with participants who came out in the 2000s, two working-class women discussed being raised in homophobic Christian households. Tre, who grew up in New York City, nodded along and added repeated "Yes" and "Exactly" replies to Kathy's story of growing up in the suburban Midwest. Kathy, who is white, described how she hadn't come out because her "parents [would] try and use [my] thirteen-year-old [sibling] as the weapon, like, 'You're gonna give him the gay,' or something," to which Tre, who is Black Afro-Caribbean, added, "Right!" It was at that moment that Kathy said she had come out to her parents, experiencing a sense of safety in choosing her own life path as she announced: "Well, I'm free, white, and twenty-one and can do whatever the hell I want." Kathy's white supremacist utterance elicited no hesitation or shock from the other white co-interviewees or from Tre, the only person of color present, who locked eyes with me and nodded at me for being with her in that moment. As essayist and poet Adrienne Rich wrote, "White women are constantly offered choices, or the appearance of choices. But also real choices that are undeniable. We [white women] don't always perceive the difference between the two."[86]

The rise to prominence of transgender people and newly termed tgncp identities in the late 1990s and early 2000s was a distinct phenomenon in US history. What I call the *FtM trans-surge* caused radical upheaval across the country as the women-born-women policies that had trickled down from 1970s lesbian feminist politics that brought so many together also excluded many queers as identities, politics, and relationships shifted.[87] The FtM trans-surge describes the dramatic rise in the number of masculine trans-identified and/or transitioning female-to-male (FtM) people beginning in the early and mid-2000s when it spread to New York City. New language and identities meant accumulating new spaces, relationships, language, and practices on top of old spaces and practices.[88] The phenomenon was fueled by the burgeoning trans movement, advent of queer theory and identities, and expanding availability of hormones and surgeries. After 9/11, as they navigated the same streets that had been enveloped in smoke from the city's gaping wound of the World Trade Center, I also imagine (and recall) that some felt a little more desperation and determination for New Yorkers to embrace life on their own terms. Historian Emily Hobson makes a parallel argument that, after the 1989 San Francisco earthquake, the lgbtq movement's energy slowed and narrowed the focus of activism in the Bay Area.[89] For many lgbtq people, this meant having their bodies, pronouns, and identities reflect their genders and sexualities, which may have also lessened the energies lgbtq New Yorkers put into national queer concerns that had yet to account for trans issues.

At the same time, newer lesbian-queer masculine identities such as aggressives, bois, fags, fairies, futches (fag butches in 2008, or femmey butch or butchy femme now), and dandies expanded female masculinity and trans masculinity. These identities emerged alongside butches and studs recalling midcentury female masculinities that did not always ascribe to men's-only fashions.[90] The FtM trans-surge was often dominated by white voices, although, in the years since my research, groups like bklyn boihood have expanded the discourse by making a community for "masculine of center* bois, lesbians, queers, trans-identified, studs, doms, butches and AGs of color through online media, events, workshops and collaborative projects" (figure 1.8).[91]

The multiplicity of shifting gender and sexual identities is and always has been racialized and classed, and also specific to generation. Most importantly, the new rise of aggressive identities (a.k.a. AG, pronounced "a-gee") to uniquely define Black and Latinx, working- and middle-class, masculine lesbians received less attention in mainstream lgbtq media. Afro-Caribbean, middle-class Alex, who grew up in Bed-Stuy and came out in 1998, shared about the independent film *Pariah*:[92]

> Essentially, it's talking about this girl who's coming out, she's seventeen. She lives in the Bronx. She goes to a club and she's with her club friends. She's like a really dark-skinned Black girl. . . . And it was actually like about her being on the subway—or being on the bus—and changing from like her doo-rag to her earrings when she went home because she couldn't be that way at home. And that's the *complete reality* of my world. . . . I live two realities when it comes to the LGBT-queer umbrella.

Mixed-race/Black, working middle-class Bailey, who came out in 1995, said she first heard "aggressive" used as an lgbtq-related adjective in 1999, and then as an identity in 2004.

Figure 1.8. bklyn boihood 2012 fundraising calendar, front and back covers

Some participants were eager to support trans people in lesbian-queer spaces, while others had arrived in full support after a strong reluctance. A few participants felt more safe clinging to long-held identities and practices, or said they needed more time. Eva, who came out in 1998, described an older lesbian friend's reaction to this change: "It's not that she's anti-trans at all . . . she said, 'In the eighties, they were just baby dykes! I don't understand!' . . . She's like, 'And now I'm sitting there, and you know, we're at a potluck and everybody's talking about what pronoun they are and I'm just, "Aaaagh!"'" While most participants were or tried not to be "anti-trans," a handful faltered (sometimes cruelly) while learning to be inclusive. Those who were remiss in recognizing trans people as members of the lesbian community fixated on this shift as inducing a state of dispossession rather than recognition and inclusion.

Trans women, however, remained largely absent from lesbian-queer spaces per my participants, which they connected to generations of shunning and rejection of this group from lesbian spaces such as Michigan Womyn's Folk Festival.[93] Trans women often went unmentioned or were presumed to be elsewhere, a geographical absence that my participants recognized as exclusion only through their conversations. Women-born-women lesbian separatist politics usually defined who could enter lesbian bars during my period of study. A few participants vividly recalled refusing lesbian-identified trans women and tgncp assigned male at birth into their spaces, primarily in the 1980s.[94] Noelle, who came out in 1983, recalled, "The trans were crashing . . . into the women's community, into the lesbian community. We're like, 'No, you can't be in our space.' But they're like, 'But we're lesbians!' Like [*waves arms*], 'You're *guys*!' . . . we didn't know how to handle it." As participants described, sometimes with remorse, they had yet to address these transphobic, essentialized arguments to claim visions of a unified women's identity (or womyn or wimmin) in women-only rhetoric and women-only spaces—and many have still yet to. As a trans masculine person who was still finding my own path and identity, I recall these hurtful comments, but I also remember how I had attached myself to the same (both outward- and self-focused) transphobia in years past. I also suspect, and in some cases know, that many of my participants have grown in their understanding of lesbian, queer, and trans identities, as well as structures of race and racism, since this research.

## The Method of Collecting Lesbian-Queer Historical Geographies

As a trans butch queer dyke myself, I found it vital to make certain this project examined the everyday lives of lesbians and queer women *with* them, rather than merely *about* them. Just as lesbian and queer spaces have been largely "invisible" to heterosexuals, gay, bisexual, and queer men, and even to other lesbians and queers, so have many of their significant community events. Therefore, I prioritized the everyday lives of participants—Berlant calls this the "crisis ordinary" affective life in the modern state—rather than larger scale or "major" lgbtq events, or popular narratives about lesbians that forefront activism alone.[95]

I wanted to try to make sense of how the lgbtq community could go from a period of what writer and activist Sarah Schulman calls the "overt and vulgar . . . oppression against gay people" of the 1980s, a time when you called your spouse a "friend," to the liberal 2000s of sometimes being out at work and the fight for same-sex marriage.[96] I begin the study in 1983 because four influential texts on lgbtq spaces and their economies were published that year: Castells's sociological project of mapping lesbian and gay "neighborhoods" rather than "ghettos," D'Emilio's and Bérubé's historical analyses connecting how gay and lesbian cultural and political growth relied on burgeoning American wartime capitalism, and Jonathan Ned Katz's sweeping history of US homosexuality.[97] These texts mark watershed renegotiations of sexuality and gender in the United States, even as some of these works and most early lgbtq studies were written by cisgender, white gay men and tend to prioritize their experiences.[98] The endpoint of 2008–2009 afforded participants the opportunity to compare their past to the liberal present; it also marked the foreclosure/financial crisis and election of President Obama.

To articulate the generational differences and similarities in lesbian-queer spaces, I crafted a qualitative, mixed-method, multigenerational approach of gathering women's and tgncp's stories in their own words, through interviews and archival research. I led a series of twenty-two multigeneration group interviews with forty-seven self-identified lesbians and queers, each with mental-mapping and artifact components. All of my participants had spent most of their time since coming out in New York City, and all identified as coming out between 1983 to 2008. My generational approach does not assume any sort of linear progression but rather accounts for "the entanglements and configurations of multiple trajectories, multiple histories."[99]

To queer notions of community and connection, this study does not use age alone as a primary marker of generation but rather foregrounds the year in which participants came out. A self-defined practice and moment, the participant's coming out year is noted after each participant's name (e.g., Jack '91, as I'm identified in interview dialogues); participants were given pseudonyms. Mental maps are an individual's or group's hand-drawn or -labeled maps of what is in their minds. Each participant was asked to draw their own map of important lesbian and queer spaces and bring them to our conversations, and some cross-generation group interviews also involved producing group mental maps or filling story sheets comparing experiences when coming out and today.[100] I asked participants to bring artifacts that were important to them when coming out; they shared photos, 1980s buttons, 1990s plastic rainbow jewelry, the first season of *The L Word*, books like Leslie Feinberg's *Stone Butch Blues*, Sarah Waters's *Tipping the Velvet*, and Audre Lorde's *Zami: A New Spelling of My Name—A Biomythography*, movies like *The Hunger, Desert Hearts, The Watermelon Woman, Bound,* or *Pariah*, CDs, mixtapes, things ex-girlfriends left behind, and handmade tokens from activisms.

All of my forty-seven participants were invited to take part in three types of interviews: (1) group interviews with a within-generational cohort; (2) group interviews with a cross-generational cohort; and (3) follow-up, private, collective, online conversations. Wanting to amplify the marginalized voices within my research, I organized a group interview for women and tgncp of color. Masculine-presenting and butch participants, who were also underrepresented, could not find a time to meet as a group. I derived the generations in this book by identifying trends in participants' own stories, which I draped over the details of the events, spaces, and organizations I found in archival records.[101] Over time, I expect that we may determine that the "post-Stonewall" generation ended with the onslaught of the AIDS epidemic and the radical activisms that accompanied it, and another generation emerged as those politics waned and conditional acceptance for some lgbtq people grew.

To speak to my participants' experiences as they framed them through politics, economies, media, activisms, geographies, and a general sense of lesbian/queer-ness, I refer to three generations, identified respectively with the 1980s, 1990s, and 2000s, and cleaved by two periods of intense change: 1991 to 1995, and 2001 to 2003. I rely on these generations to tell my participants' stories of their constellations over time.

A participatory action research approach of studying, again, *with* rather than merely *about* my participants throughout our conversations helps to bridge the turns of history with everyday memories. At the conclusion of group interviews, I presented my summary findings to participants via a private, password-protected blog. Echoing performance studies scholar José Esteban Muñoz's appreciation of his queer research subjects, the "theoretical conceptualizations and figurations that flesh out this book are indebted" to my participants.[102] Nearly half of the participants critiqued and commented on my early theoretical arguments to collectively formulate the ideas you are reading about now.

While the interviews and maps are powerful, I wanted to situate my participants' stories in their time and to situate me in the past of New York City as well. To that end, I conducted in-depth archival research of organizational documents and publications at the Lesbian Herstory Archives (LHA). The LHA, in Park Slope, Brooklyn, is the largest collection of materials by, for, and about lesbians in the world. The LHA materials detail the everyday facts, events, and economic and political sea changes of participants' stories and help to assuage concerns around the potential distortions of memory and nostalgia with contemporaneous, experiential accounts.

The final dataset included 1,400-plus pages of transcripts, 47 mental maps and personal artifacts, 391 organizational records, and 26 years of publications, along with census data, policy documents, blog posts, and newspaper articles. Because of the sheer wealth of data available and my determination to prioritize my participants' experiences, my participants' own words and mental maps are my primary object of analysis, alongside archival documents and photos, GIS (computer-drawn) maps, data visualizations, and thick description of the city's queer landscape. The combination of maps and stories allows the historical geographies to be rendered most clearly by putting the spatial and textual versions of participants' narratives in conversation. I provide more extensive details of my methodology in appendix III.

I do not want to idealize these interviews. At times I found them inspirations but I also remember questioning exactly why I was so empathetic to each breakup narrative or story of provocation—but then I read again and again how the steady undercurrent of harassment, violence, limited access, policing, unaffordability, displacement, disinvestment, dispossession, loss, and absence flowed in the proverbial lgbtq hub that is New York City. Worse, as I transcribed interviews, I became aware that I nodded or even laughed along to accounts of particular tactics of survival in the face of the homophobia, transphobia, racism, patriarchy, colonialism, and misogyny that structure queer life, and my queer life as well.

Most importantly, I came to see that women and tgncp of color's experiences of violence, as well as those of lgbtq working-class and poor people and lgbtq disabled people, are often not just obscured but largely obliterated in lgbtq history, except through word of mouth. The opportunity to speak intergenerationally among lesbians and queers of any race, class, or gender is rare, and, in the women and tgncp of color group interview, my participants told me that they had never had a multigenerational space to share their stories. Naomi '89 stated, "I doubt we'll ever have this again," and everyone nodded. I hope this book is a way for many people to have this space again and again, and many more to learn about lesbian-queer world-making.

## How to Call Them by Their Own Names

Jackie '85 put it best: "I don't even think there *is* an average dyke." Lgbtq people, like any group, are not uniform and they have varying levels of access to power or resources.[103] I posted thousands of flyers at lgbtq bars, events, stores, archives, centers, and other places, and handed them out at the Dyke March and Pride. I intentionally recruited across age, race, ethnicity, class, geography, and gender. I also emailed listservs and key individuals, and posted to social networking sites.

The range of participants' experiences offered a breadth of insights into lgbtq geographies. My participants came from all five boroughs (counties) of New York City, with wildly varying yet interconnected experiences, occupations, passions, and identities. Like lesbian-queer places, their identities are not stable. Since participants answered a call to participate in research about "lesbians and queers," I primarily describe them using those sexual identities. At the time of our interviews, they primarily employed the sexual identifiers of lesbian (25) and/or queer (18), as well as dyke (2) and gay (2).[104] Gender identities of participants also varied, though most identified as woman or female (30), while other participants chose not to identify their gender (5), or identified as femme (5), genderqueer (4), androgynous (1), fluid (1), and butch (1). Only one participant used pronouns other than "she/her/hers." On average, participants came out around age 20, and took part in the project at age 32. Aged 19 to 56 at the time of our interviews in 2008 and 2009, two-thirds of my research participants (including myself) were born before 1983 when my study begins, and therefore are witnesses to these decades of homophobia and heterosexism whether as children, teenagers, or adults.

Ten of my participants identified as Black, Latina and/or Hispanic, mixed-race, or multiethnic, and thirty-seven participants identified as white, white Jewish, or white Armenian.[105] The lack of racial diversity is one of the greatest weaknesses of my project, which I believe was rooted in my recruitment process. My use of recruiting "lesbians and queers" who had "come out" may have left some trans, non-binary, antiessentialist, people of color, and/or Indigenous people feeling welcome. As American studies scholar Carlos Ulises Decena writes, there is a "tacit" understanding of a person's sexuality among their family and friends for many Latino gay men and many other queers of color—including women and tgncp, as my research shows—whereby not publicly defining your sexuality does not equate with being silent and those who identify as queer are not the only legitimate queer subjects.[106]

Most participants had attended some college and/or had an advanced degree, one was finishing high school, and eleven were at work on bachelor's or advanced degrees. Twenty-nine identified as working middle-class, seventeen as middle-class, and one as upper middle-class. Most US citizens identify as middle-class regardless of income or education, making the qualitative study of class distinctions difficult.[107] (No upper-class women volunteered to participate in my study.) Most 1980s-generation participants identified as middle-class, suggesting that my participants saw class as related to the (varying) accumulated wealth that comes with age. The lack of diversity among my participants spurred me to further amplify the marginalized voices and hold accountable the dominant ones.

While I never asked about religion, it came up often throughout our conversations (as queers of color scholars have also found), whether in its rejection or connection.[108] Some participants felt supported in

Reform Judaism, the Metropolitan Church of Christ, or Unitarian Universalism. Some were determined to produce change from within houses of worship that had refused them, specifically the Roman Catholic Church, Southern Baptist Church, and African Methodist Episcopal Church. All the participants who cited a religion identified as Jewish or Christian. Kathy '05 recalled that the first time she hooked up with another woman, she dreamt that "Jesus came to the foot of the bed, and said, 'What's wrong with you?' . . . I woke up later and I sat up and said, 'Oh, shit.'" Most hauntingly, white, middle-class Janice '79/'91, a staunch Catholic throughout her early life, had first come out in 1979 but was convinced by a psychiatrist that she could be "cured" of her homosexuality through electroshock. She came out again in 1991. I list Janice with both of her coming out years in order to respect both distinct moments and the insights they produced.

Employed participants worked in nonprofits, social services, arts, business, or education, while others were full-time students. Over half of the participants held multiple part-time jobs to keep afloat. Like most New Yorkers, all relied on the city's public transportation system, and none mentioned owning a car. Seven participants were not out to their families; all of these participants still lived at home or were under the age of twenty-five. While the 2000 US Census suggests that one-third of partnered lesbian households have children, only three participants had children and one was a grandmother.[109] Just under half of my participants mentioned a girlfriend or partner. One participant identified as a disabled person. That I did not offer sign language support, note wheelchair access, and so on may have implied to some a lack of disability support. I regret not asking my participants about their immigration status and how that affected their experiences, although it often arose on its own throughout our conversations. At least six participants mentioned being first-generation Americans.

While some participants asked for their real names to be used when I completed the research in 2009, given that my book will be published during a regime of white antiqueer nationalist power a decade later, all participants were given pseudonyms to protect their identities. Some of my participants' identities have changed since I conducted this research—including my own, as I describe in the preface—and I rely on the terms they used to describe themselves. I list my participants and their identities in appendix II.

## A Note on Terms

Around the time I conducted my research, scholars and my participants suggested that older women more closely identified with second-wave feminism and use *lesbian*, while *queer* tends to apply to younger, third-wave feminists who also refute the application of gender norms to their own bodies and others'.[110] While this distinction often held true among participants, "queer" was also used by participants across generations by those who identified their sexuality as beyond categorization and/or to encompass gender non-confirming, non-binary, and/or transgender individuals.[111] My participants shared these identities, and they can change based on context, era, experience, and life stage. In fact, participants were likely to use multiple terms (two to six) to refer to their sexual identities, often depending on the people in their groups with whom they were speaking.

I also deploy the notion of queer and queering to mark that which is outside of norms and refute binaries and norms held in place by dominant power structures. Queer is, in the words of anthropologist Martin Manalansan, "an unsettling mode of analysis, one that disrupts and unsettles the blissful tidiness of the normal."[112] By the 2000s generation, most participants said they felt detached from the essentialized lesbian identity defined by the female gender.[113] Yet there was also an understanding across generations that my participants were tied to that identity as a form of ancestry.

*Dyke* was used by some participants from each generation to mark queer feminist resistance under neoliberalism. Willey writes that dyke is an "explicitly politicized category that lends itself differently from 'lesbian'" that "emerges out of and evokes histories of sexism/homophobia/transphobia that cannot be parsed."[114] Sexual identities are always imbricated with racial and class identities, as well as one's age, generation, and geography.

All participants identified as female at birth (what has come to be known as "afab") and were raised as girl children. A few also identified as transgender (the term "cisgender" was not yet in wide circulation), but this was not their primary or public identity as they saw transgender (then) as linked to having taken hormones or had gender confirmation surgery. When I did speak to transgender masculine people about the study, they said they did not feel comfortable being in a "lesbian and queer study," because they said they did not identify as lesbian since they had taken hormones or had surgery. As not all of my gender nonconforming participants identified as transgender, I use both terms.[115] My reference to my participants as women does not mean a particular participant identified as a lesbian, and queer-identified participants did not necessarily identify as gender non-conforming or non-binary. I do not speak to the experiences of trans women because none participated in this study.

Some of my participants described having sex and/or relationships with both cis-men and -women, but only a handful identified with the ever-contested bisexual identity. Further, the terms I define here as related to New York City may not relate to other places. As sociologist Japonica Brown-Saracino found in her research of lesbian, bisexual, and queer residents of four small cities, "the idea that one is a 'dyke' [or any lgbtq identity] and that being a dyke means that you share interests and concerns with other dykes . . . varies greatly by place."[116] I use "lesbians and queers" and "women and tgncp" to reflect my participants' own naming of their identities, and "lesbian-queer" to describe the experiences of this group of women and tgncp in a time of extreme change. I embrace this ever-evolving terminology with a mix of hesitancy (as a social scientist) and dedication (as a queer feminist scholar), knowing it is the best shorthand discursive depiction possible.

Linda '96 paused in response to my question about which words she used to describe herself and blurted out, both joking and serious: "Oh my God, they've changed *again*?!" As the very basis of queer life is gender and sexual flux and/or refusal of binaries and norms, identity terms are always shifting. For example, the use of "being in the life" for queerness or referring to one another as "family" remained popular with Black and Latinx, as well as working-class, participants, but less so among white, middle-class participants who came out after the 1980s. The terms I use are thus meant not to fix identities but to be sturdy enough for a shared understanding. For more on identity terms, see appendix I.

### Making Queer Time to Understand Queer Space

Since the turn of the century, queer theorists have been keen to theorize queer time. Lesbians and queers are situated in the non-cis-heteroreproductive rhythms of in vitro, co-parenting, adoption, wider age gaps in partners, choosing not to have children, polyamory, and so on.[117] But you cannot make queer time without making queer space. In other words, how we theorize queer space requires theorizing queer time in order to understand queer lives, knowledge, and spaces over time.

Lesbians and queers often lack the political and economic power to leave a physical, public legacy or pass on their knowledge. Feminist historian Joan Kelly-Gadol argues that the periodization of mainstream history invisibilizes women—a phenomenon that Rich found holds especially true for lesbians.[118] For example, when we add in the pattern of lesbian-queer U-hauling (moving in together shortly after beginning to date) and the breakups that often ensue against a backdrop of ever-increasing housing costs, the social geographical dimensions of lesbian-queer lives reveal themselves as equally important to urban political economy.

Along with other recent lesbian generational studies by sociologist Arlene Stein and literary scholar Elizabeth Freeman's theorization of the fuzziness of lesbian-queer generations, this project finally marks a change from the situation LHA co-founder, activist, and writer Joan Nestle wrote about in 1978: "We [lesbians] have never had the chance before to listen to a full generational discussion, to argue with or refine the visions that worked for one age but not another."[119] Most work on lgbtq lives and spaces in the social sciences pays special attention to a given research study's own moment—e.g., a year's study of a Pride march, a decade's worth of census data—while the larger historical context is often lacking. This project's period of study spans twenty-five years (1983–2008) in order to grasp urban lesbian-queer everyday experiences over generations.

Lesbians and queers find other ways to produce cultural models of kinship that give weight to their history and claim a continuum through generations. Like other queer theorists and lgbtq studies scholars, I apply a generational framework to mark the passage of time.[120] Literary scholar Carla Freccero argues that "generational succession can be seen to produce queer community" in shared practices and places if not shared lives.[121] At the same time, many lgbtq activists, researchers, and theorists bemoan a gay "generation gap" whereby lgbtq people who came out in different eras tend not to understand the experiences of those before or after them.[122] Likely, as my nuanced generational analysis shows, this gap persists in part because of the overly general pre-/post-Stonewall generation framing that is still prevalent.

With that in mind, while I pay special attention to how lesbian and queer spaces change over time, my participants were firm that some cultural codes, styles, and places seemed eternal and could not be mapped on to any one generation. Was there ever a time since the 1980s or even before without flannel? No. Without the lesbian-queer music of Ani DiFranco or her equivalent to sing along with? Nope. Without Riis Beach, the gay seaside playground of the Far Rockaways? No way! And without experiencing harassment, violence, romance, hot sex, bad sex, no sex, the closing of a bar, and gentrification—as both the gentrified and gentrifiers? Not at all. It is through these women's and tgncp's appearances, styles, identities, body modifications, purchases, activisms, codes, places, terms, jokes, and practices that they knit and keep knitting together lesbian-queer spaces and places.

Given lesbians' and queers' limited access to the public, material, and now online spaces that often define (often white, middle-class, able-bodied) gay and queer men's lives, I suggest that there is a related yet distinct swath of place-making and -connecting practices and meanings to recognize across and within generations. My use of generation as a form of succession defined by my participants does not seek to promote simplified narratives, or what Jackie referred to as a "myth of progress," but rather to recognize queerness as always in process.[123] Further, my research findings make clear the importance of examining which spaces promoted justice at which times and under what conditions. I seek to counter the time-indifferent interpretation of lgbtq and lesbian neighborhoods and bars, as well as the emphasis on feminist time as waves and intergenerational conflicts, while putting a much-needed focus on queer space and time.

My focus on the coming out period in our interviews had the unintended effect of revealing the generational framing of participants' stories and the breakdowns between them, which are heavily framed through the coming out period and racial, gender, sexuality, and disability identities, especially during adolescence or early adulthood. Rothenberg noted similar patterns in her early 1990s study of lesbians and queers in Park Slope, Brooklyn, observing a generational split "between women who grew up and came out under lesbian-feminism and younger lesbians (in their mid-20s and younger) who have come out in the age of AIDS and gay (or queer) activism."[124]

Queer origin stories are often filled with as much joy and loss as nostalgia. The distinct generational rifts structured by white cis-heteropatriarchal capitalism require attention. Women and tgncp described aging out of the bar/party scene in their thirties, which they connected to deepening relationships, midcareer commitments, and/or drinking and staying out late less and less often. Generational rifts emerged as women and tgncp frequented certain spaces less and others more, as spaces closed, scenes shifted, and political economies rose and fell. Constellations are always racialized, classed, and shaped by generation. As women and tgncp aged and were displaced with few ways to share their stories and no public outlets for recording their history, their knowledge and culture dispersed with them. Without generational exchange, *A Queer New York* also reveals how generations rewrite or never learn their histories let alone see the constellations that accrue across generations.

## A Constellated Outline for the Book Ahead

*A Queer New York* unfolds in the same way that lesbians and queers make constellations: through the accumulation of spaces, capital, and experiences, however fleeting, fragmented, and unrecognized by mainstream society they may be. The chapters each contain mental maps, GIS maps, graphs, and/or images from publications and activisms to afford a visual-textual dialogue. Using the central thematic of constellations, I tell the stories and experiences of my participants across and in the neighborhoods they often mentioned, lived in, or spent time in. It may seem contradictory to the logic of my project to write around and in neighborhoods, but my participants kicked off our conversations with a discussion of neighborhoods—before they critiqued the limitations of these spaces and wrestled with their role in neighborhood gentrification. The assumption that a gentrified claim to property-owned territory as a path to queer feminist liberation requires radical rethinking and intervention. To that end, I chose a selection of spaces most important to and frequently mentioned by participants to address in three central chapters: Greenwich Village, Bed-Stuy and Crown Heights, and Park Slope. In my fifth and final chapter, I reflect on how constellations are produced over generations across the city—in, across, and beyond New York City neighborhoods. Through constellations, I reflect on the relationship between queer feminist theory and queer and feminist geographical studies.

These neighborhoods serve as the most salient cases of the fragmented, fleeting, and embodied qualities of urban lesbian and queer life. All of my case studies are about race, gentrification, women and tgncp, and queerness, but the alignments of these concepts switch in each chapter. In revealing constellations in and across these neighborhoods, I follow queer feminist theorist Sara Ahmed's method of tracing "what allows other ways of gathering in time and space . . . [to] generate a queer landscape, shaped by the paths that we follow in deviating from the straight line."[125] As I show in *A Queer New York*, there are many queer tales of the city held, hidden, and revealed in tracing constellations that, in all ways, deviate from straightforwardness if not straightness.

2

# Belonging in Greenwich Village and Gay Manhattan

"Before coming out, I spent a few evenings walking up and down Christopher Street waiting for a girl to talk to me," Bailey shared, recalling the fearful, awkward spring of 1995 when she was sixteen. Still living at home in Washington Heights, mixed-race/Black Bailey told her co-interviewees about her journeys to Greenwich Village to walk its queer boulevard, site of the Stonewall Inn, in order to find others like her:

> I used to get . . . *real* dressed up. [*group laughter*] Stockings, boots, skirt, and gloves [*pretends to put on elbow-length gloves*] . . . and trench coat! . . . It was the nineties [so] I tried a choker or something. . . . I would get on the 1 [subway] train and take it all the way down to Christopher Street. I would, literally, just walk up and down Christopher Street waiting for someone—a lesbian—to invite me into one of the bars or stop and talk to me. It never happened. I don't know why I thought that was going to happen.

Bailey didn't care that she had to covertly travel from her uptown home to the clubs and parties of the Village. Others had moved and would move thousands of miles for this chance. The Village was and is for Bailey, for all of my participants and so many other lgbtq people, the home of the brightest stars in New York's constellations. Across races, classes, and generations, participants painted the Village idyll they found or imagined as a place of absolute queer belonging: rainbow flags waving over a historical, multiracial street life of lgbtq bodies, businesses, and organizations with a seemingly classless structure. Yet while the geographical imagination of the Village is eternally a better place, an Oz come to life, my participants' constellations reveal that lesbians and queers come home but do not stay in white, wealthy Greenwich Village. Instead, perpetual lines of return by multiracial, multiclass, gender-ranging lesbian-queer bodies to their star-like places creates the vibrant stars and lines of constellations in and beyond the Village so that the lgbtq Village is reproduced through multiracial, multiclass lgbtq places, bodies, and memories that can only visit, in the past and present.

Participants equally described the gentrification of businesses, heightened consumerism and tourism, invisibility, policing, and/or hypersexualization of queer bodies, ever-increasing rents and prices of necessary goods, a steady stream of racism, more visible bodies of and venues for white gay and queer men, the dissolution and/or defunding of organization after organization, and the absence of promised connections. All of these neoliberal trends made the Village hostile to most queer bodies' inclusion as residents or, more often, as visitors, especially queer bodies of color. At the same time, the city requires the presence of these visible queers in ever-present lgbtq spaces to demonstrate its liberal superiority and maintain its gay and lesbian tourist economy. Lgbtq people simultaneously have come to serve straight tourism engines so that they may merely be seen to some as the perpetual extras on the set of *the* lgbtq neighborhood, evoking queer geographer Natalie Oswin's notion of "value-added queerness."[1] I also know this to be true as a white, trans, butch dyke who occasionally passed as a cisgender man on the streets of New York City. At times, I also felt welcomed and even marketed to in the Village but could not afford to stay. The double-edged sword of property ownership promises belonging and takes it away.

Greenwich Village sounds and feels like New York City. It is one of the oldest white-settler neighborhoods in Manhattan, the central island around which the other boroughs wrap themselves. My participants described the neighborhood as buffered by Houston (pronounced "HOW-stin") and 14th Streets, and the Hudson River and Broadway (figure 2.1).[2] The side streets are dominated by nineteenth-century brownstones mixed with early-twentieth-century apartment buildings; since the 2000s, there is the additional smattering of look-alike condominium buildings that haunt every city (figure 2.2). The black iron fire escapes of three- and four-story buildings brightly gleam as the sun slides between them from late morning until early evening. Greenwich Village is a bustling place, but it's also seemed to me to never be too loud, as honking and chatter ricochet up and out into the ether or are caught in the trees. It is the center of Manhattan's clusters of lgbtq life—present, past, and assumed future—surrounded by the East Village/Lower East Side, Meatpacking District, Soho, and Chelsea neighborhoods.

The catch is that, as a lgbtq person, *you* are told that *you* belong *here*, whether you are from "here"—New York City, the United States—or not and whether it's 1983, 2008, or today. By whom? Your friend or some ex-lover. The proximity of most of the few lesbian bars in the city (two to five) and parties (a handful at any time), and a host of gay men's bars. New York City's Lesbian, Gay, Bisexual, & Transgender Community Center. Advertising. Rainbow flags. The camp and/or protest of the annual Halloween Parade. Tourist guides. Stories in the *New York Times* and *Village Voice*, or whichever newspaper in whichever city localizes queerness to the Village. Restaurants. Lgbtq historical geographies. TV shows. Movies. The history and lore of Stonewall, Sylvia Rivera, Marsha P. Johnson, Stormé DeLarverie, beatniks, and bohemians. Where the Pride March begins or ends, depending on the decade, for over (now) fifty years and the Dyke March ends for over (now) twenty-five years. And the range of lgbtq places and bodies, before and since.

The lgbtq history and lore of New York and the Village proved central to my participants' place attachment.[3] A small number of protests, riots, and acts of resistance in multiple US cities, largely conducted by working-class and poor Black and Latinx lgbq people and transgender and gender non-conforming people (tgncp), paved the way for the celebrated Stonewall riots on Greenwich Village's Christopher Street in 1969.[4] Buoyed by the reputation of the Stonewall riots—and the Village's bohemian, beatnik, and earlier gay history, all too often erroneously portrayed as stories of solely white, male rebellion—the neighborhood has hosted an increasing number of lgbtq restaurants, bars, organizations, businesses, and cruising grounds since the 1970s, as well as lgbtq tourism.

Also since the 1970s, as historian Christina Hanhardt describes, gay and lesbian calls for policing and claims to gay "neighborhoods," including Greenwich Village, have been legitimated by their liberal, white, middle-class demands for "safety."[5] With these claims comes the displacement, disinvestment, and ejection of most working-class and poor people, people of color, drug users, sex workers, tgncp, homeless people, and others who are marked "deviant," a term once applied to and still (of course) including (certain) homosexuals.[6] In 1980, over 60 percent

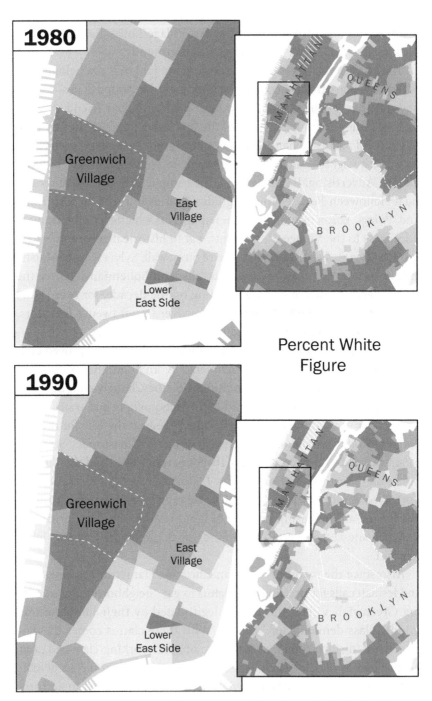

Figure 2.1. Census maps showing white percentage of population (with details of Greenwich Village), 1980, 1990, 2000, and 2010

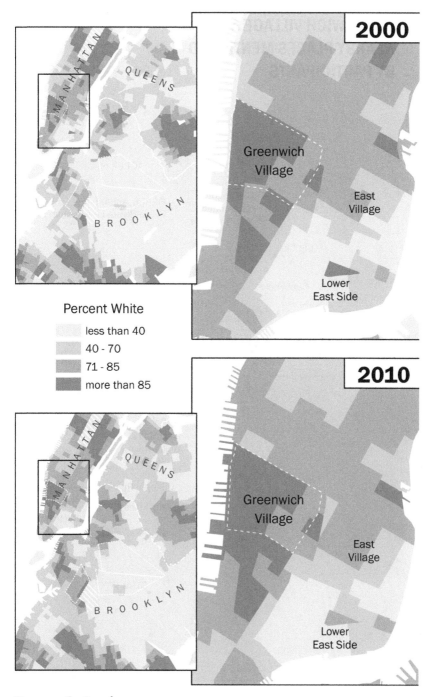

Greenwich
Village

East
Village

Lower
East Side

Percent White

less than 40
40 - 70
71 - 85
more than 85

2010

Greenwich
Village

East
Village

Lower
East Side

Figure 2.1. *Continued*

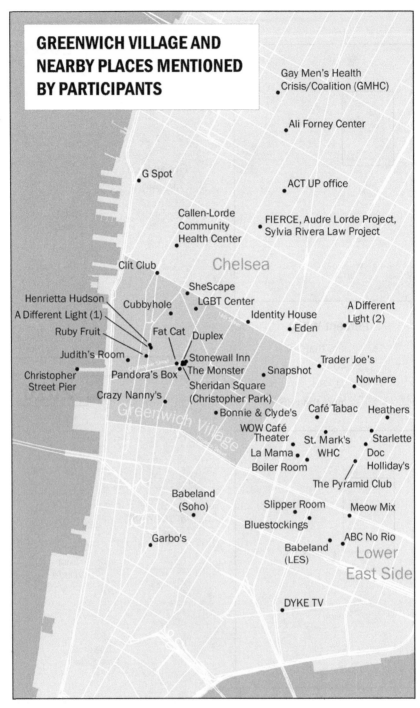

**GREENWICH VILLAGE AND NEARBY PLACES MENTIONED BY PARTICIPANTS**

Gay Men's Health Crisis/Coalition (GMHC)

Ali Forney Center

G Spot

ACT UP office

Callen-Lorde Community Health Center

FIERCE, Audre Lorde Project, Sylvia Rivera Law Project

Chelsea

Clit Club

SheScape
LGBT Center

A Different Light (2)

Henrietta Hudson
Cubbyhole
Identity House
Eden

A Different Light (1)
Ruby Fruit
Fat Cat
Duplex

Judith's Room
Stonewall Inn
Trader Joe's

Christopher Street Pier
Pandora's Box
The Monster
Snapshot
Nowhere

Crazy Nanny's
Sheridan Square (Christopher Park)

Greenwich Village

Bonnie & Clyde's
Café Tabac
Heathers

WOW Café Theater
St. Mark's
Starlette

La Mama
WHC
Doc

Boiler Room
Holliday's

The Pyramid Club

Babeland (Soho)

Slipper Room
Meow Mix

Bluestockings

Garbo's
ABC No Rio

Babeland (LES)
Lower East Side

DYKE TV

Figure 2.2. Map of Greenwich Village and nearby places often mentioned by participants

of city residents were white and 23 percent were foreign-born ; by 2010, the share of white residents had decreased to 44 percent while that of foreign-born residents had increased to 28 percent. Yet it went unmentioned in our discussions that over 85 percent of Village residents have been white *since* 1980, and an average of less than 18 percent were foreign-born (figure 2.3).[7]

Under the thrall of the false promise of neighborhood liberation, my participants could not see their queer feminist resilience and resistance in constellations. The myth of neighborhood liberation emerges through white, middle-class, homonormative promises of the American Dream. Greenwich Village is another gayborhood where, as performance studies scholar Charles I. Nero puts it, "gay strategies have focused on integrating into the middle classes . . . [and perpetuating] white hostility toward African Americans"; indeed, he argues, these strategies "are actually interdependent and, historically, have reinforced each other."[8] Yet the property ownership, visible community, business development, and home renovations required to secure the realization of this myth were beyond the means of almost all of my participants and many other lesbians and queers. To disrupt this myth, I believe that queers must

Figure 2.3. Greenwich Village's Gay Street, seen from the corner of Christopher Street

question property-owned neighborhood imaginaries of "place-based political collectivity" in order to confront how such "queer imaginings can normalize [white] settlement."[9] Looking at the city for constellations, in and beyond the Village, queers the American Dream model of neighborhood liberation to recognize and resist paradigms of white, masculinist property ownership as defining success.

While queer geographers Catherine J. Nash and Andrew Gorman-Murray argue that many lgbtq neighborhoods have become "networked entertainment districts" and lost their hold as a "territorial foundation of a political movement," the Village, in some measure, maintains itself as both.[10] My participants described the Village's residents in the 2000s primarily as cisgender, white, wealthy men—some of whom are gay, many of whom are not—who often have privileged access to resources and power (based on gender pay inequity), number of dedicated spaces (evidenced in my archival research), and public spaces, as well as the support of marketing, tourism, and policing engines. As cultural historian James Polchin wrote in the 1990s:

> Admittedly, there are many "invisible" bodies on Christopher Street. The lesbian body and bodies of color only nominally appear in the storefront aesthetics and the heart of street life. Christopher Street, with its specialty stores and gay bars, reflects the economic strength of gay men.[11]

I sought neither to compare my participants to gay-queer men, nor assume that there is a monolithic white, rich, cisgender, gay male defining the gayborhood, although I do attend to how my participants usually expressed both solidarity with gay and queer men and frustration with their vaster territorial claims to space. Like Oswin, I believe it is key to "explore the 'cultural work' that the figure of gay white affluence does rather than assuming its alignment with contemporary capitalism" for "he" is not "the only queer figure embroiled in a complicit relationship with postindustrial capitalism."[12] My research demonstrates how lesbians and queers are equally entangled in and also resist larger structural oppressions.

Urban geographer Gillian Rose argues that a feminist "sense of space which refuses to be a claim to territory . . . thus allows for radical difference."[13] She coined the feminist concept "paradoxical space" to make sense of the "dynamic tension" in women's space between attributes that "would be mutually exclusive if charted on a two-dimensional map . . . [but] are occupied simultaneously"—i.e., margin/center, prisoner/exile, inside/outside, and, especially, belonging/visitation.[14] After our interviews, Birtha '84 sent me a note: "[B]ack then, apart from bars, the [Christopher Street] pier, taxi cabs, and knowing about courtyards in certain buildings came in handy. Personally, I felt that the entire West Village was ours." While Birtha is white and middle-class, the sentiment that the Village was "ours" was shared across races and classes, even while women and tgncp of color and working-class women and tgncp described having markedly different access to fewer stars and lines between them there. All along, Birtha and the rest of my participants described a paradoxical homeland they could only visit.

## "It Had to Be in the Village" in the 1980s

In 1983, a star was born that would become the center of the Village's homo orbit. The *New York Times* announced "Sale of Site to Homosexuals Planned" in Greenwich Village.[15] It made sense to place the new facility, the Lesbian and Gay Community Center of New York City (now the Lesbian, Gay, Bisexual, and Transgender Community Center, a.k.a. the Center) in the Village. No other location was mentioned as often in participants' stories or maps as a site to orient to and from, making the Center the perpetual North Star of lesbian-queer life in New York City. As Wanda '85 said, "The Center was, like, the pinnacle. I worked there. I lived there. I played there."

The Center served as the hub of the politically queer and queerly political Greenwich Village, facilitating activisms that grew stronger alongside drag queen bingo nights, twelve-step meetings, art exhibits, installations (like Keith Haring's full-room, pro-sex mural in what used to be a second-floor bathroom), and groups for people of different races, cultures, abilities, interests, ages, and geographies (figure 2.4). The renowned GLAAD (Gay & Lesbian Alliance Against Defamation, 1985–present), ACT UP (AIDS Coalition to Unleash Power, 1987–1995 NYC), and Queer Nation (1990) had their first of many or many of their meetings at the Center, among hundreds of other groups such as the Lavender Hill Mob, Dykes Against Racism Everywhere (DARE), Senior

Figure 2.4. Keith Haring mural in the second-floor bathroom at the LGBT Center. Courtesy of the author

Action in a Gay Environment (SAGE), Lesbian Sex Mafia, Hispanic United Gays and Lesbians (HUGL), New York City Bi Women, and the Metropolitan Community Church of New York. My review of Lesbian Herstory Archives organizational records indicates that nearly one-quarter of the city's lgbtq organizations that existed between 1983 and 2008 met or held offices at the Center, which indicates the importance of this space, as well as the limited number of lgbtq spaces available to be rented or borrowed in the city.[16]

The LGBT Center, alongside other left-leaning and radical organizations like the nearby all-welcoming Judson Memorial Church, gave more lgbtq people reasons to come to the Village beyond nightlife alone. During the height of the AIDS epidemic, the Village continued its role as signifier of lgbtq homeland, action, and community. Even as fewer lgbtq people lived there in the decades that followed, queerness became forever associated with the area.[17] While the Center was described as the most hospitable of lgbtq stars, the same lgbtq people who define what it is to be lgbtq for any one event also can exclude others even at the Center, as queer New Yorkers have pointed out.[18]

In the 1980s, unlike the Stonewall era, my review of LHA organizational records also revealed that most protests, interventions, and zaps (queer activist actions and demonstrations) in the city took place *elsewhere* than the Village. My maps of lgbtq organizational meetings, mailings, and zaps reveal a distinct pro-queer landscape in the Village as well as the homophobic and/or heteronormative geographies of other areas of the city (see jgieseking.org/AQNY). Placing visible, loud lgbtq activists beyond the bounds of Village into the white, cis-heteropatriarchal capitalist hallmarks of the entrance to the New York Stock Exchange on Wall Street, the base of Midtown skyscrapers, and the steps of City Hall made queerness legible across the city. In other words, lgbtq people's sense of place attachment to the Village as "our" stronghold also emerged because it was a place they came from and returned to when taking action and often residing elsewhere.

The sense of belonging in, if not to, the Village permeated my interviews, especially among participants who came out in the 1980s. Poignantly, only white, middle-class, butch Chris '86 actually resided in Greenwich Village. At the time of my interviews, she still lived in a rent-controlled apartment she secured shortly after coming out:[19]

> [Now, the LGBT Community Center] . . . anchors [the neighborhood] as any kind of queer space at all. [In the 1980s, the places I put on my map were] Judith's Room . . . and Identity House . . . and the Duchess. That's sort of it. I haven't covered too much ground. But it was definitely: you want to hold hands? It had to be in the Village. You couldn't do it in any of these other neighborhoods.

In Chris's story, we see a constellation of fragmented spaces that define what Birtha earlier called "ours": bookstores (Judith's Room), bars (Duchess), organizing spaces and centers (Identity House, the Center), and certain places (and, although unnoted, certain times) in which gays and lesbians could publicly display affection. These spaces are also fleeting: only the LGBT Center still remains as is, and Identity House now uses LGBT Center space. The sense of belonging to this cluster of celestial objects also produces a sense of territoriality in the lines drawn *between* such spaces in a collaborative and rarely visible queerness.[20] By "clusters," like the stars of the Pleiades constellation (Seven Sisters, Seven Dancing Girls, etc.), I mean the (rare) physically close groupings of lesbian-queer places and imaginaries tied together by lesbian-queer physical paths and intersecting social networks, all of which amplify the sense of belonging to a neighborhood. Chris's comment that "you couldn't do it in any of these other neighborhoods"—demonstrating public affection, being confident in her masculine appearance and identity—suggests that the Village, material and imagined, afforded a unique place where all lgbtq people could claim both private and public spaces. Yet the possibility of residing there was an exception for most.

This geographical imagination of "ours," as Birtha put it, is based upon Chris's, Birtha's, and other participants' white privilege. The racist restrictions that shape the geographies of women and tgncp of color reconfigure any "romance of community."[21] African American, middle-class Naomi '89 held up her map to her co-participants (figure 2.5), and said,

> It's something I actually do to this day . . . apparently there's a spot, and my girlfriend finally pointed it out, where I would drop hands as I would get closer to my house. . . . One day, she was like [*pounds fist*], "Why'd you do that, you're not proud of me?!" [*Annabelle '97, Rachel '00, Holly '03 (white, working-, and middle-class): "Mm-hm" (nodding)*] . . . I didn't even realize. I had trained myself that just, if you're walking you just drop hands because . . . once I hit Sixth Avenue in the Village you drop hands . . . Then you get to the East Village and you can hold hands again. [*group laughter*]

I laughed along too, feeling that in-group sensation of recognizing another queer body only intermittently belonging in the city. Yet in transcribing and hearing forty-seven lesbian-queer voices repeat stories of rejection and hurt, it was clear the racism that women of color and tgncp face makes their claims to the city even more fleeting and fragmented, even as they travel the same or similar paths between these claimed spaces.

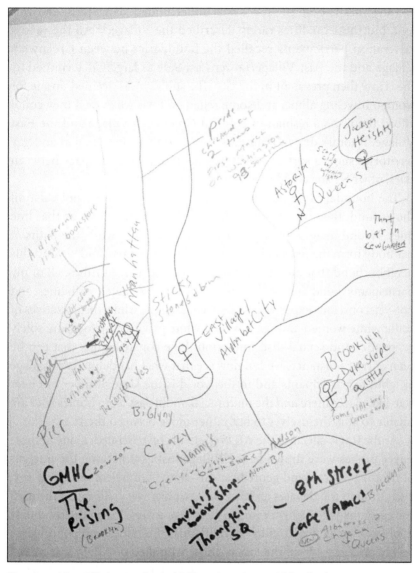

Figure 2.5. Naomi '89's mental map (African American, middle-class)

New York City in the 1980s was underfunded, dangerous, and violent, but these qualities rarely described the Village.[22] All the 1980s-generation participants recalled the boundaries between Greenwich Village and the East Village/Lower East Side as largely determined by the crime then prevalent in the city. The subway was deemed unsafe for women traveling alone, and some relied on taxis when or if they could afford them. As a lesbian of color in Greenwich Village and the East Village, Naomi's drawn boundaries around these two lesbian and gay territories show a sort of interstellar medium, the dark space between stars, of where she could and could not be herself.

The boundary line that runs down Naomi's map does not exist on the ground: there is no actual street or border that flows as that line does. Naomi imagines a supportive neighborhood, while the paths of her body form the lines of her constellations in, across, and beyond this neighborhood that nurture her as it also limits her. At times, all of my participants found humor in their survival tactics, muted visibilities, and not-yet-conscious experiences of violence; all the while, the narratives of some white women and tgncp veiled white privilege by focusing solely on gender and sexual discrimination. Like constellations that can be seen only at a distance, we can now see that what has defined the Village as lgbtq to participants and to the world is the large number of queer star-like places there *and* the multiracial, multiclass lgbtq bodies who are unable to affix themselves to but rather move between them.

As the tragic effects of the AIDS epidemic reverberated, many of these queer bodies were drawn to the Village just as it became the nucleus of death, activism, and gentrification—and, by implication, queer sex, even though the debates around the sex/porn wars still raged through the early 1980s.[23] As historian Laura Briggs writes, "Even the resolutely apolitical bar crowd couldn't entirely miss the rallies and contingents in gay pride parades. [The loss of those who died of AIDS] was a grief th[at] permeated gay communities."[24] Chris had moved to the Village, desperate to find a safe haven for her white, butch body. She embraced activism as she came out, as she also experienced the unraveling of the lgbtq neighborhood:

> In the eighties, when all of those gay men died who lived in the Village, there was a huge influx of breeders [i.e., heterosexuals] because the apart-

ments came on the market. That's when the Village changed. By the end of the eighties, early nineties, the West Village was barely even a gay space anymore. And my flower guy and my dry cleaner and the mom and pop stores went out, everyone you used to wave to at night on your way out of work, gone [i.e., died of AIDS or gentrified out]. So it was the end of that neighborhoody feeling. . . . For a while there, it didn't even feel safe in the West Village to hold hands.

Activist and writer Sarah Schulman records how the practices of city policy makers and developers took advantage of the AIDS epidemic to drive up rents. This pattern created a "dynamics of death and replacement" in the "gentrification of AIDS."[25] Each emptied apartment was a faded but still-extant star that went to market rate, eliminating another rent-controlled space as partners and lovers without their names on leases were forbidden to inherit or stay on. The focus on AIDS, which visibly affected gay men disproportionately, surely also attached male bodies foremost to the geographical imagination of the gayborhood.[26]

Ever-increasing waves of gentrification produced a space that was inhospitable and, at times, outright perilous to lgbtq people. A *New York Times* article bragged that the Village was "virgin territory" for further property development in the early 1980s, while acknowledging that "young people and Bohemians, who have traditionally given the Village its flavor, often have a hard time paying such prices."[27] Lgbtq people went unmentioned as sources of that Village "flavor." "Breeders," as Chris calls them, sought bohemian lifestyles but also often to reproduce white, middle-class, heteronormative family models, framing other sexualities and modes of kinship as distasteful. Meanwhile, the Village's role as a refuge to return to in memories of the past, as well as in everyday life in the 1980s for its sociality, services, and activism made it all the more central to participants' constellations. The neighborhood landscape must be read through the lens of a once-unstoppable disease and the painful death sentence it carried: both the spiraling fear, pain, and violence it reaped and the deep sense of loss and kinship it instilled in lgbtq people.

The cruel, homophobic reactions to the AIDS epidemic—which became an anti-sex campaign in the city under Mayor Ed Koch—intensified the state of vulnerability at home, work, and in between. Like several other participants, white, middle-class, and butch Gloria '83 was sexually harassed at work and "evicted from an apartment for being gay." Without legal protections (which most lgbtq Americans still lack throughout the country), "there was nothing [she] could do except quit" and move. As many died or were pushed out of residences, the average Greenwich Village rent went from an estimated 44 percent to 66 percent above the citywide average between 1980 and 1990 (see figure 2.6).[28] The decision in the 1989 *Titone, et al., v. Stahl* Greenwich Village housing case was the first in US history to conclude "that same-sex relationships are entitled to legal recognition and protection."[29] For many gay conservatives like libertarian pundit Andrew Sullivan, the case showed how lesbians and gays were just like everyone else.[30] Yet for most lgbtq US citizens and newly arrived immigrants, refugees, and undocumented workers, legal protections were a dream.[31] As of 2019, employment protections for sexual and gender identity still varied by jurisdiction.

Dyke anticapitalist politics were attached to Village feminist spaces of socialization and resistance, especially those with the sliding-scale or no entry fees, potlucks, and discounted costs common to lesbian-queer events. A group of feminists, many lesbians among them, led the St. Mark's Women's Health Collective in the nearby Lower East Side since 1974. Janice '79/'91 recalled how she had her first pap smear there from lesbian doctors as "they served me chamomile tea," and "You had access to your file!"[32] In 1985, the collective closed, citing lack of funds.[33] Lgbtq health funding largely migrated to the Center in the Village and groups like Gay Men's Health Crisis (later Coalition, or GMHC) and the Callen-Lorde Community Health Center in nearby Chelsea to combat the AIDS epidemic. Historian Katie Batza argues that it was lesbian and gay clinics of the 1970s similar to St. Mark's that afforded an infrastructure to care for people with AIDS (PWA) in the 1980s.[34]

While anticapitalist dyke politics created more spaces for women, they often proved financially impossible to sustain. Naomi humorously recalled, "Lesbian clubs were a sliding scale: 'Give me what you can! Give me a dollar. Give me what you got. What, you got a recipe?'" Indeed, women's (and tgncp's) labor is routinely done in the service of others. As feminist economist Rosemary Hennessey wrote, "Women provide most of the world's socially necessary labor—that is, labor that is necessary to collective survival—but much of it is rendered invisible, both in and outside the value system of commodity exchange, not least of all to women themselves."[35] These places were the stars that every lesbian or tgncp made her/his/their way to, drawing invisible lines in the wake of their paths that bound their constellations to others. The wide and wild range of such spaces (and the financial and emotional donations lesbians made to support them) cannot fully be accounted for here.

Another type of lesbian-queer space was often mentioned: feminist bookstores. As with its multiple lesbian bars, New York City became one of the small number of cities in the world to host multiple feminist and gay bookstores. Participants who came out in the 1980s often mentioned A Different Light and Judith's Room, both in the Village, and Womanbooks on the Upper West Side. Feminist bookstores empowered women to record and express their histories. As poet Carolyn Kizer writes, "We are the custodians of the world's best-kept secret: Merely the private lives of one-half of humanity."[36] Feminist as well as lesbian and gay bookstores produced lesbian space both in their physical locations and in the books, magazines, comix, and zines on their shelves, which made their ways into women's and tgncp's lives, libraries, archives, and classrooms.[37] Texts and ideas spread, and the lights from these stars continues to expand as knowledge, connection, and a sense of belonging. As library studies scholar Kristen Hogan writes, "A desire for ownership and recognition at the bookstores lives in tension with the anticapitalist goal of the bookstores as sites of resistance, socialist feminism, lesbian separatism, or other theoretical experiments."[38] While most feminist bookstores have closed, the antiracist, anticapitalist, and solidarity-building feminist politics—what I am calling dyke politics—that guided the founding of these places lives on. In a way, the knowledge and politics produced from each of these books and bookstores—which is spread in the stories lesbians and queers tell each other to make sense of themselves over cocktails or coffee, or on park benches or under the sheets—is like the light that arrives on Earth long after a star has died out.

Participants often mentioned the comparative lack of women's and tgncp's spaces (like their, then, two bookstores, three lesbian bars, and a handful of parties) in the Village versus the plethora of gay and queer

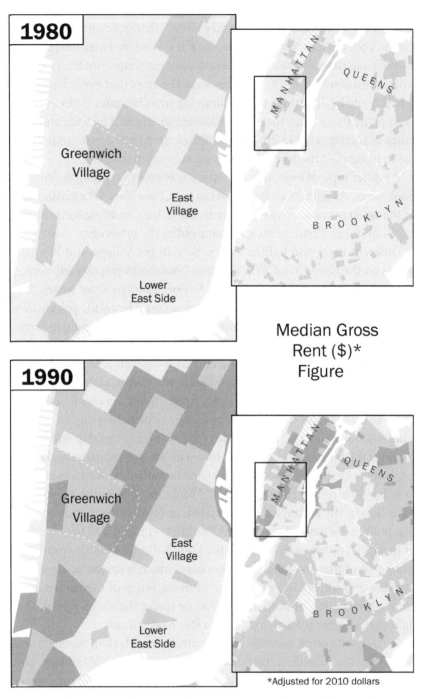

Figure 2.6. Census maps showing median gross rent (with details of Greenwich Village), 1980, 1990, 2000, and 2010

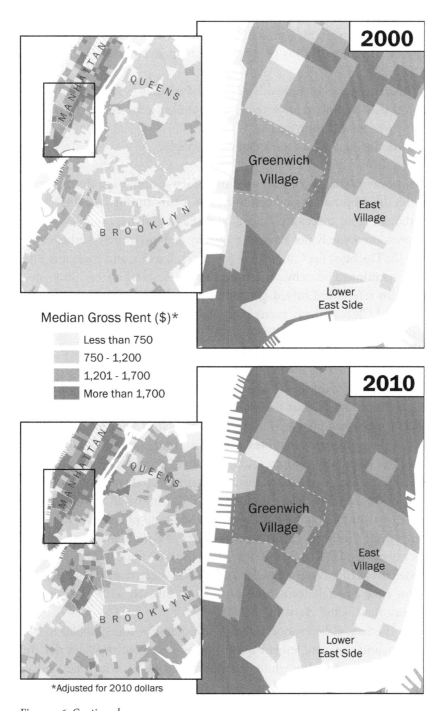

Median Gross Rent ($)*

- Less than 750
- 750 - 1,200
- 1,201 - 1,700
- More than 1,700

*Adjusted for 2010 dollars

**2000**

Greenwich Village

East Village

Lower East Side

**2010**

Greenwich Village

East Village

Lower East Side

Figure 2.6. *Continued*

men's spaces (often measured in bars, parties, and visible bodies on the streets). A group of 1980s-generation participants recalled:

> BIRTHA '84: [Gay neighborhoods] were dominated by gay men.
> YASMIN '83: They're always going to dominate the spaces. There seems to be more of them than us.
> NOELLE '83: . . . I just think they're more visible.

Unlike my participants, who aged out of bars around age thirty-five, it is not uncommon for gay men to frequent bars throughout their lives. Although lgbtq spaces are shaped by white patriarchal capitalism, such oppression is surely not extolled by all gay and queer men. Lesbian bars like the Duchess, Fat Cat, Bonnie & Clyde's, Bacall's, and Pandora's Box were mentioned often by participants as key "lesbian" spaces. Their stories also referenced mixed-gender gay bars like Tracks, Monster, and Pyramid Club, and gay men's piano bars like the Duplex and Marie's Crisis, among other spots.

At least half of my 1980s-generation participants described fighting back against racism in state protests as well as in lesbian places. The Committee of Outraged Lesbians (COOL) brought a successful discrimination suit against the Shescape party for denying admission to Black and brown people in 1985.[39] Dykes Against Racism Everywhere (DARE) co-organized to protest racial discrimination at the Village lesbian bar Bacall's in 1991 around matters of "dress code." In response, Bacall's owners issued a statement regretting "that any women of the gay community feels [sic] they have been discriminated against."[40] This statement shifted blame onto women and tgncp of color by focusing on patrons' "feelings" rather than the facts of Bacall's own discriminatory behavior. DARE's position was that the bar's imposition of a "dress code" invoked a range of racist and classist stereotypes. Such stories show how constellations have been both infused with and formed against racism and classism.

In the face of heteronormativity, homophobia, transphobia, AIDS, racism, and classism, lesbian-queer bodies were continually at risk. In an interview with other white participants, Jackie '85, who identified as upper middle-class, shared her experience of being attacked "that happened . . . in the Village," as if this geography was impervious to violence:

JACKIE '85: I mean, this was . . .'87, I suppose. And my girlfriend and I would just walk the street holding hands and kissing there [in the Village]. Just *fearless*. Although we did get spat at a few times. [*laughs*] And she got hit.

LINDA '96: Oh, *wow!*

JACKIE: [*laughs*] . . . now that I think about she got punched in the face once.

LINDA: Oh, my God.

JACKIE: Yeah. And people would yell at us. It was like water off a duck's back. I mean, it was kind of scary. But, actually, I was more angry. And that happened actually in the Village.

KATHY '05: [*wide-eyed, leaning back from the table*] Wow.

Through the 1990s- and 2000s-generation participants' mutual shock that this "happened actually in the Village," we see how the recognition of physical, emotional, and psychological violence against lgbtq people began to change over time, at least for some white, middle-class, cisgender-presenting bodies. We also see the white settler privilege that acts as both buffer to and obfuscation of the greater violence lgbtq people of color face every day.

In Jackie's security in her own survival ("like water off a duck's back"), we also see how the violence of heteronomativity and other oppressions has yet to be fully addressed, as with Naomi's line of where she can or cannot hold hands. I saw this phenomenon not only among those who came out in the 1980s but in all of my participants, and even in myself. This queer practice is reminiscent of what women's and gender studies scholar Lisa Diedrich writes about the "deeventualization" of AIDS in queer theory, what she understands to be a mutual forgetting of and distancing from AIDS.[41] How could we forget that conservatives even called for people with AIDS to be tattooed? The paradoxical space of belonging/visitation in the Village also fits into why deeventualization makes sense as a tactic of survival. Hatred against lesbians, queers, women, and tgncp accumulates in and on their bodies that wander the city seeking territory and instead produce constellations. All stars need not shine in memories or recognition, but disavowal of the experience does not erase it. Such hurt or "shame" never fully fades to many; it is its own light of ache, loss, and even desire that shines into future generations.

## The Lesbian-Queer Expansion during the Affordable, Revanchist 1990s

Like Naomi, white, working middle-class Sally '96 had drawn a distinct boundary in her map separating the Greenwich Village and Lower East Side neighborhoods (figure 2.7). But, unlike Naomi, she had also drawn a small, distinct line *connecting* them in the late 1990s:

> I have the route from Meow Mix [on the Lower East Side] over to Henrietta's and Rubyfruit [in Greenwich Village] and that whole area. 'Cause [*laughs*] how we were gonna get from the Lower East Side area over there, it was always like, "Are we going to take a cab?" "We never take cabs!"

This is a complete remapping of Naomi's vision of lower Manhattan: Sally's visible line depicts how she now can easily walk between the Village and Lower East Side, although usually with friends and without paying for a pricey taxi. Sally's white body and the bodies of her friends are then part of the gentrification of the spaces African American, middle-class Naomi could not walk a decade before. Urban planner Kristen Day writes that women's fear in public space "is typically constructed from a white perspective, which reinforces prejudice and ignores the role of race in the experience of fear."[42] Lesbian-queer bodies, especially white, cisgender, femme bodies like Sally's, mark a space as "safe" to the public. Under the logic of neoliberal capitalism, there is the sentiment: If (white, middle-class) women are "safe," isn't everyone?

That sense of the Village as "ours" also always existed alongside the violence against women and tgncp, as Jess '96 said about the East Village: "You got a little bit of harassment, but it was nothing compared to everywhere else. It was so ever-present, it was like it didn't matter. It was everywhere." Attacks from the religious right such as Pat Robertson's 1992 Iowa fundraising letter spurred more lgbtq people into action: "The feminist agenda is not about equal rights for women," he claimed. "It is about a socialist, anti-family political movement that encourages women to leave their husbands, kill their children, practice witchcraft, destroy capitalism and become lesbians."[43] Quotes like Robertson's were repurposed as calls to action by the ever-increasing nonprofit industrial complex, as well as the burgeoning lgbtq market.[44] I still recall how this

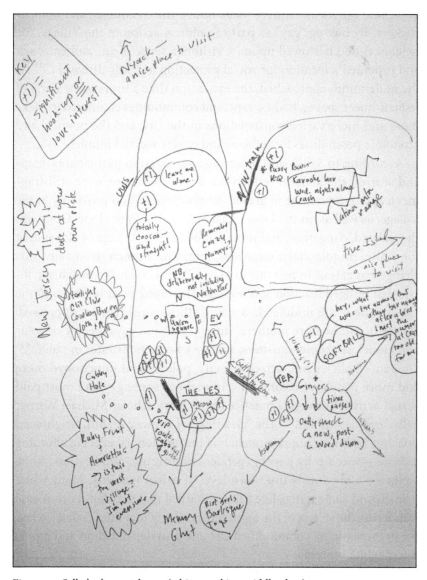

Figure 2.7. Sally '96's mental map (white, working middle-class)

quote and others like it were made into T-shirts, buttons, and bumper stickers. By buying "gay" as part of political action in the Village, the neighborhood bestowed upon its visitors a sense of an "authentic self and provided a location for social protection and self-discovery."[45] As the millennium approached, the expansion (like a universe of stars) of lesbian-queer spaces, bodies, zaps, and commodities continued to make more and more varied constellations in the city, and the political and economic possibilities for lesbians and queers seemed infinite.

According to Sally's and other 1990s-generation participants' maps and stories, the stars of lesbian-queer constellations were still fragmented, but now shone in greater number, range, and proximity in the Village, as well as on the Lower East Side and in Park Slope. Gone was the isolated, dangerous, and more bounded lgbtq Village of old, at least for white, middle-class, cisgender, feminine women. Ironically, this change was at least in part due to Mayor Rudy Giuliani's revanchist policies that bridged reaction and revenge. He waged a war to "reclaim" the city for the white middle class against those already most oppressed: "workers and 'welfare mothers,' immigrants and gays, people of color and homeless people, squatters, anyone who demonstrates in public."[46] Giuliani's policies militarized the city, policed and imprisoned more and more people of color, and criminalized some gay and most paid sexual activity through a practice that literary scholar Michael Warner calls "zoning out sex."[47] The "cleaning" of subway graffiti, heightened policing, and mass imprisonment had the unintended effect of affording lesbians—specifically passing, gender-conforming, middle-class, white women—a previously unknown level of urban mobility. Many white women and some tgncp, like Sally, remarked that they felt more at ease wandering the streets in the 1990s, not realizing that their "safety" relied on an increasingly commodified city and also depended on and reproduced white supremacy.

This lesbian-queer geographical expansion, which seemed to my participants to mark the spreading of justice and social change, related not only to Giuliani but also to the markets. After the October 1987 market and real estate crash, there was a pause in real estate investment until the mid- to late 1990s.[48] Between moments of disinvestment and "reinvestment," lesbian-queer expansion filled many buildings and streets with low-cost spaces and events, organized by (often) visibly queer bodies.

Lesbians' and queers' antiracist and anticapitalist activism continued in feminist spaces, especially racially and class diverse plays, exhibits, and performances at WOW (Women's One World) Café Theatre, La Mama, and ABC No Rio on the Lower East Side. Lesbianism itself was a core component of these places: "At WOW lesbianism is a *given* rather than an issue to be addressed—a given *not* in the sense of being mandatory but as something unremarked upon, a syllable not stressed."[49] (For many years, this given also generated anxiety about the possible presence of trans people at WOW, as was true in most other lesbian spaces.) Participants' stories show how their everyday geographies visibly multiplied and expanded, connecting more stars in Manhattan and Brooklyn in brighter constellations, and to other boroughs, so that women came into many urban rooms of their own.

Queer geographer Julie Podmore writes that in Montréal in the 1990s lgbtq groups began to question how territorialization "revolved around 'ghettoization.'"[50] These groups argued that the "use of 'territory' to build community" depended on "internal inequalities" like those race, class, and gender to divide the lgbtq community-for-all.[51] Still, across US and Canadian cities, the promise of a queer urban homestead was both popularized and increasingly indicative of (white) lgbtq people's strategy for survival. As author Armistead Maupin wrote in his *Tales of the City* series about gay life in San Francisco: "If I had my way . . . we would lock ourselves away from the madness out there."[52] Extending their constellations still meant their queer compasses pointed back to Greenwich Village as a shared lgbtq true north homeland in the city and, however briefly, invoked a sense of belonging that obscured the fleeting quality of queer stars in and beyond cities.

Thanks to the arrival of a mixed cocktail of drugs, by 1996 HIV/AIDS was no longer a death sentence for some people in the United States, namely those who could geographically and economically afford to seek treatment as well as housing and basic needs. From their homes or the Center or a nearby Chelsea office, ACT UP members led years of guerilla actions at sites ranging from the city's St. Patrick's Cathedral to the Centers for Disease Control in Atlanta and the Republican National Convention in New Orleans, and produced series of videos that "represented what producers Jean Carlomusto and Gregg Bordowitz described as 'a guerrilla-type production of safer sex "propaganda."'"[53] The intense energy and innovation that drove anarchist, creative, and militant ACT UP NYC also led much of its core group to slowly dissolve over infighting, per my participants, about how to serve the needs of its very diverse members after achieving their primary goal of securing drug trials in 1992. The disbanding of the city's first chapter that same year began to unravel the purported sense of total community that preceded it—one that, in actuality, had never been fully achieved. (ACT UP would reband multiple times over the years and some argue that it never ceased organizing.[54]) While the stigma remained, queer life felt, at times and to some, much more bearable for participants.

My reading of the Lesbian Herstory Archives' organizational records reveals that racism and classism splintered ACT UP as much as the tensions between gay men and lesbians did.[55] Queer radical activisms that aimed to produce radical justice were (and are), as political scientist Cathy Cohen observes, primarily a white platform that pitted queers against all heterosexuals without attention to the ways race, class, disability, immigration status, and so on shaped queer life.[56] Literary scholar Chandan Reddy writes of the late 1990s figure of the gay Pakistani asylum seeker who was forced to endure "heteropatriarchal relations [that facilitated] the recruitment and socialization of labor while justifying the exclusion of immigrant communities from state power through a liberal language of US citizenship as the guarantor of individual liberty and sexual freedom."[57] New Yorkers joined existing lgbtq groups, and developed well over a hundred local lgbtq organizations in the 1990s, some of which expanded across New York City, the United States, and beyond. Even in the face of uneven support, and regardless of race, gender, or class, this political and geographical expansion infused many of my participants' geographical imaginations with a sense that their constellations were, at times, boundless.

All of my 1980s- and some of my 1990s-generation participants joined or attended events hosted by what many believed to be the most important group of the period in New York City for lesbians: the Lesbian Avengers. Founded in New York City in 1992, the Avengers focused explicitly on lesbians' and women's concerns that had been ignored or slighted in most ACT UP and Queer Nation "zaps." After many earlier attempts to organize, Maxine Wolfe and other lesbian activists called yet another meeting over the lack of concern for lesbian issues. Wolfe recalls saying, "I can't believe that I'm sitting here and there's not one person in this room who is talking about what a lesbian issue is. Are you all out at the workplace? Are you all getting decent health care?"[58] They were not. Drawing on the activist energy of the period and the determination to finally attend to lesbian issues, the group collaborated for almost a year to form the Avengers.

The Avengers' radical activism depended upon inserting women's bodies in public space as gendered and sexualized objects of their own construction.[59] As seen in figures 2.8a-b, two of the fliers used to "recruit" Lesbian Avengers visualize New Yorkers' first attempt to define and work solely on lesbian concerns through guerilla activism and media-savvy techniques. The first Avengers zap responded to efforts to suppress the multicultural "Children of the Rainbow" curriculum in white, middle-class Middle Village, Queens—members of the group handed out balloons to children that read "Ask about Lesbian Lives," all the while followed by a marching band.[60] While ACT UP had focused most local efforts in Manhattan and other major US cities, the Avengers and a multitude of other organizations brought 1990s-era lgbtq activisms to the outer boroughs and less cosmopolitan places (like school board meetings and the Staten Island Ferry) more regularly and more publicly. Thus, the Avengers, with other groups, expanded the range of lesbian-queer justice and made the lines of lesbian-queer constellations more visible (see jgieseking.org/AQNY). A 1988 event designed and led by the ACT UP Women's Caucus (AUWC) was one prominent exception: the group organized a mass distribution of condoms at a major league baseball game at the New York Mets' Shea Stadium in Queens, holding up signs (with recently coined slogans like "No Glove, No Love") from the upper bleachers, and arranging for the LED scoreboard to announce that AIDS kills women.[61]

Among other actions, the Lesbian Avengers organized the first NYC Dyke March in 1993, inspired by the twenty thousand lesbians whom they organized to march at the March on Washington for Lesbian, Gay and Bi Equal Rights and Liberation in 1993. When asked what she got out of being part of the Avengers, Wanda '85 smiled and replied, "I learned how to eat fire," referring to the empowering, in-your-face, and usually bare-breasted practice of fire eating with which the group would begin all of their zaps. The practice of eating fire was a lived metaphor of

Figure 2.8a-b. Lesbian Avengers fliers, designed by
Carrie Moyer, 1992

not letting homophobia and patriarchal hatred and fear erase and deny lesbians, but to confront it by taking "the fire of action into our hearts and into our bodies . . . and make it our own."[62] The Avengers also organized a skate-in at Rockefeller Center—holding hands and kissing in public was then a more radical than sexualized act—and erected a statue of Alice B. Toklas next to the one of her partner Gertrude Stein in Bryant Park, followed by a lesbian waltz.

Lesbian, bisexual, and queer women who contracted HIV/AIDS through sex with men or needle use received little attention until the AUWC and the Avengers, and other groups soon joined in. In 1994, the group DYKE TV issued a press release for the cable network show titled "Because If We Don't Put Ourselves on the Air Nobody Else Will." The isolation lesbians felt in DYKE TV's organizing was best summed up in a 1994 letter from their executive producers to the publisher of *OUT* magazine, a national monthly lgbtq magazine, regarding fundraising for the Stonewall 25 anniversary and Gay Games in New York City:

> By turning the planned 16 events [of *OUT* in 1994] into fundraisers that will exclusively benefit AIDS charities, *OUT* is shutting out lesbians and their concerns. Furthermore, by funneling the estimated $1 million the events are expected to net through two big, established, mainstream AIDS charities with no roots whatsoever in the AIDS community— DIFFA and Broadway Cares—*OUT* is denying the lesbian com[m]unity access to funds that we urgently need to build up our institutions and support our priorities.
>
> AIDS is a horrific disease which has decimated the gay male community. Lesbians have been in the forefront of the battle against the disease both as AIDS activists and as caretakers . . . in the community. But AIDS is not the foremost priority of the lesbian community.
>
> We feel that by inviting DYKE TV . . . *OUT* magazine is attempting to legitimatize [*sic*] events which, once again, would mobilize the lesbian community to support the gay male establishment with little regard to lesbian needs and concerns. . . .
>
> Too often, lesbian needs have been subsumed in the generic causes of the gay (male homosexual) community, or the generic causes of the women's (straight women's) community. While we have been quick to

lend our solidarity to others, reciprocity has been rare and lesbian concerns still are never addressed by anyone but ourselves.

We are disappointed that *OUT* magazine's consciousness is mired in
the politics of exclusion and discrimination. We hope that you will recon-
sider your position.[63]

The common narrative that lesbians devoted themselves to gay men's
concerns foremost during the worst years of the AIDS crisis was true
for many of my participants. But the fixation on the epidemic as a gay
men's disease obscured lesbian issues, and enabled a general lack of
reciprocity that would leave many lesbians and gay men at odds and
divided. The DYKE TV letter also exposes the multimillion-dollar market (hoteling, tourism, events, shopping, food) that already fed the mass
commodification of lgbtq people and events even in the 1990s. While the
mainstream media reduced lesbians and queers to sexualized bodies—if
they mentioned them at all—radical media organizations like DYKE TV
created their own voices and visions of lesbian-queer life by filming in
a tradition of independent media in the "context of queer narration and
cultural recognition."[64]

It was not just the Avengers' and other organizations' activisms, like
those of SALGA (South Asian Lesbian and Gay Association), WeWah
and BarCheeAmpe, and GLSEN (Gay, Lesbian and Straight Education
Network), that brought a mass of lesbian-queer bodies onto New York
City streets and led to a greater claim to public space. Women and tgncp
across classes, though primarily white, claimed an even deeper sense of
"home" in public parks and stoops in and around the Village and Lower
East Side in the 1990s; tgncp mobilities would blossom to a degree in
the 2000s. White, working middle-class, genderqueer Jess '96 was a Riot
Grrrl who went to Sleater-Kinney, Bratmobile, L7, Tribe 8, Heavens to
Betsy, Le Tigre, Team Dresch, and Butchies shows and made zines in her
free time. Many participants described how the radical feminist punk
and largely white Riot Grrrl movement gave them a way to be publicly
heard and seen.[65] Jess also spent her time leading

safer-sex outreach to queer youth . . . and basically my territory was the
East Village, because that's where the young women were hanging out. . . .
This is 1998 and it's . . . my little world. [*points to her map*] Tompkins

Square Park. Kate's Vegetarian and St. Mark's Place and the Cube [public art installation at Astor Place], and where you could get cheap Doc Martens. Washington Square Park. And I slept with some girls at NYU.

Jess later said lesbian-queer territorial claims were impossible due to men's control of most public space but, in the late 1990s East Village, she had a kind of "territory" and her own "little world."

The same year, mixed-race/Black, working middle-class Bailey '95 had a home of her own across Manhattan in the Village: Crazy Nanny's. She spoke passionately about Nanny's:

Well, I was twenty-one. I was working there and everyone there was in their thirties, forties, fifties. So it wasn't *my* age group but it was a bar that was primarily African American lesbian. Didn't used to be. All the way back. But there were a lot of Latin women, working-class white women. [*Wanda '85: "Yeah!"*] A *lot* of working-class white women would feel comfortable there. And downstairs it just had that cool, Megatouch bar feeling, you know? And upstairs it was like a big dance club and bar upstairs. It was like Cheers for me. . . . I remember sitting in there writing a paper on Lil' Kim . . . telling the bartender to put on Lil' Kim while I wrote my paper. [*group laughter*] While I write my paper and drink soda. Because when I was in there I was like . . . *home*. You know what I mean? [*collective nods*] So when it closed—I worked there for five years. But also that community was there. And now people don't know where to go.

Nanny's was an incredibly important space in the Black queer geographical imagination and material history of New York City, because it was the *only* long-term lesbian bar primarily serving women and tgncp of color in Greenwich Village. American studies scholar Nikki Lane, quoting performance studies scholar Fiona Buckland, writes that queers of color in New York City in the period before and after Nanny's,

denned their own club spaces, away from fanfare or mainstream vehicles of publicity. News of these spaces spread by word of mouth; therefore, these spaces had underground cachet. This epithet held value in being outside of mainstream vehicles of publicity and the types of club populated by tourists to the city.[66]

In her research focusing on the Washington, DC, scene, Lane also writes, "The scene spaces that [Black queer women] create are often not recognized as 'public,' because they are not connected to mainstream LGBT sources of visibility and power."[67] In New York as much as in DC, "the organization of gay and lesbian clubs" orbited "around whiteness and middle-classness," as well as aspects of cisgender male identities.[68] Thus, there is a sense, per Lane, that Black queer women and Black queer women's spaces "both exist only in private (read here, 'secret' or 'underground')."[69]

When some of the "mixed" bars in the Village, Lower East Side, and other Manhattan neighborhoods did welcome large numbers of Black and Latinx lesbians and queers, it was often on less popular weekday nights or on weekend nights right before they closed.[70] In their 1980s-generation conversation, white Jackie '85 remarked the Duchess went "all-Black for a very brief time before" it closed, to which Black/Cuban Wanda '85 nodded and replied, "Right before it sank like a ship." My participants of color described the repetition of this play by racist capital generation after generation.

Still, Bailey's "home" in Nanny's is tied to Jess's "little world" on the Lower East Side, as both women's experiences are fueled with notions of a claim to the Village and a broad sense of lgbtq community that blossomed during the time of lesbian-queer expansion, i.e., the birth of more lesbian-queers stars with more lines to be drawn between them. Lesbian-queer expansion involved women and tgncp's short-lived ability to financially, politically, and socially produce more fixed, visible, and seemingly long-term places (businesses, publicized events, informal gathering hubs) in more areas across the city than at any other point in its history. Poignantly, the return of street patrols in the 1990s, like the Queer Nation's Pink Panthers, with their bright stickers proclaiming "Queers Bash Back," marked a shift from legal to extralegal gay oppression.[71] Along with the Christopher Street Patrol—which was founded by business owners and residents—writes Hanhardt, there was also "an appropriation of (and identification with) national-juridical modes of *redress*."[72] In other words, while queers were once police victims and outlaws, now they adopted the legal code and took up policing to prove their place in the city.

That women of all races, classes, and genders felt a sense of belonging in the Village speaks to the political and economic conditions that allowed lesbians and queers to feel at "home," albeit impermanently. The "world" and "home" they made there was only as visitors, even as it felt that Greenwich Village was truly "ours." And what is "ours" remains rooted in structures of cis-heteropatriarchal, racial, colonial capital. In New York City, such place-claiming would prove useful to processes of gentrification whereby some younger women and tgncp, often white and middle-class, claimed public space. Black, brown, and Latinx women and tgncp and working-class women across generations claimed even more semi-public spaces like bars in the midst of the Village. While far from constituting liberation itself, in retrospect, these shifts still evoked the promise of imminent *neighborhood* liberation. The multitude of increasingly proximal lesbian-queer places and bodies made the ever-clustered stars of Greenwich Village shine brighter for its beckoning stars than ever before—and it has never had as many places for lesbians and queers since then.

One particular star's implosion was heartfelt by my participants in the 1990s. A Different Light Bookstore closed on the Village's Hudson Street in 2001 as feminist and lgbtq bookstores across the country began to shut down en masse. Vanessa '93 recalled, "What I used to do is I'd sit there and read and drink coffee. And I'm so sad—I'm *still* sad that that bookstore closed." Participants longingly described past feminist and lgbtq bookstores, spaces that blended socialization with optional consumerism (hence their closing). They also described the sensation of being recognized, or at least sold to, in 1990s mainstream chain stores. When Gloria '83 said, "Barnes & Noble got a gay and lesbian section there—," Wanda interrupted with, "It's not the same!" Gloria responded, "I know it's not the same! But you walk in and it's like, 'Wow! I'm represented in *here.'*" At the same time, the excitement was tinged with trepidation. Noelle '83 remarked how much "you didn't want to be seen" around the gay shelf of alternative bookstores in the 1980s and 1990s for fear of outing yourself or being harassed. In fact, lesbians who thought they were "courageously" beginning to be "represented" were actually a niche market for capital.[73] As literary scholar Alexandria Chasin writes, "If validation were all that gay men and lesbians missed, then enfranchisement might mean equality and market accommodation might mean freedom. If all gay men and lesbians were white and middle class, and if lesbians were men, property rights might be what they most needed."[74]

Lesbians then possessed a record high of five bars in lower Manhattan—Henrietta Hudson, Cubbyhole, Crazy Nanny's, Meow Mix, and Rubyfruit Bar & Grill—and a series of renowned party venues like Clit Club, Café Tabac, and Shescape, and unnamed parties at bars like Wonder Bar. The scarcity of comparable parties and bars in Uptown and Midtown Manhattan then or in days past—i.e., aside from a few spots like Julie's and Sahara, and the continually popular Latinx lgbtq bar Escuelita, which also just closed as I finished writing this book—made the Village star cluster shine all the brighter. Indeed, this may be the largest clustering of lesbian bars that ever existed in one city in the world at any given time. Jackie '85 related, "I spent a lifetime at the Community Center in meetings, political meetings. And then [after meetings], we'd go to the Clit Club. Which I guess was near-ish." For those who went out often, it also became apparent that the many lesbian-queer spaces and places still existed only on a weekly or monthly basis, which prompted the sensation of a queer space in dispossession and iteration rather than permanence. In 2019, the only two lesbian bars in Manhattan were Henrietta Hudson and Cubbyhole. Both were founded in the 1990s and continue to serve as two of the brighter stars of lesbian-queer constellations by which to navigate the "lgbtq" Village and the white cis-heteropatriarchal sea of the greater city.

## The 2000s: Queers against and within the Manhattan Machine and Its Pinkwashing

In the mid-2000s, as more and more lgbtq people reaped the mixed blessings of pinkwashing, queer theorists David Eng, Jack Halberstam, and José Esteban Muñoz penned an influential article titled "What's Queer about Queer Studies Now?" They wrote, "If mainstream media attention to queer lives and issues has helped to establish the social and legal foundation for the emergence of gay marriage, family, and domesticity, what are the social costs of this new visibility?"[75] Homonormativity promised relief to white, middle-class, cisgender lesbians and gays acting "normal" by claiming a "just like one of us" assimilationist status: nestling in the arms of property ownership, privatization, gentrification, consumerism, and other forms of neoliberal racial capitalism.[76] As participants' stories related, homonormativity was not new and often not so simple.[77] Those stories grew more pronounced in the 2000s along with debates about who truly had queer interests at heart.

Participants often mentioned the Human Rights Campaign (HRC) gay and lesbian lobbying group as long epitomizing the cis-homonormative element of the movement, but many of my white 2000s-generation participants felt they had no other recourse but to financially and socially join in. White, middle-class Kristene '04 said, "It's pretty hard coming out in 2005 when you don't have the Lesbian Avengers . . . or you're too old to do GLYNY [Bisexual, Gay, Lesbian, and Transgender Youth of NY]."[78] After listing organization after organization that had shut its door and/or run out of money, she said, "HRC was my only option. At least they were doing *something*."

Belying the notion that activism was just a thing of the past, Jackie '85 shared with her 1980s-generation co-participants, "I think for us, in the eighties . . . [we were] coming out in a moment that was more conservative culturally, more homophobic, more racially divided. . . . And this is why I think it was easier for us—to get involved in that kind of activism, for me, at least because I didn't have a myth of progress." To which Wanda '85 replied, "Right. Which begets complacency." I am unsure if Kristene was merely complacent, though, when up against the forces of media, tourism, and the nonprofit industrial complex. The multimillion-dollar budget of the HRC allowed them to take center stage (often literally at concerts and galas they sponsored) and dominate the movement's message and focus. I remember my own awakening when I eagerly attended the Millennium March in DC and the accompanying HRC-sponsored Equality Rocks concert thereafter (featuring Melissa Etheridge, Tipper Gore, Ellen DeGeneres, George Michael, Chaka Khan, and Garth Brooks, among others), only to find my search for radical community had been repackaged into hundreds of mass-produced rainbow goods and a marriage/military movement.[79] As many of my 1980s- and 1990s-generation participants wondered: where was the radical difference queerness claimed to celebrate?

White, working middle-class Faith '03 was thirteen years old and not yet out when Ellen DeGeneres came out on national TV in 1997, the same year the first iteration of the Avengers disbanded. Like the rest of her generation, she encountered everyday places where she recognized others as outwardly queer—middle- and upper-class, primarily

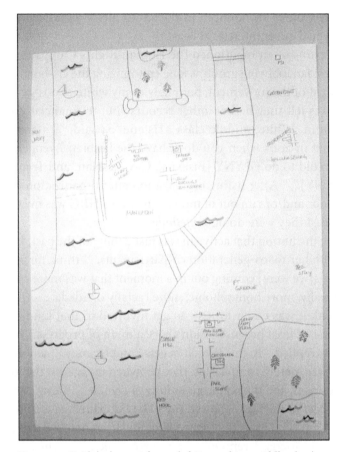

Figure 2.9. Faith '03's mental map (white, working middle-class)

white spaces (reflecting her own identity). Her mental map recorded a date at the PS1 contemporary art museum, and acknowledging or spotting other queers at Trader Joe's ("one of the gayest places") and the Park Slope Food Co-op ("also gay") (figure 2.9). The streets Faith walked down on which she saw others like her, around the aforementioned places, were also part of the lines and stars of her constellation. The wider, expanding stars of lesbian-queer spaces are still connected, thereby forming constellations in the invisible lines she walks and rides to navigate between them. Yet gone (again) from Faith's map is the visible sense of connection evoked by the line Sally drew to connect the

Village and the Lower East Side or disconnection as seen in Naomi's line down the center of her map. Race, class, gender, and generation help us read the ways that structural oppressions and generational moment structure constellations.

Framed through her white, middle-class privilege, Faith's experience of places in which to socialize and shop rather than organize (as she saw it) made few places "gay": "I didn't really have a coming out map because I didn't really do anything gay." Similarly, white, middle-class Kristene '04 professed a post-gay politics about her coming out when she said, "I'm no different than any other person." In fact, the use of identities such as the political "queer" along with the reactionary "post-gay" both suggest that sexual orientation and lgbtq places such as particular neighborhoods no longer defined a person's identity. However, both women frequented queer spaces and mourned the closing of Cattyshack, a lesbian bar in Brooklyn, as a personal loss. Later on, Faith looked at the places she included in her map and added, "These are almost all bars [the Cubbyhole, Henrietta Hudson, and Metropolitan, and the Heathers party] . . . with the exception of the LGBT Center and Bluestockings." When she found out that Cattyshack, the first lesbian bar she went to in the city, had just closed a few weeks prior, she was in shock: "Shut. Up. I was just there, like, for, for—are you serious?! Cattyshack closed?!! . . . Oh my God!" To Kristene, it was "a place [she] could go if I wanted to be around gay people." Yet as white, cisgender, feminine women coming out in the 2000s, Faith and Kristene evoke a paradoxical space of claiming a post-gay identity: people whose white privilege and class status can override their sexual identity while desiring lgbtq spaces.

To be clear, I am not chastising younger generations for their lack of activism—though some of my older participants did, often while no longer engaging politically themselves. Instead, I hope these stories show what they were up against, and how complicated this time was. Bailey '95 remarked that, as access to public spaces and the number of lesbian-specific public-private spaces waned, there were always other venues: "And now there are WNBA games and people go out after that.[80] There's no *activism* in the same way, but there's like activities usually . . . [and] people are still outside flyering." In the face of ever-increasing gentrification, the paradox of belonging/visitation makes things more tenuous and complicated for lgbtq people—and even more so for queers of color and working-class and poor queers—seeking their Oz. As documentarian Marlon Riggs said about the racism and exoticization he experienced as a gay Black man in San Francisco's Castro neighborhood, "Something in Oz and me was amiss, but I tried not to notice."[81] Scholars continue to write of the mutual, ongoing exoticization and exclusion of Black, brown, Latinx, Asian, Native American, and Indigenous people, and people from the Global South from such gayborhoods.

Many lgbtq activists fought back against the mainstream nonprofit industrial complex, through which volunteerism and philanthropy purportedly replaced the deconstructed welfare state of the mid- and late twentieth century with a limited range of services for a limited population.[82] At the same time, queer identity, increasingly prevalent in the 1990s and 2000s, afforded a claim to radicality for many of my participants that was incongruous with gay and lesbian acceptance. Queers for Economic Justice (QEJ) launched in 2002 and their founders, the Queers for Economic Justice Network, held meetings at the Center before working from a founder's home and then securing a space of their own. They espoused anticapitalist, gender-liberated platforms, as expressed on one flyer: "Capitalism got you down? Do gender binaries cramp your style? Get rowdy with queer fists!"[83] QEJ's fists were policy oriented: they took the unique approach of producing research at the intersection of issues of policing, homelessness, incarceration, poverty, and racism.[84] QEJ and other new New York City organizations like it—the Audre Lorde Project, Sylvia Rivera Law Project, FIERCE, and Ali Forney Center, among others—sought to respond to the needs of working-class, poor, and homeless communities, especially communities of color and tgncp among them. As the HRC and other "well-resourced," majority-white, national organizations dominated, it became the work of local groups to address concerns of those who remain the most vulnerable to violence, including people of color, immigrants, refugees, disabled people, working-class and poor people, tgncp, youth, and/or the elderly.[85] While some 2000s-generation participants reveled in the coded secrecy of the HRC equality logo sticker, some of my participants also recalled clearly how the rainbow sticker was replaced by the less "in-your-face" equality logo sticker (a yellow equals sign on navy that premiered on a car near you en masse in the early 2000s).

Figure 2.10. *En Masse Sunners Seen from Pier 45*, 1982. Photo by Frank Hallam

The 2000s saw the 1990s-era expansion shrink as participants possessed fewer lesbian-queer spaces. They came to the Village and nearby
Lower East Side for bars like Meow Mix (which closed in 2004), Henrietta Hudson, Cubbyhole, Nowhere Bar, and Rubyfruit Bar and Grill
(which also closed as I was conducting my research), parties like Starlette on Sunday nights at the Starlight Bar and Monday women's night at
cowboy bar Doc Holliday's, and, of course, the Center. But if the Center
was the queer North Star of the Village, the Christopher Street Pier—
known as "the Pier" or "the Piers" to lgbtq New Yorkers and repeat local
visitors—was the star that shines just as bright, if you knew where to
look in the night (figures 2.10 and 2.11). The Pier juts out into the water,
toward the equally (gentrified) bright shores of New Jersey, beckoning
those less welcome across the river to the shores of Manhattan. (The
Pier was talked about with so much reverence and/or nostalgia across
generations, that I capitalize it here.) Even with the rise of the internet and smart phones, the Pier continued to be a well-known gathering
spot, social space, and cruising ground for lgbtq people as it had been
throughout the twentieth century. While some saw this space as belonging primarily to gay men in the past, particularly white gay men, Black

Figure 2.11. FIERCE protest at Pier 40 and FIERCE rally poster, 2008.
Photo by *The Villager*

participants who came out in the 1980s through the mid-1990s mentioned it often as a uniquely welcoming public space for all lgbtq people, particularly those of color:

NAOMI '89: I remember going . . . and we'd walk for hours . . .

WANDA '85: Or you'd stand still and talk shit!

BAILEY '95: People would put up *music.*

WANDA: Yeah, there's a boom box! And queens were voguing down! [*vogues*] . . .

BAILEY: A *lot* of sex. Rats, too. The Pier was *enormous.* Before you had just these huge wooden planks and you could sit on the edge. You could jump in the water if you wanted!

WANDA: Imagine the most fabulous broken dregs. The most fabulous Blacks. The very young Black skinny boys with cheekbones to die for. Just straightening their hair. And then totally cracked. And then to the big Mohawk fabulouso. It ran the gambit. Big bad motherfuckers. . . . A gay man cursing out a lesbian. And back and forth! . . . an aggressive getting up all in the face of *cops.* Everybody just be like, "Whatever!"

NAOMI: It was dark. There were no lights. . . . So sometimes you'd just—the cops would just come and like put the lights on. And you'd be like, [*strikes freezing pose*] [*group laughter*].

As backdrop to scenes from queer media classics like the drag documentary *Paris Is Burning* and the Village People's "YMCA" music video,
the Pier, and places like it, were a space for validation and gravity of
innumerable queer lives, a public sort of room of one's own to determine
who they are. The vibrant life of the Pier represents a rare, long-standing
lgbtq space where people across races and classes could come into contact for prolonged periods of time.[86]

The Pier became one of the last places for cross-racial and -class interaction and public sex in the homeland of queer life. By the turn of
the century, what remained of the rotting Pier had become a particular
gathering place for poor lgbtq youth of color who possessed no other
informal spaces for connection and belonging. Two white, working-class
participants spoke about how queer youth of color, especially homeless
trans youth, were targeted:

> KATE '03: And now the kids at the Piers, sort of the—what's the
> phrase? What was Giuliani's phrase?
> HOLLY '03: [*using air quotes*] "Quality of life."[87]
> KATE: [*sarcastically*] Quality of life, ha, yeah. Like kids being harassed
> and arrested on the Piers . . . where are they gonna go? And *whose* life?

In the 2000s, the multimillion-dollar, private-public partnership
Hudson River Park Trust sought to redesign and upgrade the rotting
Pier using private funding to determine usage plans and maintain public lands. But such a redesign wasn't for queer youth of color, or lgbtq
adults, but instead aimed to improve property values for primarily
white residents, and increase the number of high-priced condominiums, trendy businesses, and tourists in the area. As Hanhardt writes
about the Pier specifically and the rest of the Village generally, the suc-
cessors to the lgbtq undesirables and "deviants" of the 1970s Village
were still harassed and persecuted in the new millennia if they were
not white and middle-class.[88] The Neutral Zone and Hetrick-Martin
Institute drop-in centers that supported lgbtq youth of the 1990s had
closed in the neoliberal paring down facilitated by the nonprofit industrial complex.[89]

In 2006, FIERCE (Fabulous Independent Educated Radicals for
Community Empowerment), a radical lgbtq youth of color group,

began the Safe Place to Organize Together (S.P.O.T.) campaign to stop the drastic renovations of the Pier, encouraging lgbtq nonresidents and residents to lay claim to the historic site and the entire Village neighborhood more generally.[90] Unfortunately, the renovations proceeded and the Pier was closed to the public for years. When the Pier reopened in 2008 as the Hudson River Park, police began circling on Segways before, during, and after the park's 1 a.m. curfew. I watched this racism, classism, and transphobia play out one late night in 2009 when tgncp youth of color were especially targeted, and the police ignored the white, thirty-something bodies of my femme date and my white, trans butch self. A few months later at Pride, in humidity and high temps, I stood with friends for hours among a crushing throng of sweaty lgbtq bodies, mostly Black and brown, waiting to access the cool breeze of the Pier—but they kept it closed for a private event. In step with the citywide privatization of public parks and services, white, adult, cisgender, middle-class lgbtq people were granted more acceptance citywide and found stars to gather around other than bars, parks, and organizations. Desperate for the community and space to spread out among others queers, I sensed that the Pier may never come back to lgbtq youth of color. After the expansion of lesbian-queer visible proximity in the 1990s, the intensified sprawl of gentrification in the 2000s was a supernova that exploded the clustering of lesbian-queer places.

While five of my participants mentioned having sex on the Pier in the 1980s and 1990s, Wanda '85 had recently and unsuccessfully tried to do it again. Gloria '83 replied, "They're too well lit!," referring to the lights that once dimmed—to afford what historian George Chauncey called "privacy that could only be had in public" for gay men in the early twentieth century—which now stayed turned on (in the wrong way) all too long.[91] As I witnessed street lighting brighten the dark, small, gentrifying streets of New York during the Giuliani era, I also observed Mayor Bloomberg's corporatized engine of police surveillance fill the Pier with even more blinding lights to further police lgbtq youth of color, sex workers, drug users, and homeless people.[92] The lights that literally shone so bright often blocked out the constellated light of the Pier for queers who sought to use it. Afro-Caribbean Tre '02 told me that most queer of color youth she knew had migrated into the crowds of Times Square, but the police continued to regulate, harass, and arrest them there too. The lines of queer of color constellations were again required to reorient themselves to navigate the world that white cis-heteropatriarchy defined. Indeed, "non-white, non-middle-class, non-gender-normative queer and trans people are *invisible* as good gay citizens and consumers."[93] The anonymity and acceptance of difference afforded in city life play an equal role in shaping the urban landscape as well, and changes in surveillance and technology greatly shifted this possibility over my period of study.[94]

A couple dozen blocks east on the Lower East Side, the giant glass window of Bluestockings Bookstore invokes openness and visibility to bustling Allen Street. The volunteer-organized, co-op bookshelves still feature labels such as Global Justice, Transgender Studies, Feminist Masculinity, Police & Prisons, Queer Studies, and Feminisms, Violence, & Trauma.[95] White, working middle-class Kate '03 shared that "though it's no longer specifically a women's bookstore, it's still very feminist and a queer-friendly space." Participants in the 2000s generation felt at home there, finally seeing so many feminist and queer texts in one bookstore.

Yet participants who had come out in the 1990s and earlier bemoaned Bluestockings' shift from an explicitly feminist bookstore to a radical bookstore in the 2000s. I still frequented the bookstore but shared in the sense of loss. While book clubs, spoken word gatherings, conferences, and stitch-and-bitch circles persevered, the depth of its queer and feminist devotions, as well as its commitment to women generally, wavered in the eyes of my participants who had come out around the time Bluestockings shifted its focus from the concerns of women foremost. ("It used to be gayer," Faith '03 had heard.) As 1980s-generation participants pointed out, younger women and tgncp had never experienced a *world* of feminist bookstores. Antimilitarization, antixenophobic, socialist, and anarchist conversations took center stage in post-9/11 city politics and laid the groundwork for the Occupy movement, while also contributing to Bluestockings' redefinition. For some, the star of Bluestockings had faded; others felt it still burned bright. This generational distinction shows that constellations are read differently based on where, who, and when you are coming from to see them.

And then there was the redefinition of gender itself and, with it, debates around the places and people that "count" among their constellations. The lesser number of visible butches and increasing number of passing trans men (although some people were and are still both) contributed to changing the signposts for queerness away from essentialized lesbian/ woman identities. The loss of women's spaces weighed more heavily on 1980s- and 1990s-generation participants, who often placed the blame for this loss on what I call the female-to-male or FtM trans-surge. As Tre '02 put it: "That's what I think has defined our time! Right? The whole trans is the new movement." With greater availability to hormones and surgeries, as well as activism, positive media, and digital and in-person support networks, more people assigned female at birth began to transition and/ or identify as transgender or gender non-conforming.

The 1970s lesbian feminist rhetoric of "women-only" spaces required redefining and reworking, and sometimes closing, lesbian spaces, and creating non-gender-specific queer spaces. Butch, middle-class Chris '86—who also identified as trans in our phone intake—asked, "Where have all our butch brothers gone?" expressing the sense of loss many older generations felt in the FtM trans-surge, which contained a mix of transphobia and a sense of loss for a certain lesbian geography and "community" definition. The dispersal of trans stories and knowledge afforded piecemeal sight to guiding stars. (Around midnight one drunken evening, I was invited to take T [testosterone] with some fellow butches after dancing on the bar at Doc Holliday's women's night. I replied in all seriousness, "I just *adore* Earl Grey." My friend suggested I attend their gathering another time, as I was clearly unaware that I had been invited into an underground hormone exchange.) The constellations of old required attention to apparent and underlying transphobia, and reorienting claims to sisterhood as a catchall for a community that still had never fully attended to the politics of race, class, or gender.

Participants drew on feminist terms and ideas to discuss the patriarchy and misogyny of catcalls, threats, verbal harassment, and other forms of rape culture. Yet they rarely granted their own stories a place in the same sense of structural violence. Ironically, my participants focused on the harassment and violence faced by gay and queer men. Quoting an article by planner Micky Lauria and queer geographer Lawrence Knopp, feminist geographer Tamar Rothenberg wrote in 1995 that "'women have always been given somewhat more latitude to explore relationships of depth with one another than have men.' Therefore, gay males may feel more of a need for their own territory, a safe haven, than might lesbians."[96] My participants concurred about the limits to expressing public affection. I reread these sentiments through the lens of cis-heteropatriarchy: by the 1990s and 2000s, lesbianism in public was highly sexualized while public displays of affection by gay men were scorned. In other words, my white, cisgender participants described how the heterosexual male gaze and hypersexualization of—or inability to recognize—their bodies actually protected them at times from seeming available to men. My Black and Latinx participants described some protection in some crowds, but many men still assumed access to their bodies as they were denigrated, hypersexualized, and regulated.[97]

Popular representations of gay male neighborhoods as seen in the UK's *Queer as Folk* (as well as the US version) paint a world in which "gay male sexuality becomes [recognized as] mature through spatial claiming and territorialization."[98] As property ownership indicates the maturity of both individuals and groups, the privileged patriarchal viewpoint of elite, white, wealthy-enough capitalist society defines the conditions imagined to determine (spatial) liberation. Mixed-race/Black, working-middle-class Bailey '95, who worked at a bar, recalled, "The men, they go out, they spend money, they make money. So they're going to have more." Since the 1990s, the capitalist engines of city tourism sponsored "advertising campaigns, sales missions, and special events," and collaborated "with property developers in public-private partnerships to build hotels and retail malls, and finance convention centers, arts venues and sports arenas."[99] "Lgbtq" tourism and the finances poured into it almost always targeted white, middle-class or often upper-class gay men.[100] The image of an all-gender and all-race lgbtq neighborhood shone as a beacon of belonging under a pretense of ownership, but the lived, everyday constellations were more fragmented, usually temporary, almost always rented, and often white, male-owned, with sexuality unspecified although implied.

By the late 2000s, the public and even lgbtq people—including my participants—could not yet recognize constellations as the academy and media often focused on statistics that demonstrated proof of lgbtq neighborhoods, and, in tandem, the gay American Dream success story. In a now heavily Disneyfied and ever more gentrified New York City, it often felt like any sort of difference would be instantly commodified and commercialized to serve a cheery version of a city.[101] Even as she called the Village "ours," African American, middle-class Naomi '89 bemoaned how lgbtq people, especially Black and Latinx and poor and working-class women and tgncp, had begun to disappear from the increasingly sanitized, simplified, and (still) for sale streets of the Village. She said, "I did write 'Christopher Street *in general*' [on my map]. . . . I guess it's hard because I'm in the area now and like, 'Where's all the gay?'"

## Our Very Own Oz, Still over the Rainbow

What then about the Village is so gay, so lesbian, and/or so queer? The lights and lines of lesbian-queer constellations, dim and bright, vintage and only just emerging, continued to instill a sense of the Village as a queer homeland. The greatest clustering of lgbtq places—including the always important lesbian bar—has been and continues to be in Greenwich Village. Most lgbtq Americans are still without full legal protections against workplace, housing, or other discrimination, and so the Village provides a queer homeland—under the veneer of lgbtq neighborhood liberation—for what political scientist Stephen M. Engel terms "fragmented citizens."[102]

It would be absurd to think that we, queers, still don't need a home, our very own Oz. Yet, "home" need not take the traditional form of the property-owned neighborhood. Indeed, Rose writes that women—and surely tgncp as well—can refuse to "already be mapped by someone else," if they "depend on a sense of an 'elsewhere' for [our] resistance . . . [somewhere] beyond patriarchy."[103] It is both absurd and violent that queers are denied recognition of the way they produce space in constellations, and instead it is only the claims to long-term properties and neighborhoods that matter. Reading the queer landscape for constellations reveals more clearly how lesbians and queers continue to resist and rework oppression, are resilient in the face of injustice, and can even be complicit in practices of injustice as they seek their liberation.

Many participants saw New York City as affording the time-honored urban traits of anonymity, possibility, and tolerance of difference—but all noted the restrictions that women and tgncp face in cities. Even in the early 1990s, geographer Gill Valentine found that spaces central to lesbians' lives such as the parental home and workplace, as well as mixed lgbtq bars more often populated by gay men, were spaces in which lesbians could not feel safe, let alone comfortable.[104] White, Armenian, working middle-class Maral '02 still lived at home and had not come out to her ultra-religious, conservative parents. She felt certain they would disown her. She explained the stress of being out in public to her co-interviewees:

> I still don't feel safe, even in New York City. I remember when I was first coming out I didn't even feel safe walking down Gay Street [in the West Village] holding my girlfriend's hand. . . . My dad is a cab driver so every time a cab would pass by, I'd be like, "Fuck! Is that my Dad?! *Is that my Dad?!?!?!*"

Her co-participants, across races and classes, replied with exclamations of "Whoa!" "That is so stressful!" and "God!" When urban planning activist Jane Jacobs described her "eyes on the street" notion of "natural surveillance" that supported city life in her home neighborhood of Greenwich Village, she certainly did not have Maral and other queers in mind. Jacobs saw the area as being by, for, and about its white, middle-class, cisgender, and heterosexual residents.[105] In sum, what is "ours" has always been tenuous.

A neighborhood in which few working- and middle-class lesbians and queers continue to live, and few lesbians and queers of color *ever* lived, requires a rethinking of what is "ours" as it plays out in the paradoxical space of belonging/visitation. As sociologist Theodore Greene writes, like lgbtq adults' "chosen families," "queer street families affirm the symbolic value of gay neighborhoods in an era in which greater social, political, and legal recognition of same-sex marriage and 'LGBT families' has called the salience of gay neighborhoods into question."[106] In a 2010 QEJ-sponsored study, lgbq and tgncp homeless youth of color in New York City reported police were involved in over 40 percent of the incidents of discrimination against them; 29 percent reported being strip-searched and 19 percent physically assaulted.[107] Race, racism, and classism mark the Village's territorial borders—as seen through the shifting maps of Naomi's, Sally's, and Faith's constellations over the years.

On a warm August night in Greenwich Village in 2006, seven working-class, Black and Latinx women and tgncp from a working-class, Black neighborhood in Newark, New Jersey, were verbally harassed by a middle-aged, Black man—he yelled insults including "Let me get some of that!" "Fucking dykes," and, "I'll fuck you straight, sweetheart."[108] The women responded verbally and then physically fought back when the man began choking Renata Hill, and Patreese Johnson used a knife she carried for protection. Fox News pundit Bill O'Reilly picked up the story that "violent lesbian gangs" were now spreading across the United States and "raping young girls."[109] Tara '06 described how O'Reilly's coverage made her feel even more sick and angry about the event, recalling how he "even said: 'Watch out for your daughters. They're beating up "poor" guys in the street.'" Poignantly, those who are felt to be out of place are often forced to be kept "in their place." Lane writes, "In other words, while queers of colors have always been there, . . . they will be made to feel 'out of place' in white queer spaces, and they may be subject to exclusionary spatial practices on account of their race in addition to their gendered and sexualized embodiments."[110]

Four of the women, Venice Brown, Terrain Dandridge, Hill, and Johnson, were subsequently tried and convicted, and became known as the New Jersey Four (NJ4). The four spent two to seven and a half years in prison. The event played on longstanding racist and gendered fears of violent Blacks, as with the 1989 Central Park Jogger case. The latter involved five young, Black and Hispanic men who were tried and imprisoned for the brutal rape and beating of a young white woman, despite contrary DNA evidence. The boys were said to be "wilding," a term the media used to define an unprovoked gang assault on a stranger; they spent thirteen years in prison for a crime they did not commit. Five years after the release of the (now) adult men, a sensationalist *Daily News* headline read "Girls Gone Wilding," the accompanying story describing the NJ4 as "a gang of petite but ornery lesbians."[111] Reasserting the Central Park Jogger label of "wilding" was meant to strike a chord of fear in white New Yorkers, as were the "out of place" archetypes of both the racialized prison lesbian and "the perennial lesbian vampire routine" invoked in the story.[112]

When I conducted my research, the tendrils of prison violence that have always shaped lgbtq lives were unclear to me. For example, a 2015 survey of 1,118 lgbtq prisoners revealed that 85 percent had spent time in solitary confinement, over half had spent two years in solitary confinement, and queer and trans people of color were twice as likely to be placed in solitary confinement as their white counterparts.[113] The

United Nations categorizes solitary confinement as a form of torture. Further, the buildup of the carceral industrial complex deeply shapes the circuits of Black life not only inside prison walls but beyond, including neighborhoods like Crown Heights and Bed-Stuy, which are the focus of the next chapter, as family and friends are forced to negotiate the social, political, and economic situation of keeping those behind bars alive.[114]

On the one hand, tourist studies scholar Kevin Markwell writes that lgbtq identity has become increasingly bound to "neighborhoods and territories in which material and symbolic expressions of homosexuality are clearly visible" in cities marked as global gay and lesbian travel destinations in the 2000s.[115] On the other hand, Greene refers to nonresident lgbtq people in lgbtq neighborhoods as "vicarious citizens" who define a space as lgbtq by visiting its institutions.[116] My research shows that it is the lgbtq spaces *and* bodies *and* the social, political, and economic networks between them, present day *and* historical, that keep queer resistance, reworking, and resilience alive in the Village. Further, my participants' stories in this chapter show how the Village is relational to other nearby neighborhoods like the Lower East Side and so on, so that the lines of their constellations are easier to tread along to nearby stars in other neighborhoods. The steady swarm of queer bodies moving between queer and queer-friendly star-like places—personal and shared—re-constellates the Village as queer, day after day, protest after protest, Pride after Pride, Dyke March after Dyke March, hookup after hookup.

Acts of perpetual return, determined seeking, and adventurous wandering create the queer lines of constellations. Here, the Village is thus like other lgbtq neighborhoods in the early twenty-first century. Nash and Gorman-Murray find lgbtq neighborhoods now exist "as a 'place of arrival and return,' as a place for people to come out, and as a place for LGBT and queer people to gather for political and social protest."[117] And this arrival and return is highly racialized and classed within the city itself, as the visitors are often "bridge-and-tunnel" weekend visitors from other parts of New York City or nearby Connecticut and New Jersey, alongside tourists from around the world. As anthropologist Martin Manalansan writes, "The 'B and T' or 'bridge and tunnel,' which is a disparaging term used for the general population living outside Manhattan, is also deployed for queers of color from the 'outer' boroughs who are seen to frequent the venues in and inhabit the spaces of the 'out there.'"[118]

Bars, restaurants, stores, historic sites, walking/rolling tours, Pride and Dyke Marches, activist hotbeds, and actual hot beds feed not only the queer imaginary but the public's tendency to equate neighborhoods with citizenship. My participants' stories show citizenship is often more marginal and temporary. Beyond the bright rainbows and renowned lgbtq spaces, participants noted the discrete signs of mutual recognition that are still used to queer the Village. In particular, participants described how lesbians and queers read and cruise one another: eye contact, catching sight of a queer symbol on the body (Noelle '83's *Dykes to Watch Out For* button or the scrap of rainbow ribbon Ruth '90 wore for years, or the blue star tattoos, other tattoos, jewelry, or various piercings of many participants), being masculine in appearance, holding hands, sharing a kiss, or sharing even more.

My participants rely on these markers because women's and tgncp's bodies are rarely together en masse in the Village. As women and tgncp, they do not possess any consistent or full claim to public space. Further, Podmore states that "lesbian forms of territoriality at the urban scale have been relatively 'invisible' since their communities are constituted through social networks rather than commercial sites."[119] Even as they are policed, refused entry, or cannot afford to stay, lesbians and queers both resist a city and state that marginalizes and oppresses them, even as they turn a profit for the city by projecting it as a gay-friendly locale. Neither gentrification nor commerce is a tenable plan for the social and spatial liberation of urban lesbians and queers. My work thus offers a way to theorize the spaces of these women and tgncp as the spatialized networks and overlapping experiences in star-like places and line-like paths of constellations, rather than prioritizing property ownership and lesbian-oriented commercialism to mark out territorial neighborhoods.

Lesbian bars had begun to close in large numbers across the United States as I conducted my research in 2008 and 2009, and my participants read the loss of their spaces against the retention of gay male spaces. In fact, in the years since I completed this study, gay and queer male neighborhoods faced patterns of displacement, homogenization, and rebranding common to high-end neighborhoods throughout the 2010s, and gay bars frequented by mostly white patrons began to close as well.

Throughout the period of my study, the spaces of gay men of color and poor and working-class gay men (again) were unremarked upon, as they shut down in an effort to "clean up" the city.[120] Implied was the fact that gay and queer men of color's cruising grounds—rarely if ever recognized as part of a "neighborhood"—were always itinerant and under attack as they faced policing and harassment.[121] As (white, middle-class) gay men's territorial holds ebb, the queer feminist work of producing lesbian-queer constellations becomes more legible and important in sustaining queer culture and politics.

Among its peer lgtbq neighborhoods—such as the Castro, Schöneberg, Soho, West Hollywood, Boystown, Oxford Street, and the Gayborhood—the Village is still a unique case. With so little lgbtq history taught or shared in the media, the 2010s mainstream representation of that history was reduced to a few spaces, most especially Stonewall, the Village, and New York City itself. This popular mainstream telling of lgbtq history as an urban-only phenomenon recalls anthropologist Kath Weston's accounting for the US "get thee to the big city" narrative (often in regard to San Francisco and New York City) that was fed to younger lgbtq people, inspiring, again, an urban-only "sexual imaginary."[122] Into the 2010s, the attention paid to ACT UP and (always) to Stonewall in films—some whitewashing the history, others absorbing its racial, trans radicality—linked queer publics back to the New York City origins of both.[123] And then there is the annual reiteration of the Village as queer homeland across the world in Pride marches and celebrations that mark the anniversary of the Stonewall riots, and every New York City Pride historically and physically leads back to the Stonewall Inn and Sheridan Square Park/Christopher Park on Christopher Street come June.[124] The anticapitalist and antiracist Dyke March—which still takes place without a permit the day before Pride—is a line of dykes streaming down Fifth Avenue that finishes in Washington Square Park, near the Village's eastern edge. Notably, the most massive astronomical stars similarly live fast, die young, and leave an explosive course.

Like the Castro of San Francisco, once "the seedy and marginal downtown core" of the 1950s and 1960s, the Village has become the social, political, and economic "heart" of New York City.[125] I long ago lost count of the number of tourists I met—certainly from every continent except Antarctica—who asked directions of gay-looking me as I walked the

Village in the many years I lived in New York City. After my conservative cousins admitted they never had met another gay person, I took them to the Village as a representation of queer life. Among other places there, I took them specifically to the gay Oscar Wilde Bookstore, which closed in 2009, as well as, on the Lower East Side, to Bluestockings, which still stands as Bluestockings Bookstore, Café & Activist Center. Where there was once a network of hundreds of US feminist and gay bookstores, less than a dozen feminist bookstores remained in the United States in 2019, and only a handful of gay bookstores.[126]

In 2017, a *New York Times* article declared that the Village had "undergone 'straightening' recently."[127] None of my participants even questioned their role as visitors to—rather than residents of—the Village, likely because it was and remains wildly unaffordable. By the mid-2010s, the Greenwich Village median asking rent was estimated to be 20 percent higher than the citywide average, and the Village's median household income of $121,178 was more than double the citywide figure.[128] When poverty is often bound to the lives of Black, brown, Indigenous, and Latinx people, it is not surprising that the wealthy Village was recently ranked forty-ninth out of fifty-four New York City neighborhoods in terms of racial diversity.[129] All the while, the smaller clusters of lesbian-queer spaces are scattered across the city, making the "rite of passage" of "queer pilgrimage"—rather than homecoming—an everyday occurrence.[130] Constellations are still overlapping and most prominent in lgbtq spaces and areas, but their gentrified dispersal reduces the sense of community and activist urgency that proximate residency affords.

Through the rise of the AIDS epidemic, and the ensuing gentrification, militarization, corporatization, and touristification of New York City into the new millennium, lesbians and queers suffered a constant series of disinvestments. But even as the Village increasingly became the Disney version of itself—refusing its own difference to commodify a pseudo–Main Street down Christopher and Hudson Streets that erases much of its own sexual past—I sense the Village will never fully straighten itself out. Constellations emerge through and against the neoliberal capitalist processes shaping the neighborhood that claims itself as the manifestation of the geographically imagined lgbtq village to New Yorkers, Americans, and the world.

3

# You vs. Us in Bed-Stuy and Crown Heights

It was a sweltering Thursday night in July, that time of year just after Pride when the humidity stifles New York City for the summer. I met six of my participants for a group interview, in which they created a multigenerational, lesbian-queer mental map of the city from their individual maps. The stars and lines they recorded were located in what are now primarily in white and extremely costly areas south of Manhattan's 96th Street and throughout northwest Brooklyn, a region increasingly understood as the queer, or at least lgbtq-friendly, hub of New York City.

After one white participant remarked that it was a shame that lesbian-queer places were spread out and often unknown to one another, Alex '98 and Yasmin '83, Afro-Caribbean and Latina respectively, pointed out that they had included places beyond this primarily white map of "queer" New York (figures 3.1 and 3.2). Alex then said, "There's no way that the world [of queer places] can combine themselves because [they're] so far removed. There are so many places in Brooklyn . . . : they're deep in Bed-Stuy, they're deep in Brownsville, . . . places that nobody in this room would go." She paused, and then added, "Because you don't want to die, or whatever. But that's where the girls go." Now compare Alex's powerful comment to a moment from another interview composed of only white women and transgender and gender non-conforming people (tgncp), in which Jess '96 talked of the importance of "queer community" across races and classes. She then said, "Gentrification became an issue because queer spaces are gentrified out. . . . Yet, also, gentrification within queer communities is a way of making it accessible to a large part of us."

By "you," Alex is speaking to her four white co-participants and me as white convener; with "us," Jess claims to be speaking for a "large part" of the "queer community," but is merely reproducing the perspective of white privilege. This you/us dichotomy illustrates the raced and racist construction of lesbian-queer geographies, and how neighborhoods are mapped (or not mapped) as "queer." The stories of my participants of

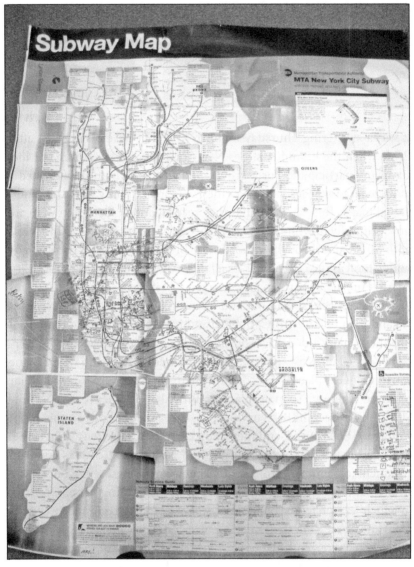

Figure 3.1. Group mental map of Yasmin '83, Susan '92, Sally '96, Alex '98, Holly '03, and Isabelle '06—full map

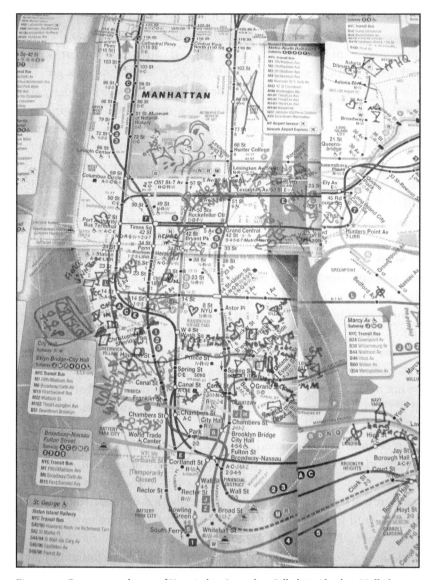

Figure 3.2. Group mental map of Yasmin '83, Susan '92, Sally '96, Alex '98, Holly '03, and Isabelle '06—detail of Manhattan and northeast Brooklyn

color—Black and Latinx women and tgncp, as well as some women and tgncp who date them—reveal how they negotiate their disidentifications from (white) queer New York in order to find their way to and produce those stars and celestial objects "where the girls go." Disidentification, as defined by performance studies scholar José Esteban Muñoz, is a way that queers of color survive by "managing and negotiating historical trauma and systemic violence of . . . the cultural logics of heteronormativity, white supremacy, and misogyny [that] . . . undergird state power" on an everyday basis.[1] In other words, to disidentify is to negotiate identifications and/or nonidentifications with different sexualities, experiences, races, interests, and so on—at times to fit in, at times to survive, and sometimes switching at a moment's notice.

Many of my white participants ignored or were unaware of the role and reproduction of white privilege. White participants acknowledged they were complicit in but largely unable to stop the violent displacement of people of color and working-class and poor people and their spaces, ranging from places like lesbian bars and parties to book clubs and basketball games, in and beyond neighborhoods of color. The "ability to not to have to take other people's existence seriously" and the "ability not to have to pay attention"—for example, Jess's claim that processes of gentrification create "queer community"—are the tactics of white privilege.[2]

In attending to the experience of participants in and in relation to neighborhoods of color in this chapter—primarily Black neighborhoods—I am able to forefront lesbians and queers of color's resistance, reworking, and resilience—primarily that of Black lesbians and queers—and to confront the white norms that structure most lesbian-queer spaces. I am keen not to repeat the narrowing and racist practice of assuming women and tgncp of color are merely to be found in Black neighborhoods, and to further the heretofore limited scholarship on Black lesbian and/or queer spaces.[3] Yet research does show that Black gays and lesbians tend to live in areas with higher proportions of Blacks, i.e., Black neighborhoods, much like Latinx and Asian and Pacific Islander lesbians and gays.[4] It follows that while there is some racial diversity in lgbtq and lesbian neighborhoods—among visitors much more so than residents, as I describe in chapter 2—these areas are primarily white. (It is also worthy of note that nearly 40 percent of the city's Black residents in the 1990s were immigrants or of immigrant descent.[5]) Further, neighborhoods of color are rarely read as queer in the mainstream media, again reconstituting the lgbtq subject as white.

In this chapter, I pay particular attention to Black women's and tgncp's experiences in and in relation to two of the most oft-mentioned neighborhoods in my research: predominantly African, Caribbean, West Indian, Black, and working-class Crown Heights and Bedford-Stuyvesant, or Bed-Stuy as New Yorkers call it (figure 3.3).[6] Crown Heights is also one-quarter white, primarily Orthodox Jewish. Including the surrounding and nearby north, east, and central Brooklyn neighborhoods of Flatbush, Clinton Hill, Fort Greene, Bushwick, Lefferts Gardens, and Brownsville, this area of Brooklyn was residence to one of the largest concentrations of Black people in the United States throughout my period of study (figure 3.4).[7] My participants of color also shared that there is a sense that you belong in Bed-Stuy and Crown Heights, especially if you are Black, African American, African, Caribbean, and/or West Indian—and more so if you pass within binary gender roles. They described the smells of fried chicken and Jamaican jerk spices that still fill the streets of Bed-Stuy and Crown Heights, alongside open-air fruit markets and dollar stores. Some local chains and one-off businesses still operated, even as an increasing number of high-end ice cream shops, new brunch spots, and hot yoga studios moved in. Still, they recalled how the sounds of hip-hop, R&B, reggae, and rap resounded from passing cars or open windows.

As for a Latinx person, my participants said that you may also be welcome but not feel exactly at home. And I already knew before they told me from my own experience that there is a strong likelihood that a white person may be read as an interloper, a threat, or both: police, gentrifier, property developer, truancy officer, social worker, etc. Some white participants presumed that women and tgncp of color felt at home in neighborhoods like Bed-Stuy and Crown Heights. In their stories, some participants of color described how they did feel at home, while others felt at times unwelcome or even disoriented, and some fluctuated between these feelings.

The ornately designed apartment buildings and brownstones of Bed-Stuy and Crown Heights built for upper-class and middle-class families

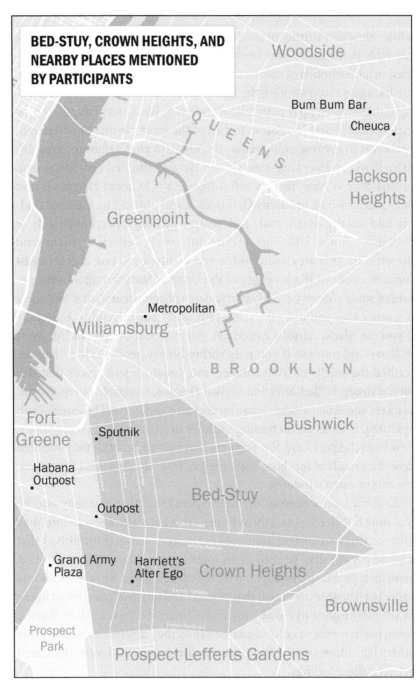

Figure 3.3. Map of Bed-Stuy, Crown Heights, and nearby places often mentioned by participants

in the late nineteenth century became, according to the *New York Times*, sought-after addresses for "back-to-the-city movement" proponents' "remodel" frenzy as early as the 1980s (figure 3.5). The same article reported, "Regarded for years as a dangerous ghetto, the central Brooklyn neighborhood now attracts many newcomers in search of affordable housing near the more prosperous Park Slope."[8] The pace of gentrification began to exponentially increase in the 2000s, with Bed-Stuy, Crown Heights, and other nearby neighborhoods of color losing over 10 percent of their Black population by 2010.[9] In Bed-Stuy, there was a significant 160 percent increase (from 5 to 13 percent) in the share of white residents between 1980 and 2010.[10]

In the multigenerational women and tgncp of color interview, my participants talked about the disconnection, frustration, anguish, and anger they often felt when listening to some white lesbians and queers, both in our conversations and in everyday life. In the middle of that conversation, two Black women turned to the assumptions that white lesbians and queers have demonstrated:

BAILEY '95: And so whiteness wasn't about ethnicity. It's about money and it's about access. And the most offensive thing to me about sitting in a room full of white people talking about sexuality is this one idea that it's so hard, that they were so disenfranchised, right? In some like amazing way—which, [*sighs*] that's unfair.

WANDA '85: Say it. Speak your mind.

BAILEY: But I feel like, it's to me—you know what? [*smacks fist into hand*] . . . If you look at the straight people in *my* community, *you* do not want to trade places with me. You do not want to have a bad education and work at Taco Bell and not be able to get up out. And be dealing with . . .

WANDA: Your second child!

BAILEY: [*nodding*]—all of the things that you have to deal with.

WANDA: Your man locked up!

BAILEY: [*continues nodding*] All of that, you know what I mean? You don't want that! And it's very hard because I go to [graduate] school now and like, you know, there's a gay group and I'm like, "That's good for them." Because let me tell you something, I'm not *just gay*. I'm biracial but I identify as Black. I have politics that are very particu-

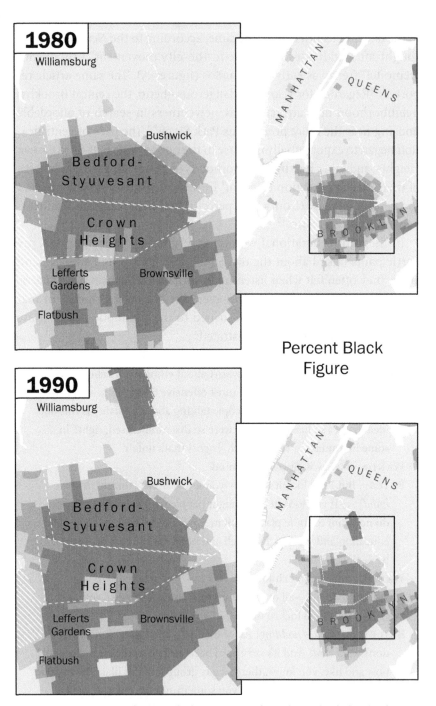

Figure 3.4. Census maps showing Black percentage of population (with details of Bed-Stuy and Crown Heights), 1980, 1990, 2000, and 2010

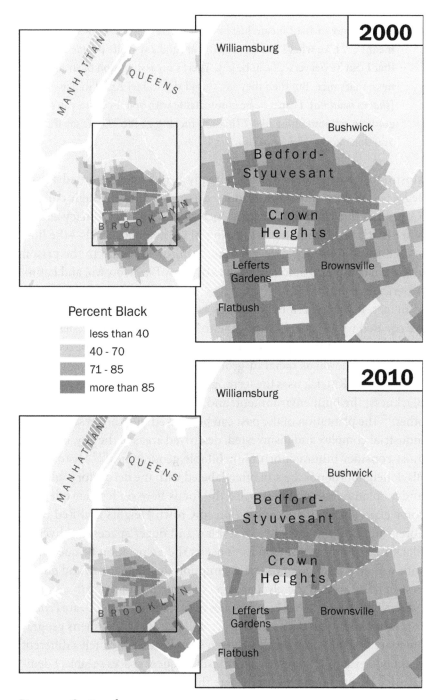

Figure 3.4. *Continued*

lar, you know what I mean. Just because *you're gay*, what does that mean? . . . Like what I like from being around gay white people is that I can be perverse, I can be gay. There's no assumption of straightness, that's nice. But then they say stupid shit to me! And I'm like [*shakes head no*], I can't . . . be comfortable with you. Because you're going to say something like, "That's so fucking ghetto." Don't say that. You don't know what you're saying.

Most of my participants of color already held bachelor's or advanced degrees and came to claim middle-class identities through college. Regardless, they witness and experience—in proximate intimacy among other Black people and in frequenting Black neighborhoods—the limited education, limited career options, and/or exposure to the prison industrial complex that touch the lives of many Black, brown, and Latinx Americans.

In fact, Bailey describes how Black lesbians' and queers' experiences are equated with spaces like the "ghetto."[11] Black participants described how this sense of belonging is fueled as much by practices of redlining and urban renewal as racial in-group identification. Black geographer Katherine McKittrick uses the term "plantation futures" to speak to how Blackness, the built environment, and the urban are bound to one another.[12] The plantation of the past can be tracked into the present prison industrial complex and disinvested, destroyed areas of the city, or "what most consider inhuman or uninhabitable geographies."[13] Historically Black neighborhoods are still often labeled with the derogatory "ghetto" under "plantocracy logics," hence the focus here on lesbian-queer of color experiences in and in relation to Crown Heights and Bed-Stuy. Foregrounding the existence of lesbian and queer spaces and lives in Black neighborhoods hopefully loosens the association of queerness with whiteness, and upends the assumption that lesbianism and queerness in these areas is merely a product of gentrification.

McKittrick writes that "geographies of black femininity . . . are *central to* how we know and understand space and place: black women's geographies are workable and lived subaltern spatialities, which tell a different geographic story."[14] To render Black lesbian-queer spaces seeable, I dedicate this chapter to describing "where the girls go." As American studies scholar Nikki Lane writes of Black queer women spaces in DC in the

Figure 3.5. Example of Bed-Stuy gentrification activism, *New York Daily News*, 2014

2010s, most Black queer women's spaces are composed of a "collection of networks and spaces those networks inhabit and produce . . . comprised of a set of constantly shifting, constantly moving scene spaces."[15] The scene in New York, like that in DC, ranged from clubs to lesbian film screenings, from performances by Black queer woman artists to burlesque shows, and from friends' parties to college basketball games. However, unlike many of the most often noted, publicized, and primarily white places in Greenwich Village, the Lower East Side, and Park Slope, this scene of "where the girls go" included stars and lines listed on maps or merely hinted at in these neighborhoods as well as Bed-Stuy, Crown Heights, or other historically Black neighborhoods.

My status as a white researcher means that my participants of color surely did not share everything they might have with me. At the same time, women of color were unable to share their experiences without describing what happens when they come up against whiteness, a systematic experience of stress and violence they detailed in our interviews. As critical social psychologist Michelle Fine writes, "Self and Other are knottily entangled. . . . When we opt, as has been the tradition, simply to write *about* those who have been Othered, we deny the hyphen."[16] In other words, my project to foreground the stories of lesbians and queers of color requires attending to the ways they navigate whiteness, and how white lesbians and queers at times perpetuate white privilege. The stories of my participants of color reveal how they relied on the practice of dis-identification to negotiate racism in queer spaces *and* heteronormativity, homophobia, patriarchy, and transphobia in spaces of color and white spaces, all the while maintaining their sense of self.

Drawing on McKittrick's point that "innovative black diaspora practices . . . spatialize acts of survival," I examine what it means to spatialize the queer of color survival strategies of Muñoz's disidentifica-tions.[17] I take a geographical reading of Muñoz's arguments that queers of color scramble and reconstruct encoded messages of "cultural texts" in their disidentifications, just as disidentifications also scramble and recode spaces.[18] Building from Muñoz's perspective, I found that Latinx women's and tgncp's stories sometimes complemented and overlapped with those of Black women and tgncp, so I include some of their stories as well. Traveling beyond the central places of white "queer" New York allows both "you" and "us" to see both the overlapping and interdependent and the unique and independent stars of constellations of lesbian-queer lives across the city.

## Home Is a Raced Place: Black Lesbian-Queer Spaces in the 1980s

A narrative of Black Brooklyn concretized at the end of the 1980s when the Bed-Stuy "ghetto" was immortalized in Spike Lee's film *Do the Right Thing*. The film records one day in the life of the neighborhood, when racism erupts into police brutality, Black murder, and, finally, a rebel-lion in the form of property destruction. On top of a city torn apart by drug wars, gang wars, and a "war on poverty," all of which just wreaked havoc upon people of color and the impoverished, HIV/AIDS arrived. By 1983, "AIDS and the medical, political, and social threats it poses had come to color all gay discourse."[19] That "color"-ing projected onto skin color as well, as white Chris '86 angrily recalled the stereotypes forced upon people living with AIDS: "If you're dying of AIDS, everyone knows

you're gay. And if you're not Haitian or a drug addict, you must be gay."
Chris speaks to the prevalent racist, colonial, ableist "4-H model" of
who was susceptible to the virus: homosexuals, hemophiliacs, heroin
addicts, and Haitians (and especially immigrants, refugees, and Blacks
and other people of color among them).[20] The Christian right, Reagan
administration, and mainstream media perpetuated the racialization
and pathologization of the disease by both stereotyping these groups
and folding them into each other. Like issues of poverty, gangs, and
drugs in the "ghetto," the mainstream (white) geographical imagination
similarly displaced AIDS as something that happened elsewhere from
whiteness.

Black/Cuban, middle-class Wanda '85 spoke with a group of white,
working middle-class, middle-class, and upper middle-class participants
in her 1980s-generation interview, including Chris '86 and Jackie '85,
who described antiracism and solidarity as core values of lesbian life:

> CHRIS: Race lines, class lines were crossed very easily in the groups
> of women I [was] among. I'm not saying that's the way it is for the
> whole world, but—
> WANDA: Why isn't it?
> CHRIS: It would be nice if it was still that way.
> WANDA: [*lightly sarcastic*] It would be *nice* if it was still *that way.*
> JACKIE: [*nodding vehemently*] Yes!
> CHRIS: It was such an improvement over the middle-class straight
> world I'd just left that it was amazing. It was mind-blowing, the way
> that people were respectful. Even if you didn't want to date someone,
> even if you thought someone was as homely as a broken picket fence,
> you wouldn't be rude. You wouldn't shun that person. You might take
> them out to coffee, you might hang out, do good work in the move-
> ment, whatever. People just treated each other like human beings.
> *Women* treated each other like human beings.

No white participants in the room seemed to notice Wanda's tonal tactic of disidentification with her white co-participants' nostalgia. While
Wanda fervently worked within the 1980s feminist and gay and lesbian
liberation movements, her tone implies that Chris and Jackie remained
attached to an idealized dyke politics that mutually transcended racism,

homophobia, and patriarchy, or, at times, at least saw difference as positive rather than negative. Both the ideal and reality of an antiracist dyke politics was the norm in the lgbtq community. In these narratives, it was lesbians (more than gay men, more than straight women) who, at times, disentangled themselves from the smog of patriarchal, racist capitalism.[21]

At the same time, I noticed that my participants' stories of their 1980s and 1990s geographies did in fact include more inter-race and -class socializing than those from subsequent years. This period was the height of the US AIDS epidemic and its immediate aftermath, which required and afforded organizing across race and class. Wanda recounted how AIDS galvanized her into a lifetime of activism, beginning with joining ACT UP:

> People were dying! There was an urgency! It was in the headlines of the paper that a prostitute was arrested because she had bit a cop, the arresting cop.[22] She was HIV positive or had AIDS—it was considered a felony . . . considering she has this deadly disease. So . . . I was like: "Oh my God. This shit is transmittable by fluids. Do you know how many motherfuckers visit prostitutes? Gay people. Straight people. Oh my God, DL [down low] people! Black people! How many of them are prostitutes? Oh my God! Black women! There's no defense! Brothers going back and forth into prison alone! Oh my God!" So I'm: "Okay, I'll be part of ACT UP! They're doing the most work. As soon as the gay boys are taken care of, we're gonna get down to the women. And it's gonna trickle down." . . . I was there with coffins! Blood throwing and shit! Got arrested. Got beat up by cops! And then they're finally going to let us do some work for the CDC [Center for Disease Control] on women's issues and we got that shit changed. Alleluia! Praise be! Now women can get insurance coverage if you have symptoms. Okay, that's awesome! [pauses] And then all that shit stopped [in the 1990s].

With a play on words, Wanda revealed how lgbtq politics worked against injustices—up to a point. Trickle-down economic policy was President Reagan's racist, classist, sexist rationale for cutting taxes for the wealthy and middle class with the promise that wealth would "trickle down" to the poor. In other words, Wanda was inspired to stand up for those that

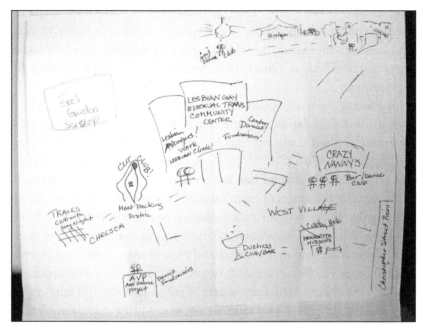

Figure 3.6. Wanda '83's mental map (Black/Cuban, middle-class)

such a trickle did not and would never reach. The breakdown of support among Black people for those with AIDS—seen as a gay men's or IV drug users' issue rather than an issue of racial justice—fractured the Black community along what political scientist Cathy Cohen describes as the "boundaries of blackness."[23] Those boundaries speak to some of the absences in participants' stories and maps, the interstellar medium between the stars of their constellations.

The connections that Wanda made in her activism reflected what many of my 1980s-generation participants envisioned in their constellations: as both spaces of coming together with other lesbians and queers, and spaces of coming apart over their differences. Brooklyn falls off of Wanda's map, which depicts stars primarily in southern Manhattan (as a central gay and lesbian locale, but also a primarily white area in the city), especially places related to the arts or activisms (figure 3.6). In her map, Wanda shows the key bars and parties of the 1980s and 1990s (Duchess, Henrietta's, Crazy Nanny's, Clit Club, Tracks), the LGBT Center and nearby Christopher Street Pier, and feminist Eve's Garden Sex

Shop, as well as her nearby college. The ability to make lesbian-queer of color spaces outside of the home was often limited. Later, Wanda would recount the segregation she experienced in mixed-race bars, even as she disidentified, as a mode of survival, from any resulting sense of displacement.

Lane found a spatiotemporal rhythm to Black queer women's spaces that worked around regulation and limitation in the 2010s in Washington, DC. For example, Black queer women's happy hours were on off-peak nights like Tuesdays.[24] With lesser access to financial and political resources, lesbians and queers of color had less recourse to produce their places in mainstream leisure spaces or create businesses, especially long-term places, meaning that the stars of their constellations often grew in the city's outer boroughs. With more distant stars to travel to and from, the lines of their constellations are that much longer and require more time, energy, and effort to forge. Further, prominent (white) lesbian-queer commercial establishments kept and still keep queers of colors spatially and temporally marginalized. As a Black gay male narrator shares to the camera in Marlon Riggs's 1989 film, *Tongues Untied*,

> There was a new club . . . we waited in line for *at least* fifteen minutes, all the while, the doorman . . . *watching us*. Ten Black men show . . . [and make the doorman] paranoid the [club] is *gonna tilt*. . . . We finally get to the door and [the doorman] says, with much condescension, "You know there's a *cover* to get in." Well, I tried to ignore her rudeness, and then she shot her arm out: "I need to see *three* pieces of ID." [*pauses*] I thought this shit was through.[25]

Gloria '83, who is white, attested to this racism in some lesbian bars: "There were a number of times there when I ran into situations where I'd be out with Black friends. And you couldn't get them in. They would have to show three kinds of ID to get into a bar." As mentioned in chapter 2, protests at and discrimination suits against the party Shescape in 1985 and protests at the bar Bacall's in 1991 fought against racist practices, and protests were led against other racist lesbian, gay, and queer venues in my participants' stories across generations.

At the same time, many of my white participants—sometimes the very same participants who brought up issues of racism—seemed oblivious to or denied their white privilege, including when it came to participants' "unintended" gentrification. White, Jewish, middle-class, femme Esther '87 talked about moving in with her girlfriend in the late 1980s, who had purchased and was restoring a house in a primarily working-class African American, African, West Indian, and Caribbean neighborhood. She found the experience to be a stressful hardship: "Can you imagine being the first lesbian couple in the neighborhood? . . . [My butch girlfriend] was the only white person on the street. And I moved in, and I'm the *second* white person on the street. She's butch and I'm femme. We're the lesbians." She went on, "It's all West Indian, Caribbean people and . . . it was *not* a nice place to live. Go to the grocery store and see how you're treated. It's like everybody knew who we were. . . . Where I lived, in my neighborhood, was not a safe place. . . . The neighborhood was a not a place where I went out. There wasn't a bar or things to do or neighbors to go do things with." Later on, Esther described herself as a "pioneer" that "settled" this neighborhood in Brooklyn—language often used in the 1980s and early 1990s, as I discuss in chapter 4—so that other (presumably white) lesbians who also needed access to affordable housing near other queers followed. As in Greenwich Village and Park Slope, lesbians and queers, primarily white and middle-class, clung to American Dream promises of neighborhood liberation to legitimate their gentrification. This settler colonial claim to the "frontier" recreates a tragic queer Manifest Destiny–like pattern of white imperialism.

At the same time, the public harassment and treatment Esther and other publicly visible queers experienced and experience, was not be bound to any neighborhood and people. As queer activist and scholar Amber L. Hollibaugh—a long-time resident of New York City and San Francisco—writes:

> We lived constantly with the rude looks and loud, bitterly spoken comments—in the restaurants where we ate, the stores where we bought our clothes and groceries. Insults could be flung at us as we walked along any street, at any time. Strolling together as a butch/femme couple, we were in an erotic, magnetic, moving target for all the sexual fear, envy, and ignorance of this culture. Our movements and our decisions were fraught with potential danger: unexpected visits to the emergency room, how to rent a motel room when we traveled, crossing a border between the

United States and Canada or Mexico, being busted at bars when the cops came for their weekly payoffs, getting an apartment. None of these acts were simple or could ever be taken for granted. . . . We fought together, we carried ourselves with our heads high, we protected the women we loved when we could—as they tried to protect us—we held each other and we didn't win, and we held each other when we did.[26]

Even in purportedly queer cities, the stress and violence of visible queer life was pervasive.

The group she spoke with was white and working middle- and middle-class, and they did not concur with Esther's (among a few other participants') seemingly pro-gentrification narrative. Two of her co-participants, Janice '79/'91 and Gretch '98, pushed back. Gretch asked Esther if she felt she had gentrified by "bringing-in of white people into a neighborhood that may be predominantly Black or West Indian or Caribbean."[27] Esther laughed off the notion: "We didn't do that!" She later rationalized her claims, saying it was gay men who increased property values. Esther also connected her liberation to claiming urban space as a Jewish woman in New York City. While making space for the marginalized and vilified religious communities like Jews, especially in the 1980s, there is also a reliance on passing as white, and being a middle-class and college-educated homeowner to lay claim to the "neighborhood."[28]

Why did some white lesbians and queers feel that their behaviors were outside of the capitalist project of gentrification? Novelist James Baldwin wrote,

> The sexual question comes after the question of color; it's simply one more aspect of the danger in which all black people live. I think white gay people feel cheated because they were born, in principle, into a society in which they were supposed to be safe. The anomaly of their sexuality puts them in danger, unexpectedly.[29]

The cruel homophobia, vitriolic sexism, and vile anti-Semitism that Esther experienced as a Jewish lesbian in most neighborhoods in 1980s New York City drove her to believe in or at least take part in the myth of neighborhood liberation, and many others clung to this myth for similar reasons. Regardless, the racism and homophobia central to Esther's narrative paints "the lesbians" as struggling to survive in working-class, Black neighborhoods, implying only lesbians can be white and ignoring the lesbian-queer Black and brown lives around her. In the next group interview, I remember how poignant it was when Alex '98, who is Afro-Caribbean and grew up near Esther's old neighborhood, said: "I live in Bed-Stuy. Which has a *huge* lesbian population."

Patterns of segregation and rejection could be found in every constellation. Wanda also shared, "Unfortunately I came out at [an elite, predominantly white college]. The only Black lesbian. . . . It was [*sarcastically*] *great*. And [long pause, becomes somber] . . . although it was *very hard racially*—it was *very, very hard*, it was *very, very hard.*" As much as she found acceptance of her gender, sexuality, and middle-class identity, Wanda was isolated as one of the few Black/Cuban women, let alone as "the only Black lesbian":

WANDA: [My first girlfriend in college] . . . was a little bit willful to [her father]. . . . So he went into her room . . . and he grabbed her diary . . . [and found out she was gay and that she, a white girl, was dating Wanda]. The shit hit all over the fan. He, like, beat her up! He broke her jaw! Took her out of college! Put her in therapy! It was really, really fucked. I was like, "Uggggh! Okay! We're not gay. This is way too dramatic for me!" And I'm a dramatic motherfucker. But, no, the end. It was too traumatizing to me. Then her father sent all of our correspondence to my mother . . . with anything that was homoerotic underlined.

CHRIS: [*still sarcastically*] Because she wouldn't have gotten it otherwise.

WANDA: The thing that saved me with my mom? Racism. "What the hell that white man think he doin'? He trying to tell me some shit about who my child is. Let's look . . . Yeah, you '*love*' her . . . I get that. There's something wrong with that bitch!" [*group laughter*] "She got some issues!" And I was like [*pause*], "I know, I'm trying to help her with her issues!" [*group laughter*]

Wanda described her and her mother's disidentification from whiteness, which her mother associated with gayness. But Wanda's mother's refusal to note her daughter's lesbianism is a "tacit" approach, per American studies scholar Carlos Ulises Decena. Writing on gay Dominican immigrant men, he found that, among some people of color and religious and conservative people, "all relatives are complicit in the public secret precisely because they are invested in sustaining an institution that makes them socially viable. . . . It is not hypocritical or unethical to wrestle with this complexity."[30]

As anthropologist Martin Manalansan writes, while there are immigrant and refugee of color families that accept their queer family members, that more often than not the family is still "a social unit that exerts an enormous amount of power over the lives of immigrants or non-white groups." He goes on to write that "citizenship for queers of color and diasporic queers is neither a birth right nor is it about the romance of dissidence and resistance, but is about struggling to create scripts that will enable them to survive."[31] Wanda's disavowed and/or unclaimed lesbianism, in the words of Muñoz, can "be understood as disidentificatory in that it is not about assimilation into a heterosexual matrix but instead a partial disavowal of that cultural form that works to restructure it from within."[32] Wanda's story emblematizes how many of my participants of color create stars and the lines between them by embracing a set of tactics that, again per Muñoz, "neither opts to assimilate within such a structure nor strictly opposes it."[33] With these insights, we understand why and how the stars and lines of Wanda's constellations are blotted out for most onlookers by the pollution of whiteness, homophobia, and sexism as she navigates the city given her disidentificatory orientation.

What McKittrick calls the "plantocracy logics" continue to shape the segregation of the city and the state also shape the production of constellations. White, upper middle-class Jackie '85 also faced discrimination for being a lesbian at home, on the streets, and throughout most of her elite campus. Yet, unlike Wanda and Yasmin related about their experiences in the 1980s as women of color, Jackie was able to build a world apart in her college apartment:

> [T]here was also this endless stream of women because . . . our roommates were kind of experimenting with non-monogamy . . . it's just this endless—but it was such a small community that you knew *everyone*. [*group laughter*] . . . It was this sort of feminist community. One of our roommates was then straight but I think now is a dyke. And another one

was—he mostly had boyfriends . . . so it was just this really kind of *Dykes to Watch Out For* kind of scenario. [*group laughter*] . . . this multiracial, multisexed, multigendered environment. And . . . I really, I really loved that apartment.

While "multiracial, multisexed, multigendered" exchange was purportedly encouraged in predominantly white, elite educational environments, these spaces draw on the white privilege of including "others" whose very "inclusion" is based on their limited numbers and power. Wanda described a similar sense of sexual openness in college, but her earlier story about her white girlfriend and her mother's reaction reveals how the white supremacy of the state and elite education spaces required her disidentifications with white privilege while claiming some power for her own.

In a striking complement to Bailey's story, Black feminist and lesbian essayist Audre Lorde drew on her own 1950s college experience when she wrote, in her 1982 mytho-autobiography *Zami,* "Downtown in the gay bars I was a closet student and an invisible Black. Uptown at Hunter [College] I was a closet dyke and a general intruder."[34] For many of my participants, like Lorde in decades previous, to identify with college as a woman of color also meant to disidentify with the white privilege that educational institutions promote to maintain their and their subjects' eliteness. Stars that burned bright from the viewpoint of white privilege may seem dim or fading to participants of color as they negotiated their disidentifications. These tactics infused Black and Latinx participants' constellations that they formed through disidentifications with commitments to biological family, Black and Latinx cultures, and religion at times, as well as families of choice, queer culture, and politics at other times—relationships and larger cultural structures that might require code switching in the blink of an eye.[35]

While the myth of neighborhood liberation would never trickle down to most lesbians and queers of color, let alone all lesbians and queers, Black lesbians flourished on the page.[36] Still, the credit due to queers of color for their artistic works and the labor that has gone into them is often as obscured as the stars in their constellations. African American studies scholar Sharon Holland wrote, "The 'colored girls' do all the soul work of the discipline, and the white women shell out the theories that decide how this soul work is going to be read, disseminated, and taught in juxtaposition to already canonized white lesbian authors."[37] Like many participants, mixed-race/Black Bailey '95 recalled a disidentification with both the "traditional" white, male heterosexual and white, lesbian canons that fueled her sense of self: "Just reading the writers. You know, Audre Lorde, and all of these feminist, lesbian writers in the 1980s, late seventies. I'm still *so* excited by it!" Felicia '89 said that some lesbians and queers get "caught up in the words and the jargon and the cool" of queer theory and Lina '05 shared, "I think some people really embrace those terms [like Butler's performativity] and some people think it's a load of crap." Participants often excitedly cited the writing and ideas of feminist lesbians of color—what would serve as the basis for queer theory and queer of color critique—like Lorde, Gloria Anzaldúa, Cherríe Moraga, and Barbara Smith, as well as white, antiracist Adrienne Rich.[38]

Such theory was also already bound to activism and also already shaped by white privilege: "White lesbian history, which just about everyone simply calls, 'lesbian history,' puts white lesbians at the center, acting as if lesbians of color did not attend the party, fight at the barricades, or form lesbian identities," writes literary scholar Linda Garber.[39] Creating their own organizations afforded many 1980s-generation lesbians and queers of color the opportunity to define their gender and sexuality beyond white "norms." In 1971, the Black Lesbian Caucus of the city's Gay Activist Alliance created Salsa Soul Sisters, Third World Wimmin Inc. One of the first lesbian organizations created by, for, and about women of color in the United States, Salsa Soul Sisters included Latinx, African American, Asian American, and Native American women. New York City was a hub for women and tgncp of color organizing, including groups like the Third World Women's Archive, Asian Lesbians of the East Coast (ALOEC), Street Transvestite Action Revolutionaries (STAR), Las Buenas Amigas, Dykes Against Racism Everywhere (DARE), South Asian Lesbian and Gay Association (SALGA), Jews for Racial and Economic Justice, WeWah and BarCheeAmpe, Somos Hermanas, Kilawin Kolektibo, Audre Lorde Project, Fabulous Independent Educated Radicals for Community Empowerment (FIERCE), African Ancestral Lesbians United for Social Change (AALUSC), Sista II Sista, Sisters Lending Circle, and Kambal Sa Lusog-Pilipinas Lesbians, Bisexuals, and Gays for Progress (see jgieseking .org/AQNY).[40]

These groups' activisms bound lesbian and queer activism to larger Third World Women's (a prominent 1980s identity conceived to promote solidarity) and antiracist organizing, recalling issue-based, social justice coalitions developed in the 1960s and 1970s.[41] Anthropologist Scott Morgensen recounts that WeWah and BarCheeAmpe was founded by "Native queer people to challenge settler colonialism and defend Native peoples within pantribal alliances."[42] He describes how the group's broad agenda inspired the founding of larger queer of color coalitions as they "drew non-Native queers of color into antiracist queer alliances committed to Native decolonization."[43] This alliance united ALOEC, Las Buenas Amigas, SALGA, AALUSC, the Astrea Foundation for lesbian concerns, and other groups to recognize and support lesbians of color.

Antiracism also remained the focus of many devoted white lesbians and mixed-race groups. Beyond their protests of racist practices at Bacall's bar, the activists of DARE, for example, marched and/or organized against South African apartheid, US support for the Nicaraguan Contras, and the Ku Klux Klan, held potlucks to support women in New York State's women's prison, and launched anti-right-wing critiques in response to attacks upon women, especially of the Third World. While my participants did not mention all of these groups, the work they did filtered down like stars to eventually light and inspire other queer paths.

## The Lesbian-Queer of Color Private Spaces of the Gay Public 1990s

Wanda '85 and Naomi '89, both Black and middle-class, reflected on their lifelong inability to access parts of the everyday city landscape, where Blackness read as "dangerous." When Naomi shared that "we'd use someone's whiteness to get a cab. Or boobs. You need whiteness or boobs," Wanda replied: "White boobs are even better." Both women enacted a disidentification by borrowing white privilege and making use of the male gaze—and their wit—to expand their own constellations. Later, Wanda brought up how navigating her constellation required being around, but disidentifying from, whiteness:

> But who I am *supersedes* my gayness. . . . As long as I had a couple of white people with me, I could get in anywhere. I feel like that access is the

same. So . . . the only places I couldn't get into were male-only places and those are some of those places I can't get into now. [*pauses*] . . . But you still couldn't get a cab.

In contrast, white, feminine-presenting Birtha '84 discussed (white) women's fear in the urban public sphere: "I remember that I had to structure certain events that happened in the city late at night around taking a cab home [to Brooklyn] because I really didn't feel safe taking the subway at all." In contrast to Wanda, who "still couldn't get a cab," Birtha's story shows how white privilege shapes both the stars of constellations and the lines between them, and reveals how white lesbians and queers fail to acknowledge the labor of disidentifications Wanda must enact for her survival.

Cabs are merely one slice of city life that attests to racist urban policies, many of which were reasserted or amplified by Mayor Rudy Giuliani's 1990s plantocracy logics, realized in his administration's militarization of the city.[44] He extolled "broken windows" policing, in which the residents of poor neighborhoods—usually neighborhoods of color like Bed-Stuy and Crown Heights—suffering visible blight were targeted for increased policing, surveillance, and incarceration since the 1980s. When the crack epidemic slowed in 1990, policing continued to "protect" new stores, property renovations, and real estate developments. These actions were tied to the expansion of lesbian-queer places outlined in chapter 2. The word "ghetto" appeared less often in the media, but mainstream, negative imagery of Black neighborhoods still fed some of my white participants' fear and distrust of those places, and their treatment of lesbians and queers of color. As McKittrick notes, "In many senses the plantation maps specific Black geographies as identifiably violent and impoverished, consequently normalizing the uneven production of space."[45]

At the same time, it was not until the late 1990s that the most well-known lesbian bar devoted foremost to women of color and a truly racially mixed party opened in Manhattan. The bar, Crazy Nanny's, operated for years in Greenwich Village as one of its brightest stars. The nearby, stunningly titled, and most popular party among my study's participants, Clit Club, took place on Friday nights, usually in the nearby Meatpacking District. Both remain some of the brightest stars in my participants of color's constellations. Bailey '95 discussed the mixing and segregation of these spaces:

> I'm saying the clubs *have* [*bangs hand down*] *been* [*bangs hand down*] *segregated* [*bangs hand down*]! The Clit Club would have some mixes . . . race-wise—you'll have a lot of middle-class, Black women and Asians. And at [Crazy] Nanny's, it was pretty working-class. I mean, it was primarily Black so you would have working-class and Latina and white women. But it was primarily Black.

Clit Club would last until the early 2000s, and Nanny's would close in 2004. Imbricated in racist and anti-sex policies and attitudes, skyrocketing rents in and around the Village fed and were fed by an influx of investments in high-end boutiques and high-priced condo developments. While the presence of trans people went unmentioned in our conversations, it is notable that the Nanny's promotion sticker read: "Nanny's / A Place for Gay Women / Biological and Otherwise."[46] While participants did not discuss the inclusion of trans women at Nanny's or elsewhere, this sticker may have been a reaction to 1970s white feminism that privileged the inclusion of bodies of color over exclusive identities.

Dana '98, a multiethnic, working-class, feminine woman primarily dated butches and aggressives/AGs of color. She talked at length both about the time, money, and effort required by queer women of color to find one another, and the limits to connecting to the Black and Latinx queer women's and tgncp's scene. She shared, "There's this club in Brooklyn, I think it's called the Lab. I wanted to go there because that was where the AGs of color were. Those were the kinds of girls I was into, the type of environment I felt comfortable." She then added, "But I never went because I live in the Bronx, and at the end of the day I wasn't trying to ride the train two hours to go anywhere." It would have taken an hour or more to get to the Village from the Bronx. Dana went on to describe how the negative stereotypes of Black neighborhoods as unwelcoming of queers were untrue. After "living for three years with my butch ex-gf [girlfriend] in the Bronx," she found these neighborhoods to be "the *most* accepting of aggressive lesbians." She added:

These areas have no [*makes air quotes*] "gay community" the way that . . . pockets of downtown Manhattan supposedly do, so the lesbians . . . [*makes air quotes*] "commute" [or] migrate in groups, from uptown to downtown on the D or A [subway] train, thus debunking the myth of a lack of community. Because if there are more than three of us, we got a community.

In the lines that Black and Latinx lesbians and queers—and those who shared space with them—take to find one another, the constellations in, out, and across neighborhoods of color burn bright.

All of my participants described how house parties were central to lesbian-queer life, and tended to flourish in the private spaces women, like tgncp, have been associated with for millennia. Urban planner Moira Kenney wrote of such lesbian spaces in 1990s Los Angeles: "When recognizable enclaves, analogous to gay male constructions, are found, lesbian life flourishes. When such signs are not visible, lesbian life is often considered nascent, or nonexistent."[47] Many of my participants of color and working-class participants described the role of rent parties and dollar parties; the practice, around since at least the 1920s among urban Black communities from Harlem to the South, involves a renter hosting an apartment party with food for sale at low cost in order to pay rent.[48] Historian Finn Enke writes that lesbian rent and/or dollar parties were on "the margins of—but not outside—the economy" so that "such spaces partially circumvented normative race and gender hierarchies."[49] Such an "unlicensed marketplace" of "quasi-commercial alternatives," per Enke, afforded a way for women and tgncp to produce their own spaces and economies for decades. Lesbians and queers of color produced many of their spaces in private long before they could claim long-term, well-publicized, centrally located bars.

Notably, participants' apartments and the parties within them were one of the least likely spaces to be labeled lesbian or queer on participants' maps, regardless of race or class. I believe that the fixation on claiming public space on behalf of activism and consumption obscured the role that private and semi-public spaces played. Writing about Black queer women's spaces in DC, Lane noted many women had apartment parties, with or without a fee: "As a means of bypassing systems of power and exclusion such as racial segregation and homophobia in public spaces, Black lesbians often repurposed private homes for 'semi-public' use."[50] Among the stars Afro-Caribbean Tre '02 described as "real spaces that I feel comfortable [in]" were public spots in Brooklyn, near her university, and in lower Manhattan; she then added, "Friends' apartments. We create space. The space gets created. You know?"

For queer immigrants and refugees, "home" could also be a space of struggle for other reasons. As literary scholar Chandan Reddy states, "queers of color as people of color . . . take up the critical task of both re-membering and rejecting the model of the 'home' offered in the United States."[51] Reddy speaks to the requirements of US immigration that demand commitments to family even as queers of color may need to reject or may be rejected from the family home.

At the same time, part of the production of Black lesbian-queer spaces requires safeguarding their constellations of "where the girls go" from white people and straight men. "Where the girls go" also speaks to what Black geographers McKittrick and Clyde Woods describe as "the tension, between the mapped and the unknown" or "the Where of Blackness."[52] Lane states that "the relationship that black people have to public-private is more complex than many queer theorists and lesbian and gay historians have addressed. . . . A semi-public space is only 'public' to those for whom the space is intended."[53] Black queer women's semi-publics "offer intimacy, safety, and possibilities for the enactment of discourses not available to them elsewhere."[54]

We can see Lane's arguments clearly represented in Bailey's map. Mixed-race/Black Bailey drew her childhood home in Latinx, working-class Washington Heights, where she had her first kiss and first girl-friend ("I spent almost every night here") but where she did not feel at home ("closeted and harassed by dudes"). She also drew Village bars, diners, parties, and the Pier, but left her then current home neighborhood of Crown Heights off the map. Bailey's constellation is comprised of both the city center and margins of the outer boroughs (figure 3.7). The lines that Bailey must have taken between these stars are unmapped but described in her stories. Most of her map captures the literal and figurative white space in between, an interstellar medium of surging flows of gentrification.

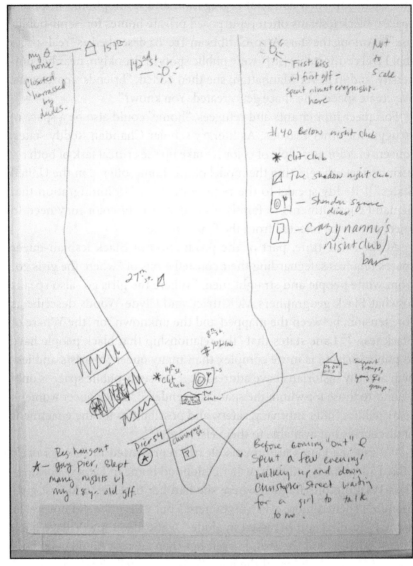

Figure 3.7. Bailey '95's mental map (mixed-race/Black, working middle-class)

In the 1990s, middle-class women and tgncp continued to describe college as a space where they could define their own lesbian and/or queer path. Yet now my participants described no longer being the only lesbian of color in college. After presenting her map, Bailey also shared, "There were a lot of lesbians [at my elite college], and so I was doing the poetry thing, right? I met a *lot* of lesbians there [*group laughter*] . . . and I never felt like I couldn't find anything, which was really nice. [I felt] comfort." She paused, and then went on, "I had this group of girls around me who were all lesbian-identified . . . it was like we lived in some TV show . . . where you didn't really feel the outside effects of the world, 'cause we all made sense to each other. Really nice. Very fortunate in that way." Bailey uses the word "fortunate" to describe the mutual ability of lesbians to make "sense to each other" in attending college and being part of the spoken word scene, but the ability to make sense of one's self as a lesbian, a woman of color, and a lesbian of color all at once should not be "fortunate," rare, or brief. While Bailey's experiences bear similarities to Jackie's experience of her queer college apartment, and both women attended prominent colleges, the white privilege that supported Jackie pushes Bailey and other women and tgncp of color to both their affective limits and the city limits.

Relieved to finally be among multiple generations of lesbians and queers of color (in that group interview), femme-identified Bailey shared about the stress of living in Crown Heights. She discussed wearing "whiteness" on her body as a disidentification strategy, before she added:

> I've never ever had a place to say this, what I'm saying here. And it's so nice. Because [straight Black] people are just like, "Oh, you privileged! They like you. They're attracted to you. You might as well take that as a compliment." Or [Black lesbian and queers], "You're not AG. You're not an aggressive. You don't know what it's like to go to the bathroom." I spend everyday thinking about: "How am I going to walk through here? Who am I gonna—? I've got to pretend I'm on the phone. I gotta pick my nose. I gotta make up stories about my man." And sometimes [I wish] . . . I could just move through the world and not think about it.

Her co-participants nodded and sat quietly making eye contact, until Wanda said, "Forget it! Forget it, forget it. You'd have to be a *straight man.*" The Black neighborhood is where Bailey must exist but often cannot be at home—where, in the words of McKittrick, she "is everywhere and nowhere."[55] Beyond this laundry list of exhausting practices—what Muñoz meant when he warns us that disidentification is "*not always* an adequate strategy"—Bailey also mentioned wearing larger clothing sizes as a way to navigate misogyny and the hypsersexualization of her body "without a man."[56]

Feminine-presenting participants described frequent unwanted and threatening attention. Feminine-presenting Black and Latinx participants relayed even more intense harassment by men of all races who felt they could claim and hypersexualize their bodies. In predominantly working-class neighborhoods of color like Bed-Stuy and Crown Heights, my participants of color raged against the male gaze, public toxic masculinity, and accompanying heteronormativity that they said all too often shaped their constellations in ways that my white participants did not describe needing to negotiate in the same ways. In her remark about aggressives or AGs—working-class Black and Latinx studs or masculine-presenting lesbians, dykes, or queers—Bailey respects and sympathizes with the violence that AGs face (some of whom are her exes). Notably, butches and AGs rarely discussed the harassment they experienced.[57]

Some white participants continued to devote themselves to antiracist work in the 1990s, like white, working middle-class, genderqueer Heather '95. They founded organizations to resist and rework the white, cis-heteropatriarchal state and city: "When the [*makes air quotes*] 'gay movement' started becoming more and more about gay marriage, money, and civil rights—that leaves people behind. . . . The lack of class analysis and race analysis and on and on." Heather later added, "I feel like transgender organizing and queer people of color organizing has been more where those edges are." As the AIDS epidemic began to slow, mainstream lgbtq organizations with more conservative perspectives grew their power and funding (the "gay movement," which participants often described as the Human Rights Campaign (HRC) and similarly large, moneyed, mainstream nonprofits). Yet lgbtq people's ability to connect sexually, politically, and socially across races and classes also planted the seeds for more antiracist, anticapitalist organizations and spaces. Like a (then) handful of other white participants, Heather's antiracist geographies bound them closely to women and tgncp of color's spaces by embracing those people, issues, and spaces pushed to the geo-graphical, political, and economic "edges" of city life.

The disidentifications women and tgncp of color used to survive often required pushing aside white noise—at times, white music and systematic white privilege—to produce their own constellations. As an Afro-Caribbean woman, Alex '98 felt rejected by queer culture when she celebrated those edges and did not participate in the visible, central-ized "queer" life: "I felt left out [of the lesbian music scene]. . . . I'd never heard an Ani DiFranco recording and when I did . . . I was just not into it. I'm not listening to this." She went on, "And then I felt like there was some, like Gay 101 that I didn't take and so I failed all the time. And I just didn't feel interesting or interested either." Some participants of color, like Bailey, enjoyed DiFranco and Melissa Etheridge (she brought Etheridge's *If I Wanted To* as her coming out artifact), and adored punk as well ("Riot Grrrl, yeah!" she said). Even as Alex often drew on lyrics from the lesbian folk acoustic duo the Indigo Girls to make in-jokes, the rise of (almost always white) women's music, lesbian folk, and Riot Grrrl artists induced a sense of disconnect for Alex from mainstream lesbian-queer culture and political economies. The popularity and largely white fan base of DiFranco, Bikini Kill, Indigo Girls, Tegan and Sara, and Sleater-Kinney, among others—all of whom sang against white hetero-patriarchy—still asserted a white bodily representation to lesbian politics. Participants mentioned Black lesbian singers like Tracy Chap-man and Joan Armatrading less often and these artists appeared less often in lesbian-queer publications.

The mainstream faction of the 1990s gay and lesbian movement ig-nored the primacy of survival for many lgbtq people of color, poor and working-class lgbtq people, and lgbtq refugees and immigrants. The state and city yet again placed stringent constraints on poor, single, Black and Latina women's reproductive, employment, and child-rearing decisions and possibilities in the 1990s. At the same time, the "in-your-face" tac-tics of queer activism also relied on the privilege of whiteness to con-front the heteronormative public and the state in (white) public space. In other words, some white, middle-class, cisgender lgbtq people sought justice based foremost on sexual identity, partaking in what American studies scholar Lisa Duggan calls "homonormativity."[58] But the radi-cal politics of queer organizing also often relied on white privilege. As

Cohen writes, "queer politics has served to reinforce simple dichotomies between heterosexual and everything 'queer,'" and, in so doing, "may have lost its potential to be a politically expedient organizing tool for addressing the needs and mobilizing the bodies of people of color."[59] The same issues Cohen outlined over a decade ago surely still define lesbian-queer lives. Justice for some or only temporarily is liberation for none.

Racist policies saturate the production of lgbtq spaces. Historian Christina Hanhardt describes how national "hate crime laws and the geography of punishment" in the 1990s were set up against white "gay visibility," which "was cast as a goal and a risk of neighborhood growth."[60] As a result, she adds, "this dual set of assumptions helped to define the essence of antigay violence as a crime."[61]

Indeed, many of my participants raged against the lack of accounting for race and racism in hate crime legislation and enforcement. White, working middle-class Susan '92 compared the attention to the 1997 beating and death of Matthew Shepard in Laramie, Wyoming, to the consistently disregarded murders of Black and Latinx queer and trans people, particularly Black and Latinx trans women:

> We've always got to look out for the "t" in the lgbt because that is policing gender behavior. . . . Everyone gets so upset over Shepard, like, "Oh, he was so cute, he was so clean cut, he looked like somebody straight," and so they feel bad about him. But [*angrily*], "[Black and Latinx queer and trans people of color who are murdered]? Who's that? I don't know."

The media and political attention granted Shepard's death correlated to his body; his white, cisgender, "cute," "clean-cut" (blond hair, blue eyes) appearance again equated gayness with whiteness. As lgbtq and labor historian Allan Bérubé writes in his essay "How Gay Stays White and What Kind of White It Stays":

> A gay rights politics that is supposedly color-blind (and sex-neutral and classless) is in fact a politics of race (and gender and class). It assumes, without ever having to say it, that gay must equal white (and male and economically secure): that is, it assumes white (and male and middle-class) as the default categories that remain once one discounts those who as gay

people must continually and primarily deal with racism (and sexism and class oppressions), especially within gay communities.[62]

Communication studies scholar E. Cram writes that the empathy and sympathy the country directed toward Shepard as "America's gay son" was equally bound to "the place of the rural American West . . . as an acutely volatile place for queer bodies, displacing attention to articulations of violence in the spaces of cities and suburbs."[63] Gay whiteness then does not need to disidentify but rather can assert an identification to gain power. In the mainstream media's and lgbtq organizations' claim to the cisgender-enough male Shepard as victim, he became a default lgbtq subject with which to identify, and the white gay urban—who, in comparison, had now survived as the exemplary person living with AIDS (PWA)—was again idealized.

In contrast and complement, communications studies scholar C. Riley Snorton argues that the media coverage of the 1992 murder of white, transgender Brandon Teena in Humboldt, Nebraska, overshadowed the simultaneous murders of a Black, disabled, cisgender man, Philip DeVine, and his white ex-girlfriend, Lisa Lambert. Snorton responds to the framing of DeVine's Black life through his murder as an example of the "wrong place, wrong time" narrative that explains Black death away as inevitable and forgettable. Instead, citing literary scholar Hortense Spillers, he argues it is a "formulation of blackness-as-waiting . . . under which 'the human body becomes a defenseless target for rape and veneration . . . [rendered as] a resource for metaphor.'"[64] DeVine's absence mirrors the similar absence of many queers of color from queer history and everyday "queer" spaces. With these absences, dismissals, and acts of violence shaping their everyday lives, Black and Latinx participants—in Bed-Stuy, Crown Heights, and beyond—produced more fragmented and fleeting star maps, with the longer lines of their paths drawn between them.

## "The Very First White People That Usually Show Up Are Queer" in the 2000s (and Always)

Conversations about race and sexuality in the 2000s immediately evolved into discussions about gentrification. A young Hispanic, working middle-class gay woman, Tara '06 grew up in New York City and was a college student who had come out less than two years before taking part in my study; her map records quintessentially lgbtq neighborhoods and the stars within them (the Village, LGBT Center ["Gay Center"], the Pier, Park Slope, East Village, Chelsea), places she gathers with others her age (Brooklyn Tech, Union Square, Queens Pride Center), and her home (figure 3.8). Bars, which showed up frequently on the maps of women and tgncp who came out in the 1980s and 1990s, regardless of age, featured much less often in the maps of 2000s-generation participants like Tara. The city's intensified policing also, finally, led to the suppression of underage drinking, especially in spaces that welcomed people of color. This shift ended the decades-long practice of lgbtq spaces' proprietors and staff "looking the other way" when young queer people came out for the evening. In the 2000s, Tara said, "there's hardly any places for people under twenty-one," but she did not know why such places felt inaccessible to her and, in turn, how generations of policing shaped her constellation.

At the same time, Tara could very clearly see how gentrification shaped her (once) Latinx and Black, working-class Brooklyn neighborhood of Red Hook. She shared that gentrification resulted in "not just the homophobic harassment" but also "a way of [my neighbors, family, and friends] talking about these *white* people coming in and bringing in their, their queer *things*." In stark comparison, during another interview, white Birtha '84 said that, after a night in a Harlem comedy club where the few, white audience members were mocked as gentrifiers, it became clear to her and her partner that they would not move there: "The message was loud and clear, 'We don't want you here.' . . . We decided not to move there *because* of that. We didn't want to gentrify the neighborhood. But look at it! Who gentrifies? The very first white people that usually show up are queer." Birtha, the only participant who described her own ability to purchase a home, faced being unwelcome. Yet Tara's story makes clear that she, as a gay woman of color, bears the brunt of gentrification in everyday distrust, harassment, and, at times, disidentification from her queer identity since—at least it appears and we are told that—"the very first white people that usually show up are queer."

Certain lgbtq people have long been sought after in the get-rich-quick-again-and-again schemes attached to the processes of

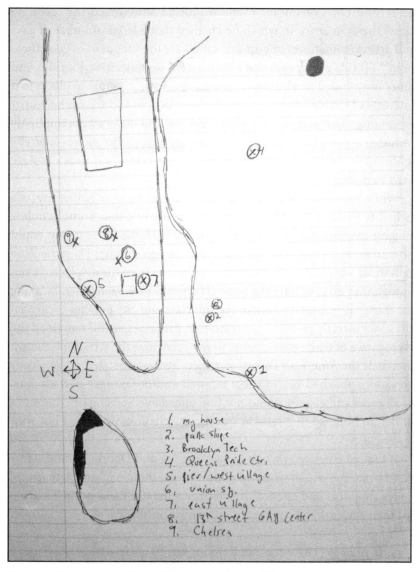

1. my house
2. park slope
3. Brooklyn Tech
4. Queens Pride Ctr.
5. pier/west village
6. union sq.
7. east village
8. 13th street GAy Center
9. Chelsea

Figure 3.8. Tara '06's mental map (Hispanic, working middle-class)

gentrification. Consultant Richard Florida announced the "creative class" thesis in 2002, in which he claimed that a larger number of gays and artists (sometimes one-in-the-same) are the vanguard of gentrification.[65] Florida even produced a "gay index" to rank cities. Florida's and other likeminded marketing campaigns paid attention to the places and interests of visible white, able-bodied gay people and the higher earners among them, namely gay men. Lesbians and queers were implicitly included among the "creatives," but claims to sexuality alone—thereby ignoring the white cis-heteropatriarchal aspects of a "gay index"—were used to mark a unique category of gentrifiers.

While two-thirds of my participants were white, over half of my participants lived in neighborhoods historically of color. Some scholars suggest that many of the white participants in the latter group could be read as "marginal gentrifiers," what urban geographer Damaris Rose calls those who are not "'structurally' polarized from the displaced" even though they do not "have the same class position as each other."[66] While the forces of real estate developers and state and city policies tacitly assist if not directly promote gentrification processes, it still remained the prerogative of white participants to not recognize the structural racism that fuels the American Dream–certified "real estate state."[67] Many conversations touched on how less monied and/or younger participants, of all races and classes, could not find affordable housing or commutes under an hour, so that lesbian-queer constellations dispersed but with fewer clusters.

A dialogue between white Magdalene '04 and Donna '05 and Afro-Caribbean Tre '02, all working middle-class, about a lgbtq party space/coffee shop that had opened in Bed-Stuy reiterates the way queers bring in "their queer *things*" as part of the gentrification process:

MAGDALENE: I have some stuff [on my mental map] in Bed-Stuy. House parties. My apartment. The [queer activist marching band] Rude Mechanical Orchestra. . . . It's just like a really queer, gender-fucking scene. Outpost coffee shop, which will always be near to my heart. Does anyone know Outpost? It's a gay boy-owned coffee shop in Bed-Stuy. And party space, too.

TRE: [*eyes wide open, in shock*] Where?

MAGDALENE: It's on Fulton Street. . . . It was, I don't know what the scene is now, but when I lived in Bed-Stuy [it] is really . . . kind of like a nice little gay haven in Bed-Stuy, so that was nice.

DONNA: Oh, I remember it. Someone was fucking with it because of the gentrification thing. Like, "Oh, they think they're pioneers, calling it the Outpost." They didn't get "out" [*makes air quotes, implying coming out as gay*].

Outpost was a delight to Magdalene and Donna, who did not account for the whiteness of this space or the privilege involved in producing it, and a cruel surprise to Tre, who enacted a disidentificiation by "recycling and rethinking encoded meaning."[68] Tre had grown up in nearby Crown Heights and only a few minutes earlier had spoken about "the gentrification of white queers" of primarily working-class, Black neighborhoods like hers. I watched her shake her head and disidentify with the conversation and sentiment.

Magdalene's description of a "little gay haven" and "queer genderfucking scene" makes neighborhoods like Tre's seem like white, queer playgrounds—one to which Tre was uninvited in her own backyard. As ironic as the name Outpost may seem to Donna, it replicates what urban geographer Neil Smith describes as the "new urban frontier" mentality among the white middle class who sought to "settle" the unknown and uncivilized "frontier" through the violent processes of gentrification.[69] The few publicized queer and queer-friendly parties like Sputnik in Bed-Stuy also targeted whites, with business names that drew on metaphors of outsider surveillance and settler claims. After walking through streets filled mostly with Black people and well-kept brownstones, I once visited Outpost and found a collective of mostly white, queer, fat femmes leading a bake sale for a sick friend. While I gladly bought a cupcake, my role as a gentrifier and interloper was clear. Through the 1990s, neighboring Bed-Stuy was known "as one of America's largest ghettoes."[70] A steady in-migration of African, West Indian, and Caribbean people balanced out the increasing displacement of African Americans from the neighborhood in the 2000s (figure 3.9). By 2013, Bed-Stuy was referred to as the "then-ghetto" of the city in the Real Estate section of the *New York Times*.[71]

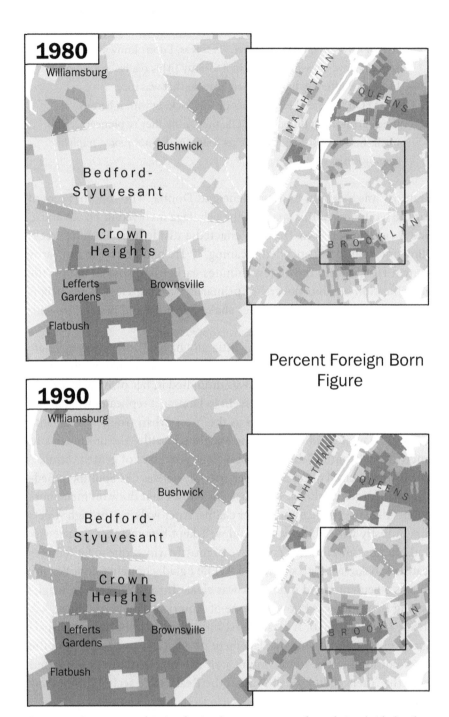

Figure 3.9. Census maps showing foreign-born percentage of population (with details of Bed-Stuy and Crown Heights), 1980, 1990, 2000, and 2010

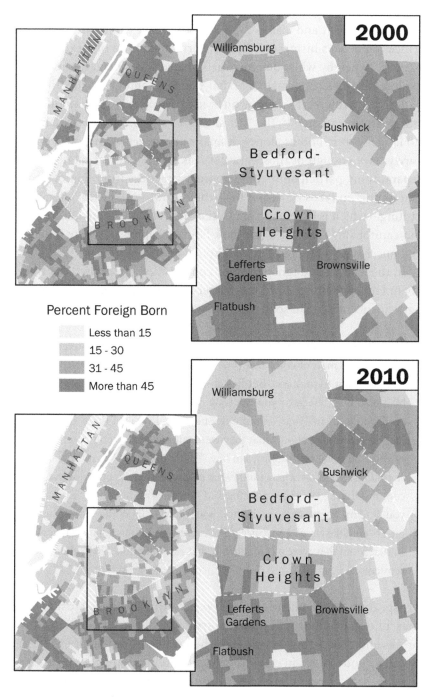

Figure 3.9. *Continued*

In this example and many others, contemporary white-on-Black gentrification evokes historian Lillian Faderman's notion of "sexual colonialism," whereby white heterosexuals visited Black neighborhoods to
explore non-heteronormative sexual practices and queer identities.[72]
Faderman wrote that "many whites *used* Harlem as a commodity, a
stimulant to sexuality."[73] The "stimulant" or aphrodisiac to sexuality is
no longer exotic bodies alone—lesbians and queer women and tgncp
surely have enough of those—rather it is affordable real estate. What
separates my participants' contemporary practices from that of white
"slumming" in 1920s Harlem is that whites now roost, instead of merely
visiting—which is different from Greenwich Village, where queers visit
but cannot stay (chapter 2), or Park Slope (chapter 4), where lesbians
and queers could find residence, although often temporarily.

In the women and tgncp of color conversation, Tre shared the story
about Outpost and spoke to the dangers of gentrification while her co-
participants nodded in solidarity:

> Let's all get this straight. When your white ass walks down the street next
> to me, he [a man of color from the neighborhood] is going to look at
> you and want to fuck you, but he's going to say to me, "Bitch, blah blah
> blah blah blah." Because you can walk down the street at 3 a.m. You can
> go, "Woohoo!" in "*your*" community now. . . . I've lived there all of my
> life. Even thinking about what they were talking about: food co-ops and
> just like building community. I'm like, "What the fuck? What the *fuck* is
> *community*?" I know where [and] what community is: it's the West Indian
> community. . . . We've got policing and now they're more pigs to protect
> you. So I'm, "Is my gayness the first issue? Hm . . .". [White lesbians and
> queers are] like [*small girly voice*], "I'm repressed! Because of my gayness."
> In that room they were putting that as that was it. Period. No hyphen. No
> semicolon.

Tre speaks to her hyphenated identity: gay–Afro-Caribbean–daughter–
masculine–neighborhood resident–young–college student, etc. The
breaks and pauses show where and when she must disidentify with her
sexuality and gender in order to navigate the racism, policing, gentrification, sexism, and classism the capitalist state tries to use to define
her. Her Afro-Caribbean community is the group who recognizes and

protects her, though it enforces cis-heteropatriarchy. Her favorite hangouts were Fort Greene Park, nearby Habana Outpost restaurant, and Harriett's Alter Ego restaurant in Park Slope, the last of which is now closed. In step with Tre's anxieties, sociologist Mignon R. Moore writes that the "concern in openly expressing a gay sexuality in predominantly Black neighborhoods is the fear of violence and homophobia."[74] At the same time, this community faces the incursion of those white "queer things," as Tara put it, and the accompanying policing and gentrification.

Fine refers to "hyphenated identities" as the juncture "at which the Self-Other join in the politics of everyday life, that is, the hyphen that both separates and merges personal identities with our inventions of Others."[75] Tre's story reminded me of Esther '87's previously mentioned story in which she described herself as "the second white person"—after her girlfriend—to "settle" a nearby historically Black neighborhood. Tre and Esther never met, but the hyphens that Tre alludes to also bind her, as othered, to other lesbians and queers. Tre's and Esther's stories show how queers of color face different, intensified forms of violence. The myth of neighborhood liberation fails lgbtq people, again and again, with particular gendered, racialized, and classed effects that violently shape their spatialities into constellations rather than neighborhoods alone.

Participants in the 2000s generation also described how they intentionally sought not to gentrify queer of color spaces. On her birthday, white, Jewish, working middle-class Lily '01 attempted to visit the predominantly Black, working-class Starlite Lounge bar and club in Crown Heights. Founded in 1962, it was the oldest and longest-lasting lgbtq bar in New York City. Drunk at the door, she and her white, queer, cis-female friends realized "they obviously didn't want a bunch of white lesbians there" and headed to Park Slope, keen to support Black, brown, and Latinx queer spaces maintaining their own desires and demographics.

The documentary *We Came to Sweat* records the last days of Starlite Lounge, which closed in 2010. At one point, a long-time patron turns to the camera and shares, "You need these kinds of places like you need churches."[76] To be clear, many Black people do understand church as a need. In interviewing Black lesbians in the US South, Black geographer LaToya Eaves writes, "The Black Church has operated as not only a place to meet religious and spiritual needs but also as an impetus for change in discriminatory practices."[77] Looking again at the city, we can see that the lines not made between stars can reflect a state of placelessness formed by acts of racism, capitalism, and violence as much as acts of solidarity, respect, and support, even when gentrification processes show no such respect. Some of the lines remain to the viewer alone to see, like the erased histories and unstated experiences that remain tacit, not silent but unstated.

A long-time organizer against gentrification, Afro-Caribbean, working middle-class Alex '98 had helped to form a number of organizations for queer youth of color a decade earlier:

> There was always all this funding to sort of capitalize—[it had] to do with the nonprofit industrial complex in the nineties. . . . Organizations were hiring and saying, "Women and people of color and lgbt people encouraged, and disability, blah, blah, blah encouraged to apply." And I was like, "That's me!"

With the mass defunding of the welfare state, the nonprofit industrial complex (NPIC) grew as the power and profit of social reproduction was privatized and placed under the control of largely white nonprofits, NGOs, foundations, philanthropic organizations, social services, and social justice groups.[78] Alex identified with how what she experienced as hopeful in the 1990s was absorbed into the capitalist NPIC by the 2000s as the funding available to Alex and others like her decreased or entirely disappeared.

When coming out, Alex had no access to the history that came before her. Hanhardt writes, "The 1980s saw the relative mainstreaming of lesbian and gay movements, as over two decades of political organizing transformed some modes of sexual deviancy into affirmative identities nominally recognized in popular culture, the marketplace, and the law."[79] Like Giuliani's militarization policies, the 1980s mainstreaming and 1990s NPIC would help to throttle radical queer politics into a simplified, well-funded, and highly consumptive message of "love wins" during the Prop 8 fights for same-sex marriage, leaving a highly weakened lgbtq movement through the 2010s. In the 1990s in New York City, Reddy writes that more churches petitioned to provide what were formerly government services, meaning that more immigrants, many queers among them, had to "access church services as their primary service provider," exposing them to many conservative churches and therefore "remarkable heteropatriarchal coercion."[80]

The Lesbian Herstory Archives' organizational records show that a small number of organizations focusing on lesbian-queer of color concerns were founded or held meetings in Bed-Stuy and Crown Heights. These organizations included stars like African Ancestral Lesbians United for Social Change and Asian Lesbians of the East Coast in the 1980s, and G.L.O.B.E. Community Center, Sista II Sista, and Sisters Lending Circle in the 1990s.[81] Many lesbian and/or queer of color organizations continued to use the LGBT Center or homes for meetings, or turned to newer community centers in Brooklyn, the Bronx, and Queens.

Along with using time-honored word-of-mouth practices to find these places and groups, many participants increasingly relied on the internet to find places, especially queer of color venues that mainstream lgbtq media largely ignored. My own white privilege clouded my assumption that people of color turned to lesbian-queer publications consistently and found equal representation there—until Lane failed to mention them in her research, and instead relied solely on a website to find Black queer women's spaces in DC in the early 2010s.[82] My 1980s- and 1990s-generation participants, meanwhile, bemoaned the dearth of local lesbian-queer publications they had access to over the years—three to zero being published at any given time.[83] In generations previous, lesbian publications allowed some of their "readers to see themselves as part of a much larger entity and to make connections with women on the local scale."[84]

Rather than a revelation, anthropologist Mary Gray suggests that new media served as a complement to everyday life for youth who grew up with the internet.[85] Gray writes that the medium of the internet afforded more realistic and varied representations of lgbtq bodies and spaces than ever before. Constellations always included physical and virtual stars such as books, music, film, and art, and the virtuality of queer space now multiplied online. White, working middle-class Kathy '05 and Afro-Caribbean, working middle-class Tre '02 described the unstated disciplinarity that shaped how they used the internet in their homes to search for lgbtq content, but they had to also obsessively delete their browsing history in order to not out themselves to their homophobic families.[86]

Tre's words to live by still echo in my brain: "Delete your history"—and I still see Kathy nodding solemnly beside her. But managing the outness of identities is hardly new. In high school over a decade earlier, Phyllis '88 cut out anything "gay-related" from the *Village Voice* and hid it in her record sleeves. Depending on their living situations, Tre, Kathy, and other queers could have access to lesbian-queer stars of connection and their line-like search history, but had to make their interests and even their own existence invisible.

The self-policing of deleted/hidden histories was just another form of policing to women and tgncp youth of color, which they especially experienced in physical spaces and surely constrained the stars and lines of their constellations. By 2008, invasive policing tactics involved stopping and frisking people on the street without cause, particularly people of color. There were over twenty-six thousand stop-and-frisk cases in the first half of 2012 alone in Crown Heights and Bed-Stuy, the vast majority of which targeted Black people.[87] The stop-and-frisk policy that politicians claimed originated in antiterrorism efforts also extended the project of gentrification entailed in state securitization, from laws like the Patriot Act to prisons like Guantánamo Bay and Rikers Island. Critical social psychologists established that lgbtq youth of color were "much more likely to have negative experiences with the police . . . compared to straight youth."[88] A study from the Queers for Economic Justice's research group, Welfare Warriors Collective, found that the majority of those stopped were poor youth of color: 47 percent of low-income lgbq and tgncp people reported being stopped for questioning within the prior two years; those who identified as female, transgender, or Two-Spirit were more likely to experience sexual misconduct and/or assualt from police.[89] Further, transgender and Two-Spirit people were more likely to be arrested or to receive a ticket or summons, and more than twice as likely to be physically assaulted by police than other low-income lgbq and tgncp people.

When violence against queers came up in conversation, I noticed that all of my participants turned the discussion to the most vulnerable subjects: transgender homeless youth of color. Legal scholar Dean Spade refers to trans people as experiencing a state of "extreme vulnerability" that is only amplified for people of color, refugees, immigrants, Muslims, and poor and working-class, homeless, and/or disabled people.[90]

This pattern echoes how Black and Latina, working-class, young women are often deemed "at risk" and a "burden to society."[91] Like these young women, Black and Latinx lesbians and queers must exert significant labor to disidentify with white, middle-class, state-certified codes, meanings, and identities projected upon them, while they turn to and produce the light of their own constellations, however partial or dispersed, regardless.

## Disidentifications: The Geographies of Coming Apart and Together

At times, participants' racial identities led them to see the same urban horizon with similar-yet-distinct night skies—and then draw different but interdependent constellations from their stars. The myth of neighborhood liberation kept many of my white participants focused on making "community" among "us" (white) queers, as Jess put it at the beginning of this chapter, while failing to acknowledge the (queer) communities of color already in place. Describing the racist dyke-chotomy undergirding gentrification in geographies of you vs. them considered in this chapter, McKittrick writes that

> the lands . . . were transformed by plantocracy logics . . . with spaces for *us* (inhabited by secular economically comfortable man and positioned in opposition to the underdeveloped impoverished spaces for *them*) being cast as the locations the oppressed should strive toward.[92]

As a result, Black and Latinx participants, like Alex, needed to point out to white participants how they failed to see their power and privilege. Many lesbians and queers of color feared that recording certain of their stars and lines would betray the ways people of color operate in their own communities. Alex's comment about "where the girls go" thus remains largely unmapped in mainstream—i.e., predominantly white, middle-class lesbian-queer—periodicals, websites, novels, stories, and other communiqués.

At times and among many white participants, antiracism was enacted and not merely extolled as part of dyke politics. As white supremacist voices and power have grown more visible to white liberals while I wrote this book, I have seen even more of my participants—and lesbians and queers more broadly—take up antiracist and anticapitalist tenets of dyke politics with a fervor I had not seen in my lifetime. Yet in the lived reality of late-2000s gentrification, some participants (usually white) described a lesbian-queer geographical imagination of community overcoming class and race oppressions.

Participants of color and working-class participants were more likely to try to remain close with their families. All of my participants of color were also from New York City, so they negotiated physical and social intimacies throughout their lives. In comparison, the stories of my white participants parallel those of Manalansan's description of immigrant, gay Filipino men in New York City who kept a physical distance from while maintaining intimate communities and relationships with their biological families.[93] However—and this is a huge however—like these men, my white, nonimmigrant participants had the privilege to do so while staying in the same country.

Latina, middle-class Yasmin '83 was afraid to come out to her biological family:

> And I [thought], "Oh, they're never gonna understand, they're gonna dis-own me." . . . It was just part of the norm within my culture, within my home, within my family systems, and I wanted to try to honor that, but I didn't want to dishonor myself. . . . I was able to eventually really embrace who I was with my sexual orientation. I had T-shirts that said, "I love to watch lesbians," "I'm a lipstick lesbian." Yeah, I just wear that. Like, so gracefully. I'm just: here I am. [opens arms with a flourish] . . .
>
> And, actually, my mother has gotten better with it. Like, she actually started to accept my partners. . . . My father's not doing too well with it still. . . . My mother [sometimes] says to me, "I don't know what hap-pened to you. You must have done some drugs with that first girl you was messing with. . . . And that's why you're the way you are." . . . Although she's receiving it a lot better and respecting it.

Structures of racial capitalism require queers of color to remain com-mitted to their biological families and communities of color, which Yasmin describes as a form of honor. Yasmin also "didn't want to dis-honor" her sexuality and relationships. This bifurcated commitment requires disidentifications from her mother's iterant homophobia and her father's decades of "not doing too well" with her sexuality. Relatedly, the dependence on the family can be all the more intensified for immigrants since, per Reddy, what is "definitional to living as an immigrant in [New York] City" often makes it an impossibility to embrace "being gay."[94]

In both parallel and contrast, Afro-Caribbean, working-class Tre described the constant back-and-forth she experienced coming out twenty years after Yasmin did:

> [My mother will] be like, "How's [name of Tre's girlfriend]?" . . . next day she'll be like, "You know, your lifestyle is causing—everything negative thing that is happening in your life is because of your lifestyle." I'm just like, "No!" I love her, but. . . . So I'm like, "What you say makes a difference in my life . . . what we say has power."

Yasmin's twenty-five years of fluctuating disidentification between her family and her sexuality is similar to the pattern of disidentification Tre has enacted decades later between her family and her "lifestyle." It was my participants of color who both knowingly and unknowingly exerted affective, social, and economic capital in order to claim their identities and spaces, to walk and roll along longer lines to reach more distant stars, to form constellations visible only to those rooted in a particular location. As Lane found, more than half the Black queer women in her study regarding Black queer women's spaces in DC "were still in the midst of dealing with their immediate family's ambivalence toward their sexuality, and rather than dealing with being exiled from family, they had to negotiate *how* they interacted with their family around their sexuality."[95] The process of "negotiation" *is* disidentification. Some of my white participants who came out in the 2000s found immediate acceptance when coming out, but most of my participants, especially Black and Latinx women and tgncp, described securing tolerance if not acceptance only through years of negotiations with their families.

At the same time, all of my participants across race and class described, at least in some measure, "families of choice," or the ability to create kinship by choosing who to call family among friends and lovers when biological family may reject you.[96] Lesbian Herstory Archives organizational records indicate that the oldest continuing lgbtq organization in New York City, Imperial Kings and Queens (founded in 1968), was a mixed-race socializing group that afforded a space for "transgenderists" (cross-dressers, drag queens, transgender people, and gender non-conforming people) and their partners to gather.[97] Trans queer of color activists Marsha P. Johnson and Sylvia Rivera founded Street Transvestite Action Revolutionaries (STAR) in 1970 as a gender non-conforming and transgender street activist coalition. As mothers of the household—much like the ball culture made public in *Paris Is Burning* and drag queen culture more recently made public in *RuPaul's Drag Race* and *Pose*—Johnson and Rivera provided housing, shelter, and support to young trans people.[98] Moore writes that Black lesbian families in New York City are "invisible families," as Black lesbianism is eroticized rather than read as familial.[99] My participants of color experienced New York City in the same way Black queer women experienced DC in Lane's study: they "are grafted into the very fabric of their neighborhoods," like constellations that can be seen only from a certain vantage point.[100]

Participants without strong biological familial support during our interviews were more likely to be raised in conservative religious households. Like generations before them who turned to books and periodicals, Tre and other 2000s-generation participants turned to the internet for answers: "I just needed to know, like, 'Can people be gay and Christian and still believe in God?' That was huge! . . . It was like, 'Where do all the gay people go living in the 'hood? . . . Am I normal? Are there other people?'" Community was often equated with the Black Church among participants of color like Tre. In her study of Black rural lesbians in the US South, Eaves writes that religion "will continue to influence the ways they think about themselves and how they choose to interact with the world."[101]

African American studies scholar E. Patrick Johnson writes that "despite the [Black] church's homophobia, it is a place of comfort—a place, ironically, where they are first accepted, where they first felt a sense of community and belonging."[102] Many of the Black women and tgncp in my research produced "where the girls go" in their constellations, again and again, both within and outside of white, middle- and upper-class lgbtq and lesbian neighborhoods. They returned to and/or lived in Black neighborhoods even when they had to disidentify as part of their everyday lives. Minding the space of the church, the family, and the Black neighborhood often meant regulating the self through doubt and guilt and limiting displays of public affection.

My participants' stories also made clear that whiteness is neither experienced as a totalizing nor a uniform privilege, particularly in regard to religion. Many white participants did not feel liberated in their queerness. For example, white, androgynous Cullen '99 shared that the Ani DiFranco album *Little Plastic Castles* kept her alive during the painful time when she was being sent to "ex-gay ministries and all of that stuff." The room of white, Black, and Latinx, working middle- and middle-class women and tgncp fell silent in sympathetic heartbreak. Shared violence against lgbtq minds and bodies brought their connections into a bright if not burning clarity. Overall, though, the racialization of constellations kept lesbians and queers apart as much as it bound them together. There are the stars that fall outside of our position at one pole or another, still more stars that can be seen only if you know to look, and lines to be walked, rolled, and ridden between them with friends, family, kin, lovers, acquaintances, and strangers.

Like the vague but certain "where the girls go" Alex see as definitive of Black lesbian-queer geographies, there is also an intentional absence I have produced in this chapter. As McKittrick writes, Black women's "bodily geographies are not only unfinished and incomplete, they must have a place."[103] I am often asked: are there Black lgbtq and/or lesbian neighborhoods, or lesbian-queer of color clusters of homes and/or businesses in the city?[104] Yes, there are pockets of New York City neighborhoods that operate exactly in this way. In reference to one working-class, primarily Black neighborhood, Wanda stated there were "*old, old, old* neighborhoods" of Black lesbians to be found there. Bailey described one area as a "lesbian haven but nobody knows about it because the people who are talking about it aren't white and aren't . . . there." I only begin to record "where the girls go" and intentionally do not name many spaces like this neighborhood so that Black and Latinx women and tgncp can name their spaces as such if or when they see fit.

Constellations at times work for but also around and against capitalist projects of real estate development, commodification, tourism, rezoning, and housing financialization that would likely follow by labeling these stars on a map. In fact, these geographic places appear already in constellations, and in those stars yet to be born.

# 4

## Dyke Slope

African American, middle-class Naomi '89 was just fifteen years old when she and her friends would secretly take the subway to the city's only lesbian neighborhood, in Brooklyn. She said,

> After BiGLYNY—Bisexual, Gay, and Lesbian Youth of New York— [meetings at the Village's LGBT Center] we would get on the [F subway] train and we would go to Brooklyn. . . . I was like [*excited, wide-eyed*], "What are we going to do?!?!" [*even more excited, bouncing up and down*] "We're going to look at *lesbians*!!!" [*sits still*] And we would just hang in Park Slope. . . . [We would] go to Dyke Slope. I actually wrote in "Dyke Slope" [on my map] [*group laughter*].

A decade later, I was as clueless as Naomi about where to find other lesbians in New York City, even though I was about to move there after graduating college. When older lesbians took one look at very butch me, they said, "Honey, you've got to move to Park Slope." And so I did. And so did a lot of other lesbians, dykes, and queers for a period that spanned at least forty years—until many lesbians and queers were forced from or made invisible in the same neighborhood that they (ironically) played a key role in gentrifying. While discussing Park Slope, some of my white, middle-class, and/or college-educated participants—non-heterosexual women and transgender and gender non-conforming people (tgncp) who also face contracted political and economic power—focused on their "failure" to keep New York City's only lesbian neighborhood. Examining both the liberatory and agonizing aspects of spatialized queer failure, I reveal how participants made, retained, and would (inevitably) lose some of the greatest clusters of lesbian-queer constellations in one of the most expensive cities in the world.

By the time I conducted my research in 2008 and 2009, Park Slope was brimming with bookstores, cafés, restaurants, patisseries, toy shops, bodegas, boutiques, delis, and high-end home stores. Picturesque Prospect Park, with its gentle hills, meandering paths, busy softball fields, and queer and trans picnic gatherings, lies at the top of the Slope. Just thirty minutes from Manhattan (and the queer North Star that is the LGBT Center), stunning three-story brownstone homes fill tree-lined side streets that bustle with the noises of children playing, the crunch of leaves under pedestrians' feet, and the periodic whoosh of cabs. Distinctions between North and South Slope and the neighborhood's borders saturated Brooklynites' conversations—i.e., not-at-all-cleverly coded status debates based on race, ethnicity, and class that asserted the white, middle-class, and/or college-educated as the default citizens of Park Slope. By 2008 and still today, Park Slope's borders were (often) marked by the thoroughfares of Fourth Avenue, Prospect Park West, Flatbush Avenue, and the Brooklyn-Queens Expressway, and the adjacent neighborhoods of Gowanus, Boerum Hill, Prospect Heights, Crown Heights, Windsor Terrace, and Greenwood Heights (figure 4.1).[1]

When we turn a feminist eye to Park Slope, another reading of lesbian-queer experience reveals itself. Unsurprisingly, most narratives of urban progress are predicated on "female disappearance," whether that be their being made invisible, slut shaming, rape culture, having their land and occupations stolen, or their outright murder.[2] Writing of women's protests on behalf of disappeared women who have likely been murdered in Mexico, feminist geographer Melissa Wright argues that

> when the women of La Paz refuse to disappear and when the human rights activists hold up their signs, they turn the valorization of female disappearance on its head and stalk the urban elites with another vision of value: a city that survives through women's reappearances.[3]

Dyke Slope is a queer failure in a radical sense insofar as it represents a refusal to suffer the call for isolation, silence, and self-blame of cis-heteropatriarchy, a refusal enacted in participants' dyke politics: in the cultural institutions they formed, in the anticapitalist economies they often extolled, in the mass of women's bodies on public city streets, and in the volunteer labor they dedicated to producing and maintaining healing spaces, supporting schools, art studios, animal shelters, nonprofits, CSAs, and in other activism. As queer geographer Lynda Johnston

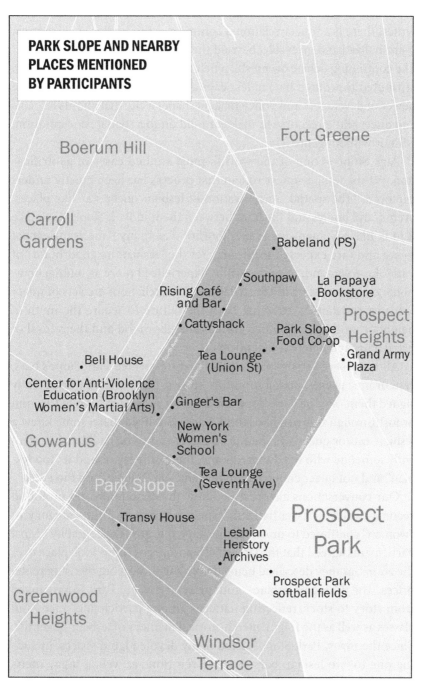

Figure 4.1. Map of Park Slope and nearby places often mentioned by participants

writes, there is a "queer relational commitment to bodies deemed most marginalized and grievable, beyond the category of lesbian," queer, etc.[4] The continuing debate over lesbian neighborhoods' decline is most often attributed to women having less capital, but we must also see how the power of developers and policy makers shapes a city that affords lesbians and queers little recourse to make or hold on to a spatial concentration, with or without gentrifying.

Park Slope is one of the world's most studied cases of gentrification, yet the lesbian-queer role in that process has been greatly underexplored.[5] The spatial concentration of lesbian-queer star-like places, events, and bodies and the lines between them in Park Slope may make it look like a lesbian-queer neighborhood as many Americans expect to see and (are expected to) desire. Yet the "lesbian neighborhood" of Park Slope was and, to many, still is experienced more as multigenerational clusters of stars in constellations. Constellations are acts of queer feminist resistance, reflecting both the failure to secure the myth of neighborhood liberation in a formal neighborhood and the refusal of patriarchal and heterosexual norms.

All forty-seven of my participants had frequented Park Slope's bars, restaurants, events, and community spaces, had a friend who secretly signed them into the Park Slope Food Co-op, or walked or rolled around or just through this neighborhood. Some had lived there, some knew a lesbian and/or queer who had lived there, and some had dated or slept with someone who lived there. Some, like Sudie '99, found it "too lesbian" and not queer enough, or, like Dana '98, "bougie" and too elitist.

Our conversations also revealed how the dissolution and profound reconstitution of essentialized lesbian identity and the category of "woman" continued to drastically reshape this group's geography.[6] Most participants agreed that the largest lesbian-queer exodus took place over the 2000s, as they described being driven out or kept out by rising rental prices. The timing of lesbians' and queers' arrival in Park Slope ranged from story to story, reflecting patterns among participants' races and classes as well as the fragmented historical memory of lesbian-queer life. Since the 1970s, Park Slope hosted many devoted lgbtq spaces, including one to two lesbian bars at any given time, as well as a gay men's bar, a women-only gym, two gay, lesbian, and/or women's bookstores (depending on who you asked), an antiviolence center, and the Lesbian

Herstory Archives (LHA). When I began my research in 2008, Dyke Slope housed two lesbian bars, Cattyshack and Ginger's; only the latter still operated in 2019. The neighborhood has hosted Brooklyn Pride marches and celebrations since 2010.

Park Slope ranks (or ranked, to some) as the only "lesbian neighborhood" in New York City. Few of these areas exist or have existed in the United States, including the likes of the also disappearing/disappeared Mission District in San Francisco and Andersonville in Chicago.[7] Feminist geographer Tamar Rothenberg, in her research on Park Slope's lesbian spaces in the early 1990s, wrote that lesbians rely on the "*spatial significance* of the lesbian 'community,'" which took the form a spatial "concentration" or "networks" rather than a formal lesbian neighborhood.[8] These concentrations are residential, commercial, or a mix thereof, but they are not a traditional neighborhood in that women did not majority-own, visibly occupy, and/or control these areas. Like the lesbians Rothenberg interviewed, my participants also described having little ability to assert outright, permanent spatial territorialization. Instead they clustered, like stars, into certain (then affordable) areas that, at times, fit their political economy and cultural values (see jgieseking.org/AQNY).

My argument here is that the (mostly white, middle-class, and/or college-educated) labor of lesbians and queers to create spatial community also generates the conditions of their own spatial demise—even as their geographical imagination kept the idea of a neighborhood intact. Extending Rothenberg's earlier insights about the patterns of lesbian-on-lesbian gentrification, I found that the qualifiers of white, middle-class, and/or college-educated are in parentheses above to indicate how the privilege that shaped Park Slope often went unsaid or unexamined in our conversations. My analysis reveals that dyke politics necessitate an active commitment to the production of certain types of star-like places: creating and frequenting community gardens, setting up community-supported agriculture (CSA) networks and produce stands, frequenting local bookstores, attending potlucks, forming health justice centers, fundraising for local nonprofits, spreading the word about brunch restaurants, participating in women's rights activism, organizing on behalf of prison abolition and local animal shelters, volunteering at (and complaining about) co-ops, and joining yoga studios. A mix of consumerism, place-making, and volunteerism, the ideal markers of lesbian-queer spatial community are both an upper middle-class family's and real estate agent's dream: where lesbian clogs, boots, and heels tread, price hikes soon followed.

Some of my participants saw the loss of Park Slope as their own personal "failure," at times a failure to hold on to the neighborhood through activism, and at times a failure to gentrify the neighborhood in order to lay claim to it. White, working middle-class Sally '96 shared:

> I would say it's hard for me to say that I've ever had a gay community. . . . I think it's something you slip into and slip out of . . . it's not a stable space. It's not like [*cartoon voice*], "Oh, now I go home to my queer community." [*group laughter*] It's not like, "Oh, I go home to my queer neighborhood." . . . We don't have . . . a town in upstate you go home to every night. You know it's like we're constantly moving in and out of queer and straight and lesbian spaces and mostly we're in kind of, like [*sighs*] . . . spaces that are heteronormative or whatever you want to call it. So I wouldn't say I really have a queer community. And I felt like it's kind of a failing on my part.

Like stars that come and go in the sky, the lesbian-queer spaces that Sally tells us that "you slip into and slip out of" are fleeting and fragmented, "not a stable space." Her story recalls cultural theorist Jack Halberstam's feminist theorization of "queer failure" as a form of liberation: "failure allows us to escape the punishing norms that discipline behavior and manage human development with the goal of delivering us from unruly childhoods to orderly and predictable adulthoods."[9] In this antisocial refusal of normativity—for example, "constantly moving in and out of queer and straight and lesbian spaces"—Sally and others like her are Halberstam's "subjects who unravel," as they fail to attend to capitalist, racist, and cis-heteropatriarchal demands to hold on to territory.[10]

My participants' stories reveal that their failures are liberatory but also harmful and even violent, causing some lesbians and queers to emotionally, geographically, and relationally unravel. They described the isolation, unease, despair, doubt, and anger, as well as the dispossession, financial burdens, and displacement in "failing." I and many of my participants connect with the celebratory, antisocial turn of "queer failure," but a geographical reading of the term also points out that the failure to enact white cis-heteropatriarchal capitalist norms can also result in depression, anxiety, isolation, and even suicide.[11] Saturated in the myth of neighborhood liberation under capitalism, my participants were unable to sustain or (re)create a long-term, territorial, lesbian neighborhood—other than renting a commercial space or a weekly or monthly event—as a "respite from an incessantly heterosexist society."[12] If we take a step back, it is clear that white settler, cis-heteropatriarchal capitalism is structured so that women and tgncp—and, differently but relatedly, people of color and working-class and poor people—were rarely if ever meant to secure the American Dream's project of territorialization through property ownership. The precarious conditions of everyday urban life and geopolitical insecurity mixed with the global housing crisis are all the more intensified for lesbians and queers.[13]

Few of my participants of color and working-class participants felt that Dyke Slope was ever theirs. Further, attending college (as in my own story) became a mark of cultural privilege that enabled participants to claim many spaces in the city, including Park Slope.[14] When we hold the liberatory potential of failure in tension with the painful loss experienced in the dissolution of and displacement from Park Slope, my participants' stories of Park Slope and other lesbian-queer "disappeared" places over generations also complicate queer failure. I also want to intervene in the "ideology of positive thinking [that] insists on success," per Halberstam, which, in my research, assumes that success through property ownership is required let alone possible.[15] It was almost always, again and again, primarily my white, middle-class, and/or educated participants who sensed that they "failed" to make a visible, physical, long-term neighborhood, while all of my participants contributed to producing the brightest clusters of lesbian-queer stars in the urban galaxy.

## When Lesbians Were "Pioneers": Early Waves of Gentrification in the 1980s

Gloria '83 moved to "Dyke Slope," as she also called it, in the 1980s. She recalled, "I told somebody I lived in it . . . and she assumed I was gay because I lived there. A *straight person*!" Gloria's map shows a clustering of friends and hangouts in Greenwich Village, and the nearby grouping

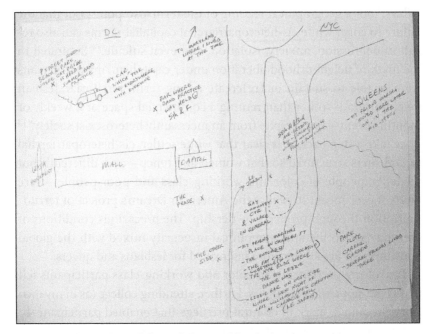

Figure 4.2. Gloria '83's mental map (white, middle-class)

of friends' homes in Park Slope, as well as a friend in Queens (figure 4.2). Describing her map—half of which focuses on her coming out in Washington, DC—she said that she included Park Slope ("of course") because "I had several friends who lived there so I used to take the [subway] train over there." Gloria's limited constellations reflect how the singular residential and commercial clusters of stars in Dyke Slope read as a neighborhood of one's own.

Poignantly, stories of Park Slope's significance to queer life in the 1980s were relayed almost exclusively by white women, which was interrupted by Naomi's story of repeatedly visiting the area as a teenager. White, middle-class, butch Gloria '83 was one of those visible lesbians that young Naomi may have seen as a role model on the streets of the Slope. This racialized distinction also hints at how the default, mainstream subject of the urban lesbian became white, both in the streets and in the historic production of a lesbian neighborhood.

Reflecting on historian Lillian Faderman's hallmark US twentieth-century lesbian history, *Odd Girls and Twilight Lovers*, urban planner

Moira Kenney describes the 1980s "lesbian community" as envisioned around a political economy "with the establishment of food co-ops, medical clinics and other social services, and independent businesses of all types. . . . [It was] the moment when lesbian politics [were] most clearly articulated and connected to lesbian urban reality."[16] Faderman may have had in mind the concentration of lesbian-owned, -run, -staffed, and/or -oriented businesses in Park Slope. The significant number of star-like places that developed out of the feminist movement were pivotal in branding Park Slope as lesbian: La Papaya bookstore, New York Women's School, the Brooklyn Women's Martial Arts (now the Center for Anti-Violence Education [CAE]), and a women's gym, as well as the Park Slope Food Co-op.

By placing cisgender "women" first, the neighborhood would also take on a radical and covertly homosexual edge in the public eye. "Women's spaces" were feminist spaces where covert and/or open lesbianism among those assigned female at birth could flourish. Most of the heterosexual population of the city—Gloria's straight friend being a rare exception—did not yet regard Park Slope as lesbian in the early 1980s. Overt lesbian claims to the neighborhood would likely have exposed women and tgncp to violence. As white, Jewish, middle-class Esther'87 shared about Sevens, a women's gym: "It was owned by two lesbians. It was run by two lesbians. . . . It wasn't you know, a lesbian gym by any means . . . it really was a women's gym." Esther's lesbian/women's space distinction also reflects the discourse participants employed in the 1980s to negotiate their place in the feminist movement and the urban landscape.

Notably, Park Slope did not yet possess the quintessential lesbian-queer hangout of a lesbian bar. Instead, my participants' stories corroborate Rothenberg's assertion that "the timing of Park Slope's gentrification and the women's movement—particularly the directions of lesbian-feminism, cultural feminism and radical feminism—was essential in creating Park Slope as the centre of lesbian population in New York."[17] In comparison to the high-density bars and places for gay men in lgbtq Greenwich Village and gay male Chelsea and Hell's Kitchen (in pricier Manhattan), lesbian-queer women and tgncp could only financially and socially afford to gather in smaller numbers and fewer places in the 1980s. As such, the constellations that formed in and across Park Slope (in more affordable Brooklyn) allowed a more varied social and political environment less reliant on catchall bar spaces.

As early as the 1970s, urban lesbians sought out ethnically mixed, working-class areas with a strong "quality of neighborhood life, low-rent housing, and the possibility of maintaining a kind of anonymity."[18] Lesbian propertied claims to land and territory have been rare, with the exception of the (largely rural) lesbian land movement, which also began in the 1970s.[19] Activist historian Joyce Cheney wrote in her 1985 book, *Lesbian Land*: "What is male has so demonstratively not worked, that it seems the only thing to do is to start fresh, with the stuff of our women's lives for material."[20] She went on to add, "We know we will not survive if we don't start to build a world as we know it can be, free of violence, suffering, exploitation." Lesbian land often evolved into an American Dream removed (from the patriarchal city) rather than deferred (by building an urban neighborhood). Those in the land movement communally buy, share, and tend to their property, particularly at times and in locations when land and housing are more affordable, but often excluded working-class and poor women.[21]

The urban lesbians concentrating in Park Slope were part of or overlapped with a national trend that urban historian Suleiman Osman describes as "middle-class migration" that "blossomed into a full-fledged back to the city movement."[22] The self-declared "pioneers" in this migration sought "authenticity" as they "envisioned themselves as place missionaries, moving into poor, increasingly nonwhite Brooklyn on a mission of rescue."[23] For this reason, lesbian land and back-to-the-city projects—developed under settler colonialism and racial capitalism—must be in conversation. Like moths drawn to flannel-tinted stars of communal hope, those building constellations of lesbian feminist politics that sought community in place had found, at least for some, their urban lesbian "land" in Park Slope.

The assumption that participants had attended college often circulated through their politics and socializing. They used their knowledge, credentialization, class, and connections as a way of claiming space. College was not an option for Latina, middle-class Yasmin '83 in the 1980s, so that when white, middle-class Noelle '83 said to her 1980s-generation co-interviewees, "We're educated. We all have graduate degrees or something," Yasmin replied, "Yeah, as of last week!"—and she meant it.

Park Slope had a largely working-class population, and around a third of the neighborhood was Hispanic or Latinx in the early 1980s (figure 4.3). The neighborhood became increasingly moneyed and white as property values and rents soared. While none of my participants spoke of embracing such a racist "mission," there was no evidence that members of their cohort had organized with or even expressed sympathy for (who they imagined to be) the neighborhood's non-lesbian or non-middle-class lesbian residents. While rents remained low across the city, Park Slope had the second largest increase in property sale prices in the city during the 1980s, a whopping 299.7 percent markup (the Brooklyn average was 180 percent).[24]

Gentrifiers in the back-to-the-city movement—many white and middle-class lesbians among them—continued to remodel landlord-abandoned buildings ("left behind" in the 1970s financial crisis) and other disinvested properties until the "renovated" brownstone look produced an increasingly refined neighborhood aesthetic. Similarly to other gentrifying Brooklyn neighborhoods, Park Slope lost 50 percent of its low-rent units in the 1970s real estate boom, while residents "anxious to preserve the neighborhood's low-rise character and family atmosphere" successfully opposed plans to construct a low-income apartment tower.[25] To amplify how gentrification became an aesthetic element of white, middle-class, and college-educated life in the city, I include the cover of lesbian activist and writer Sarah Schulman's *Gentrification of the Mind* depicting a row of sought-after brownstone homes near Prospect Park (figure 4.4).

The possibility of creating lesbian lands and the failure of most so far arose often in our conversations, with participants frequently taking sides, as in one discussion among members of a multigenerational, mixed-race, mixed-class group:

ALEX '98: Why don't lesbians all get together and move to the same area?

SUSAN '92: Right?! I think we should colonize an upstate town. [*group laughter*]

YASMIN '83: A lesbian *community*, right? [*sarcastically*] Riiiiiiight.

SUSAN: I'm serious. I'm there.

KATE '03: [*sarcastically*] That would be *totally* functional. That wouldn't *self-destruct* at *all*. [*group laughter*]

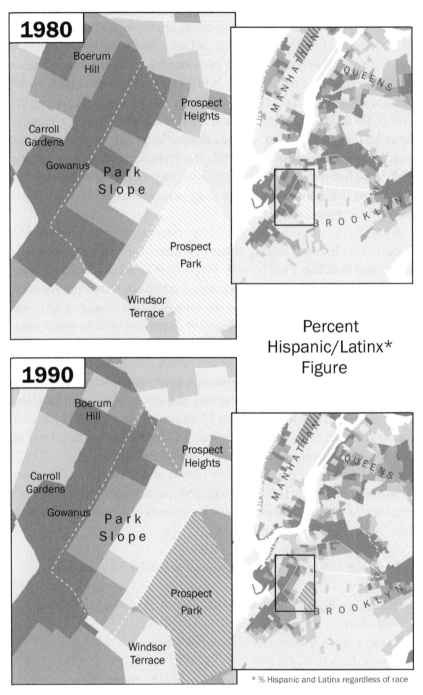

Figure 4.3. Census maps showing Hispanic percentage of population (with details of Park Slope), 1980, 1990, 2000, and 2010

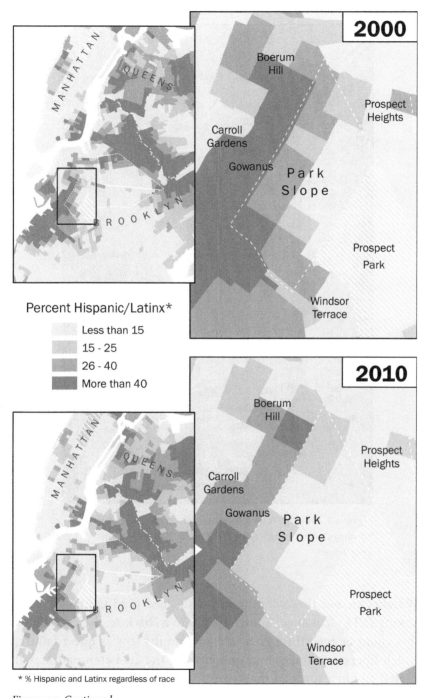

Figure 4.3. *Continued*

Figure 4.4. Brooklyn brownstones as seen on the cover of Sarah Schulman's *The Gentrification of the Mind: Witness to a Lost Imagination*

Whether or not these communities succeed (and many still do), Susan's call to "colonize" a town speaks to a "back-to-the-city" ethos that could be read through a lesbian feminist lens as queer failure, which liberates lesbians and queers from the cis-heteropatriarchal capital city in a space of their own. Such claims also rely on tactics of settler homonationalism, succumbing to "imperial biopolitics" by claiming and enacting liberal subjecthood.[26] In these conversations, there was also the tenor of antiruralism that urban settler colonialism depends upon.

Historian Christina Hanhardt demonstrates how gays and lesbians have drawn upon white, middle-class claims to safety in producing mixed gay and lesbian urban neighborhoods since the 1970s. She writes that they "merged with the goal of visibility" to "increasingly fit liberal gay politics into the broader forces of a city whose land market was ripe for new investment opportunities."[27] I found that women's spaces could flourish only by claiming space in a neighborhood already home to other marginalized people, namely the poor and people of color. My findings here extend Hanhardt's argument by showing that some lesbians adopted the same strategies in producing lesbian neighborhoods, but, as women and tgncp, had significantly less ability than white, middle-class gay men did to retain their neighborhood in New York City.

With a large number of abandoned buildings, the area was so heavily hit by the crack epidemic that Birtha '84, a white artist who then lived in Park Slope, called it a "major crack neighborhood." Jackie '85 recalled that Fourth Avenue, a busy six-lane thoroughfare that serves as the physical edge of the neighborhood on its western downhill side, was filled with "one crack-addled prostitute after another. It was pretty scary. And our car was broken into . . . we were afraid but it wasn't going to let us act any differently." While Jackie and Birtha did not racialize their stories, the allusion to "crack-addled prostitutes" evokes the war on drugs' racialization of the crack epidemic as a Black and Latinx issue. Media portrayals of the "crack mother," the "aggressively sexual black Jezebel who threatens the lives and safety of her born and unborn children," reasserted President Reagan's explicitly feminized and implicitly racialized description of poor and working-class as "welfare queens."[28] To further legitimate the destruction of the welfare state, the myth of the welfare queen and narrative of the "crack mother" ridiculed this group, claiming they preferred to take welfare rather than work. Stereotypes like these were used to legitimate Black and Latinx displacement due to processes of gentrification and policing in the neighborhood for decades.[29] As Jackie and others like her felt no urgency to "act any differently," their role in the gentrification also progressed against those bodies marked as pathologized and less grievable to the racist, settler capitalist machine.

Even with their sense of living and/or socializing in a lesbian neighborhood, women's and tgncp's claim to public space in Park Slope remained tentative and fragmented at best. Jackie recalled how her safety
and her claim to the neighborhood had to be constantly reproduced
within structures of white cis-heteropatriarchy:

> But, you know, there's been a number of times I've walked down the street
> holding hands with my girlfriend in Park Slope in the eighties, and we'd
> get yelled at. Some old, Irish guys shouted at us, "Go back to San Fran-
> cisco!" . . . Like [I respond with], "I live on St. Mark's Place [a street in
> the heart of Park Slope]! I don't know what to tell you." That was pretty
> hilarious.

Jackie uses her address in the heart of Park Slope to both laugh off a verbal assault and to legitimate her claim to the space as hers and for others
like her. In contrast to her description of her partner being punched in
1980s Greenwich Village as unsurprising (described in chapter 2), Park
Slope is a space where Jackie's white, upper middle-class body safely
belongs and the aged, white homophobe does not. Her story flips who
can claim the neighborhood, from the traditional ("old, Irish" men,
prostitutes, addicts) to the "modern" authority of what is cosmopolitan
and, in so doing, repeating many of the same claims made for the basis
of colonization. Her queer failure to refuse disciplining of her body by
white cis-heteropatriarchy still relies on white privilege to legitimate a
space of home for all lesbians and queers. "This everyday world of white
unseeing," writes literary scholar Patricia Yeager, is "a cloud of unknow-
ing that extends over everyday racial interactions."[30]

Violence also materialized in the harassment and attacks that women
and tgncp faced in the city—with consistent detriment to their mental
and physical well-being—overtly in the 1980s and 1990s, and more covertly in the 2000s per my participants.[31] Lesbian-queer gentrification
would help bring (brief) citywide media coverage to lesbian-queer concerns at the end of the decade. The New York Times reported a 65 percent
increase in attacks against homosexuals in the city between 1989 and
1990, two of which were the much discussed 1990 "lesbian bashings"
in Park Slope.[32] Rapes and shootings of lesbians in Brooklyn continued

through the decade, with little to no attention from the mainstream press. In 1994, CAE records state that an African American woman was raped in Prospect Park and police leaked false information that she wasn't raped. In 1995, they record that two women were shot in Boerum Hill, one fatally; women were robbed at gunpoint in Park Slope; and a serial rapist attacked women in Park Slope.[33] I recall being told by (other white, middle-class, and/or college-educated) women I met that, when walking home at night, I should not speak to drivers who would call out from their cars asking directions, as there were men who would grab women and then cruelly drag them along.

After discussing the gentrification of and violence against women in Park Slope, mixed-race/Black, working middle-class Bailey '95 said, "You're talking about white women that were getting attacked, right? . . . But this idea that there was a place where lesbians felt safe. *Which* lesbians? *White* lesbians." Bailey makes clear that which lesbians were given attention and where in Park Slope—the city's exemplar neighborhood of gentrification for good—reveal the white privilege in who can aspire to or attain "safety." The "word-of-mouth" culture that drew lesbians to Park Slope, per Rothenberg, also circulated understandings of how to navigate the violence they faced there.[34] Park Slope lesbians knew that bashings were happening to "some lesbians"—although their identities were unclear.

Protests against this violence came home to Park Slope as well. My review of Lesbian Herstory Archives organizational records spanning twenty-five years (1983–2008) showed that over 70 percent of groups organized at the national or citywide scale. Only one group came together to advance lesbian-queer concerns in a specific neighborhood and therefore laid claim to that neighborhood, which was, of course, Park Slope. The antiracist and antiviolence group Brooklyn Lesbians and Gays Against Hate Crimes (BLGAHC) held a few protests and marched against the attacks in Park Slope as an offshoot of Queer Nation's radical activist agenda in 1990.[35] Rothenberg wrote that her participants felt the protests were "an assertion of Park Slope as a place where lesbians *should* be able to feel safe; local lesbians were moved to action by outrage over an attack that took place in *their* neighbourhood."[36] A claim to a "lesbian neighborhood" here does not imply ownership, but it does signal how these women's ideas of shared political and social identities congeal and cohere in place.

Alongisde some participants' complicity in gentrification, the BLGAHC's protest merged a defense of territory with claims to bodily sovereignty for lesbians and queers. The sensation of freedom/fear can also be seen in feminist geographer Leslie Kern's research on women's purchase of condominiums in Toronto shows that the "gendered imaginary in revitalization and gentrification" uses "the sexual objectification of women in public space" to produce fear as "part of the social production of (patriarchal) urban space."[37] The paradox of freedom/fear and excitement/anxiety that my participants also described, per Johnston, are the same "power relations that structure contemporary gentrified urban life."[38]

Poignantly, the most active lesbian of color groups in the 1980s, like African Ancestral Lesbians United for Social Change, Salsa Soul Sisters, Las Buenas Amigas, and Asian Lesbians of the East Coast, held most of their (recorded) events in the Bronx or at Manhattan's LGBT Center.[39] When these groups met in Brooklyn outside of predominantly Black neighborhoods like Bed-Stuy, Crown Heights, and Flatbush, LHA records indicate that they did so primarily at the LHA, Prospect Park, and Women's Martial Arts/Center for Anti-Violence Education (CAE). Magdalene '04 described the mixed space of CAE, where survivors of violence still receive free martial arts, self-defense, or tai chi classes. These few meeting grounds in predominantly white Brooklyn indicate that there may have been few interracial queer spaces for organizations and activists to gather at, and that those handful of stars were to be found in Park Slope.

When women assert themselves as key constituents in a given area, a maternal, welcoming, and liberal aura is bestowed on that area in the perception of the cis-heteropatriarchal onlooker. The highly gentrifying Park Slope was cast in the public geographical imagination as the city's "lesbian neighborhood," while radical pockets of intervention also gave it the sensation of greater diversity and inclusion than it actually supported among its residents. The constellations lesbians and queers pieced together between the Co-op and dates, their own apartments and friends' homes, marches and picnics, and around the sites of attacks brought them visibly into the public streets.

## The Place Where White, Middle-Class Lesbians Felt Safe in the 1990s

The 1990s were the most visible decade for the spatializing of dyke politics in New York City's lesbian neighborhood, and, in tandem, participants who came out in the 1980s and 1990s had more attachments to Park Slope. For white, working middle-class, genderqueer Heather '95, the neighborhood was defined as lesbian-queer: "My first girlfriend lived on Sixth Avenue [in Park Slope], and she was very cool because she was already out and she was already in Park Slope. And so she was, like, *official*." Heather then described the half of their mental map that they drew in Park Slope (figure 4.5):

> The Lesbian Herstory Archives is up here and it kind of represents all the places that I'd go to do lesbian things I like to do. Oh, this is when I was doing welfare rights organizing . . . right there. And then Radical Jewish Lesbian Seder. My first girlfriend was Jewish and she just had this whole world of these incredible people who liked and found a way to bring together their radicality and culture.

Heather's map splits down the middle, with the sights and sounds of Greenwich Village as a series of fragmented places on the left, and the congealed, street layout of political Park Slope on the right. A smattering of key figures (their lesbian aunts), lesbian-queer haircuts, and books (by Audre Lorde, Gloria Anzaldúa, Cherrie Moraga, etc.) fill the space between to configure their queer identity in place.

They went on about what we called a "dyke nod" in our conversations—holding eye contact and perhaps nodding to a dyke passerby—felt easier in Park Slope:

> I like making that connection. . . . On better days I definitely smile and make eye contact. It makes me feel comfortable . . . it creates more of a shared space. I do remember being in Park Slope and doing the dyke nod . . . like if it's two of us like we're passing or we're alone . . . or going to something, and if it's more or less straight, then it's more of a solidarity thing. . . . I didn't especially do it a lot. But I did do it.

Figure 4.5. Heather '95's mental map (white, working middle-class)

The constellations Heather describes—a set of tight, multigenerational clusters of stars that they return to again and again—give the appearance of a lesbian neighborhood where everything was "right there." Like many other participants' stories, their stars of lesbian-queer places and the lines between them in the 1990s are further intertwined in a mix of radical politics, corporate consumption, and sprawling gentrification.

Participants' stories portrayed how the large lesbian-queer residential population, along with a constant stream of stardust in the paths of lesbian-queer visitors, made Park Slope its own hub of activism. Janice '79/'91, who is white, middle-class, and lives in a rare rent-stabilized Park Slope apartment, joined the popular group Slope Activities for Lesbians (SAL).⁴⁰ She recalled that the members "would meet at the leader's apartment or we would listen to kd lang, or hav[e] picnics in Prospect Park. Sometimes on the weekend we would paste the posters onto street lamps and stuff." A group of 1980s-generation lesbians—white and Black, middle-class and working middle-class—fondly recalled their experiences of SAL:

> JACKIE '85: Well, I was living in the Slope in the early nineties, and this woman . . . started this group called Slope Activities for Lesbians.

ALL: SAL! [*smiles, nodding, inaudible cross-talk*]

JACKIE: What was great about it was—I knew her already maybe from Queer Nation? Yes, that's how I met her. She had this great girlfriend who was a super butch dyke with huge tattoos who was . . . a total animal lover . . . this lovely woman.

WANDA '85: And that did something for you. [*group laughter*]

JACKIE: She looked like this tough, biker dyke.

WANDA [*sarcastically*] Who had gentle hands. [*group laughter*]

JACKIE: . . . anyway . . . they were very different people and we had one activity at our apartment. I don't know how all these working-class, Latina dykes found their way to our apartment. It was like games night or something. They were all playing Boggle together, and I was like I would never in a million years have met these women if we weren't just lesbians who wanted to hang out with other lesbians. . . . I was struck by how different [we] were. There was what I'd think of as an old-style butch/femme Latina couple, a couple of young, white women with long hair, a butch, white woman with tattoos, a Black woman with dreads, and my girlfriend and me with our short haircuts, unshaven armpits, and Queer Nation T-shirts.

The cross-race and cross-class contact—what novelist and essayist Samuel Delany describes as deeper connections than mere networking—between dykes enacted the sense of community that my participants sought in an urban lesbian land.⁴¹ The antiracist, anticapitalist activism of SAL speaks to the queer failure that refuses the white cis-heteropatriarchal state. On the heels of ACT UP and Queer Nation, and meeting at the same time as the Lesbian Avengers, SAL members could merge antiracist and anticapitalist politics, socializing, and desire to interact with people they "would never have met in a million years."

Most 2000s-generation participants idealized the "community" of the 1980s and 1990s. Through a retrospective generational lens, we can see the geographical imagination, radical crisis response, mainstream political abandonment, and labor required to produce such a space at a certain time. Geographically, SAL bridged public, affordable, and accessible spaces like parks (especially the oft-mentioned Prospect Park), low-cost gatherings in businesses, and no-cost meetings in private homes. In their vibrant constellations, these home stars were sometimes labeled

Figure 4.6. Co-founder Deb Edel in the Lesbian Herstory Archives. Courtesy of the Lesbian Herstory Archives

on participants' maps but almost always mentioned as the backdrop to stories of relationships, sex, friendship, activism, and solitude.[42] People assigned female at birth have been regulated to homes over the millennia. My participants knew how to draw lines between them as the unrecorded "anchors," the stars of lesbian-queer constellations hidden by the smog of patriarchy.

The most constant star in the Park Slope constellation is a former house that was turned into one of the most culturally important lesbian locales in the city: founded in 1974 in Joan Nestle and Deb Edel's Upper West Side apartment, the Lesbian Herstory Archives (LHA) acquired a permanent place in a Park Slope brownstone in 1992 (figure 4.6). The LHA showed up on many of my participants' mental maps; as Kate '03 put it, she included "the Lesbian Herstory Archives for obvious reasons." Like Heather's "*official*" Park Slope girlfriend, the "obvious" lesbianness of LHA marks Park Slope as lesbian too.

The Archives cost just over $163,000, purchased and paid for primarily by small grants and donations.[43] It was then and still may be the only building owned by a lesbian organization in the New York City metropolitan area.[44] Many participants repeated the story of the building's purchase, as did the women and tgncp in the minutes and flyers of organizational records, and women and tgncp in feature stories of publications. As I sat doing research in the LHA, I also heard these stories from women and tgncp who wandered through the Archives whispering to one another while holding hands, kissing, or buddying around. The LHA's building was valued at nearly $3 million in 2019.[45] While other lesbian-queer spaces disappear, early and sustained investment, dedicated volunteers, multigenerational community, and property tax exemptions (501c3) may be one of the unique combinations that sustains lesbian-queer productions of place.

The LHA is a constant, bright star to enact antiracist, anticapitalist, solidarity-building dyke politics that lesbians and queers hold dear, and a set of rooms of one's own that all dykes are welcome to share. While Rothenberg rightly contends that the LHA extended lesbian gentrification in the Slope, the founders also took the historically feminized, disempowered space of the home, and repurposed it as a radical and stable space from which to collect and share lesbian histories.[46] (On colder days, I'd take down boxes from Adrienne Rich's, Barbara Smith's, and Audre Lorde's archives to sit beside me for company; these three New Yorkers' work are stars in so many participants' constellations, including my own.) The LHA makes a space for memories and evidence of lesbian-queer lives and spaces, even if lesbians, bisexuals, gays, queers, dykes, and other Sapphic sisters can no longer afford to physically live in large numbers in Park Slope. The rarity of lesbian archives and the LHA's collections specifically—compared to lgbtq archives, which have historically tended to focus on the collections of white, cisgender, gay men (notably, men are more often taught their history and assume that it is worth recording)—mirror both the limits and affordances of property ownership under patriarchal capitalism.

In the late 1990s, Park Slope also got its first lesbian bar when the Rising Café and Bar opened. Yet it was more than a bar. The Rising bridged the two most often mentioned lesbian hangouts of the period: bars and coffee shops. Cafés became the "alternative" to (still popular) bars, supporting what Faderman calls the "culture of sobriety" that emerged in the early 1990s, what many of my participants saw as an intervention in the harmful behaviors lgbtq people suffer as a result of homophobia and heteronormative structures.[47] A local café chain, Tea Lounge, was referenced even more often than the Rising. With two of three locations in Park Slope, white, working middle-class Holly '03 said, "Only one [Tea Lounge] is queer. Because one of them is overrun by strollers, one is for hipsters, and one's really gay." I wrote some of this book at various Tea Lounges, and I had my first New York City date at one too. Latina, middle-class Yasmin '83 often used Tea Lounge as a place to meet for dates because, as a femme of color, she felt that she and her butch dates would also feel at home there. She added, "I went to Tea Lounge on my first date with my current partner. We've been together almost five years." White, middle-class Noelle '83 went so far as to explain where she lived in reference to Tea Lounge indicating how much being around other lesbians and queers is central to queer constellations.

The ability for some of my participants to openly express one's sexuality—compared to when, in their living memory, gays and lesbians were regarded as "deviants" who had to meet under cover of night—made these affordable-to-some café haunts central to constellations. Places for both day- and night-time socializing, cafés were open year-round, unlike public parks and most pools. The emphasis on "women's safety" grew in step with Mayor Giuliani's "zoning out sex," anti-homelessness policies, and focus on "broken windows" policing in the 1990s against the backdrop of a world soaked in rape culture, patriarchy, and white supremacy.[48] Kern writes that the culture of women's "fear is integral to the success of revanchist tactics and neoliberal agendas."[49]

It is not just chance that such claims to women's safety emerged during strong eras in the feminist and lgbtq movements, as well as a surge of mainstream media that billed a hypersexualized, white, middle-class "lesbian chic."[50] Art historian Tara J. Burk states, "Perhaps unsurprisingly, the escalation of violence against lesbians in the early 1990s was coextensive with their unprecedented visibility in realms of culture, society, and politics."[51] Activist art collectives like Fierce Pussy and Dyke Action Machine! (DAM!) wheatpasted critical commentary to demand recognition of lesbian lives, bodies, and spaces. Kenney and Faderman poignantly also recorded that the 1980s lesbian activism and community in the urban sphere gave "way to a more market- and media-driven community" in the years that followed, fueled equally by consumerism, commodification, and processes of gentrification.[52] However, as neoliberal politics spiraled, lesbians and queers created their own world that attempted to also thwart these processes.

In the early 1990s, New York City's young and hip began to move en masse to affordable Brooklyn as gentrification in lower Manhattan raised rents too high for too many. Similar price hikes came to Brooklyn by the end of the decade. As white, Jewish, working middle-class Susan '92 shared with her mixed-race, multigeneration co-interviewees:

> I didn't discover Park Slope until '97 or '98. Like I heard rumors—[*group laughter*]—that [there] were like greener, gayer pastures. But I didn't make the move [there] until '98 . . . to about, maybe 2001 or 2000. I sort of watched the gentrification *skyrocket* in those couple of years. . . . My landlord . . . said, "I did renovations! I can triple, quadruple, quintuple your rent!" [*collective "mm-hm"*] So I was like, "Okay. [*sighs*] Time to go!"

The participants laughed, identifying her loss as their own. Others, like white, working middle-class Vanessa '93, shared with shaking fists that she found the "expensive" apartments to be "so small" in the late 1990s that she didn't even try to move to Dyke Slope, and all of her co-participants nodded. Both stories by white, middle-class, and college-educated participants express how, in a quick decade, the claim to an urban lesbian land began to slip away, even as they had more places across the city, like a seemingly expanding galaxy that only spreads stars farther apart. Yet even as fewer of the lines between stars extended toward and from Park Slope, they still expected to turn in that angle, like a gravitational pull back to a mythical dyke homeland—if not a residential neighborhood.

In fact, Park Slope underwent some of the most intense gentrification in New York City history: the median household income was an estimated 32 percent *below* the city average in 1990, and 40 percent *above* average just ten years later (figure 4.7).[53] The processes of gentrification that brought participants into the neighborhood began to quickly overlap with their gentrification out of the neighborhood; the sensation of the fleeting lesbian-queer geographies resonates with their urban political economic conditions.[54] The queer failure to secure a spatial community became clear. Yet the long-term effects were not yet clear to lesbians and queers in the 1990s who still clung to the geographical imagination of an urban lesbian land, clouding out the view of their consistently dazzling constellations.

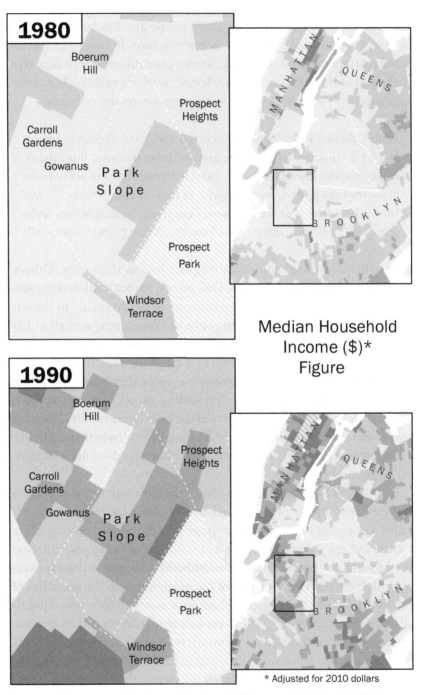

Figure 4.7. Census maps showing median household income (with details of Park Slope), 1980, 1990, 2000, and 2010

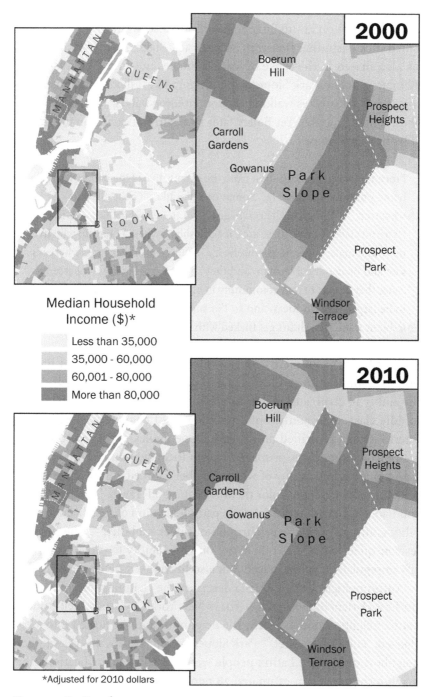

Median Household
Income ($)*

Less than 35,000
35,000 - 60,000
60,001 - 80,000
More than 80,000

*Adjusted for 2010 dollars

Figure 4.7. *Continued*

The fixation on an idyllic neighborhood also whitewashed the racism and classism that fueled it. Mixed-race/Black, middle-class Bailey '95 also shared in the sense of loss: "It makes me angry, because I remember going to Park Slope and it looking like a dyke neighborhood, you know? Like dykes walking around, holding hands. . . . And now it's like: straight, yuppie." Yet Bailey later spoke to the exclusionary aspect of lesbian Park Slope:

> I mean, *I* look at gentrification from the perspective of the people who are being pushed *out*, right? . . . Sometimes I'm like, "Great! Starbucks!" or whatever. . . . Who had the privilege to live there and get to go to Rising [Bar and Café]? 'Cause there are a lot of lesbians where I grew up who live there and make a way for themselves. . . . There *are* other places where it's safe and okay to be a lesbian, and they're not experiencing violence because they're part of that community in other ways. . . . Fifth Avenue used to be largely Puerto Rican and so I'm sure that there were Puerto Rican lesbians there who didn't get fucked with.

Both of Bailey's comments contest the myth of neighborhood liberation as a solution for all lesbians and queers, and again amplify how the ability to claim success or failure is often the purview of the white middle class. Poignantly, only participants of color remarked on the Puerto Ricans gentrified *out* of Park Slope. Bailey speaks in solidarity with the working-class, primarily Puerto Rican and other Hispanic and Latinx populations, many of whom had been forced out by processes of gentrification. Queer of color theorists Fatima El-Tayeb, Jin Haritaworn, and Paola Bacchetta write that "the pathologization of racialized immobility contrasts with the celebration of queer mobility."[55] The lines of lesbian-queer mobilities reflect not only the ability to move about the city unregulated and unpoliced, but also to choose where to live.

Anthropologist Arlene Dávila describes the "Latinization" of El Barrio/East Harlem in the 2000s, perhaps New York City's most well-known Latinx neighborhood, whereby the neighborhood was turned into a racialized, "cultural" market.[56] Park Slope, in comparison, was yet another neighborhood where Latinx people were erased by gentrification. The neighborhood was an estimated 28 percent Hispanic according to US census data in 1980; that would drop to 15 percent by 2010. The Puerto

Rican community who lived in Park Slope indisputably hosted Hispanic and Latinx lesbian gathering locales, but I found only one recorded to sit alongside my and my participants' memories: Queers for Economic Justice had a local lesbian/queer support/social group at a women's shelter near the LHA.[57] I do remember a bar that held weekly lesbian nights filled by Latinx and white women on Eighth Avenue and 15th Street in the early 2000s, but I never could find or find anyone who recalled the party's name or if it had a name. The absence of Puerto Rican lesbian-queer stories in this book amplifies how constellations can be found only if you know when and where to look, and how racialized and classed constellations are.

Latinx geographer Lorena Muñoz writes in her research with queer street vendors in Los Angeles that she "perpetuated understandings of immigrant vending landscapes as heteronormative, thereby rendering queer Latinas . . . invisible in the streets."[58] As a result, she found that "embodied practices inform how street vending is practiced . . . [and are] entangled with embodied heteronormative ideologies that discipline queer bodies in space."[59] While many Latinx voices are absent from this project, Muñoz's insights point to how constellations are intentionally produced with stars and lines hidden or out of sight for survival for many women and tgncp of color and working-class women and tgncp. While Park Slope was one of the city's many historically segregated neighborhoods (99.7 percent white in 1950), US census data indicates that the neighborhood's white population went from an estimated (post–"white flight" and –"urban renewal") 6 percent to a drastic 64 percent higher than the citywide averages between 1980 and 2010.[60] The ensuing whiteness, education, and class privilege that (again) defines Park Slope continues to be similarly premised upon settler colonial promises of innate belonging in gentrified places.

Due to the processes of gentrification, fewer and fewer lesbians and queers of all races and classes could afford to stay in the spaces they helped to create or mark as queer. When I moved to Park Slope in 1999—white, newly middle-class, college-educated, and in my early twenties—I delighted in walking through streets of row after row of elite brownstones, with grand staircases leading up to each, peering in to see built-in bookcases, fireplaces, and stunning lighting. Like many other similarly identified participants, I thought that this is what lesbian-queer life was like until I watched gentrification make my apartment in South Slope unaffordable as well. I performed my own queer failure by being a very visible butch body on the streets of Park Slope. I succumbed to the American meritocratic myth even while I financially struggled to make ends meet. What else could lesbians and queers do, many of us thought, but continue to dream the lesbian land version of the American Dream—white, middle-class, and college-educated all along—into the next century?

## The 2000s: If That's Moving Up, I'm Moving Out

Of all New York City neighborhoods at the turn of the century, participants described the gentrification of Park Slope as especially drastic. The forces that made Park Slope available to some lesbians pushed or kept them out. Like most of my participants, white, working middle-class Holly '03 described how hard it was to afford her life as a New Yorker. Holly told me in her phone intake that she lived at home with her parents to make ends meet as she launched a new career. Like most of my participants, especially those under the age of forty-five, she felt these financial limitations of precarious neoliberalism related to her sense of failure to secure a "whole neighborhood." Structural oppressions that had long fed and were fed by the gentrification of Park Slope structured Holly's and all of my participants' lives. The lesbians and queers who once shared the proximal density of their clustered stars in Park Slope were forced to spread out farther, often into Brooklyn, Queens, and northern Manhattan. Now in step with rather than at the forefront of patterns of gentrification, a pattern of queer failure to secure neighborhood liberation in the form of a "lesbian neighborhood" became increasingly evident as time passed. Instead, the places of lesbian-queer life had always been created in practice and revealed themselves diagrammatically as more resembling the scattering of stars in the sky.

While she spoke of a range of lesbian and queer places across the city, her map shows the same steady geographical imagination of queer New York as Gloria and Heather (who did not grow up in the city), made five years after coming out (figure 4.8). Holly's map includes a series of bars and the LGBT Center in Greenwich Village, and the bars and LHA

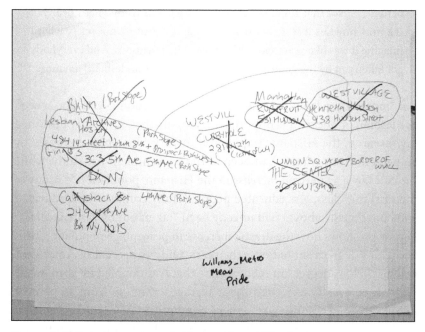

Figure 4.8. Holly '03's mental map (white, working middle-class)

in Park Slope, as well as the lgbtq Metropolitan Bar in Williamsburg, Brooklyn; she crossed out each place as we talked in our group interview. Many would return to or discover Dyke Slope as visitors in the 2000s, invoking the same paradox of belonging/visitation my participants used to describe Greenwich Village.

By the mid-2000s, small, multigeneration local businesses were replaced by up-and-coming stores along what the *New York Times* now billed "hot Fifth Avenue."[61] The increasingly white Fifth Avenue was recently the center of the neighborhood's working-class Puerto Rican and larger Latinx community just a few years earlier. Fifth Avenue now housed Ginger's Bar and would soon be the site of Brooklyn Pride. Holly grew up in a nearby neighborhood, and thought of this gentrification as both positive and negative:

> Gentrification is a mixed blessing. . . . On some levels in some ways, gentrification does make places more queer-friendly . . . but with gentrification, you get more sometimes intelligent people . . . and it does make it

better. . . . Not that I remember that far back, but from what I heard in the mid-nineties it was very dyke-friendly. . . . But it's not really what I imagine it was like years ago, with whole neighborhoods. And everybody got taken out by the gentrification, so I don't see it [as lesbian] anymore.

But "more queer-friendly" and a "blessing" for whom? And who is seen as a lesbian or queer? It is important to amplify that, soon after I finished my research, the Hispanic population in Park Slope had *decreased* by 46 percent from what it had been at the beginning of my study, while the city saw a 37 percent *increase* in the Hispanic population.[62] Many of the working-class, less educated people (Holly confuses well-educated and "intelligent" above) had *already* been "taken out by gentrification." Figure 4.9 shows how the drastic increase in percentage population with bachelor's degrees shifted over the years. Only 15 percent of Americans held bachelor's degrees in 1980, a share that had doubled by 2010, while Park Slope greatly exceeded these averages, ranging from 36 percent in 1980 to 70 percent in 2010. These numbers do not demonstrate that lesbians and queers tend to be more educated (a common assumption among participants), but rather that lesbians and queers tend to live in areas with people who are more educated.

Further, the views of Park Slope as a place with a "family atmosphere" and a hub of "very dyke-friendly" lesbian-queer life are not opposed. I am not picking on Holly, for I (and many of my participants) also once believed (and many may still believe) the same racist, classist, colonial, and elitist tropes. By 2010, residents of Park Slope had an average household income of $95,212, 75 percent greater than the citywide average.[63] Park Slope's gentrification exploded in the property developers and real estate agents seeking to place the mass of twenty-somethings who arrived in the city in the 1990s. A decade later, this group sought the best schools, parks, and services in a ready-made "community" and "family neighborhood" close to southern and central Manhattan. Park Slope had the largest neighborhood increase in households with children since 2000, some of whom were lesbian households.[64]

The women and tgncp of color I interviewed, all of whom were in college or held bachelor's degrees, described a paradoxical sensation of safety/whiteness in Park Slope. Bailey '95 shared with the women and tgncp of color group interview about the sense of crossing from

Crown Heights, Bed-Stuy, and other historically Black neighborhoods into Park Slope, which women who had come in the 1980s and 2000s had also felt:

> BAILEY: Honestly, I'm not around a lot of white people. I don't have white people in my life like that. So I feel weird to say [*pause*], "I feel so safe in Park Slope." But I *do*.
> WANDA '85: And it's wonderful she said it *that way*! She got her *privilege*.
> ALL: That's right. [*collective nods*]
> WANDA: As soon as she crossed there, it was, "Ahhhh." Because whatever you bring, I can handle it.
> TRE '02: That shit is *fucked up*. But it's true!

Yet later on in the same conversation, Tre, who was in her early twenties, eight years younger than Bailey, talked about being policed as suspect in Park Slope, about the resulting sense that "you shouldn't belong here. . . . And that's not sexuality, that's Blackness." All of the participants nodded again, but did not discuss how their education and class also gave them a claim to "feel so safe" in Dyke Slope. There are so few clusters of lesbian-queer stars and claims to comfort in public spaces between them that participants of color were forced to put up with whiteness, as well as the disidentifications, policing, isolation, and racism that came with it.

In fact, I found that the contemporary image of the noble lesbian (à la "her" dyke politics) was used as a symbol of cultural capital to whitewash and pinkwash narratives of Brooklyn's racist and disinvested past. Brooklyn borough president Marty Markowitz went so far as to name Brooklyn the "lesbian capital of New York City and the Northeast" in 2013, surely inspired by Park Slope's racialized financial boom.[65] The measured contributions lesbians and queers made to the neighborhood's, borough's, and city's economy cannot be traced, but Markowitz added, "They made unbelievable contributions to the quality of life in our city and our borough." The median household income shifted from 7 percent below the citywide average in 1980, to a striking 133 percent above in 2010. The neighborhood's average rent rose 47 percent from 1990 to 2010, the fourth largest increase in the city and over double the citywide average.[66]

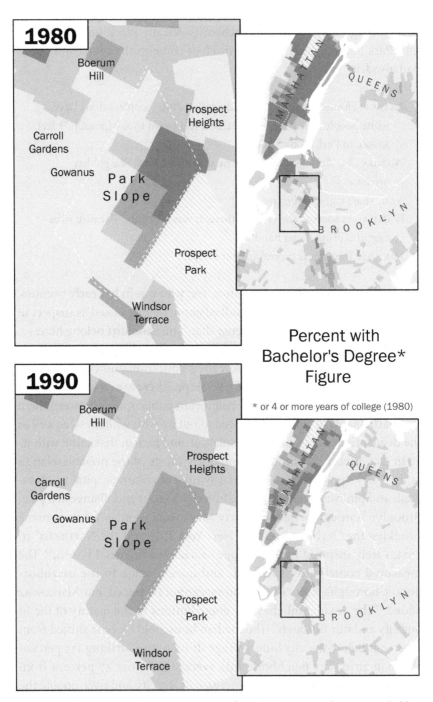

Figure 4.9. Census maps showing percentage of population twenty-five years and older with bachelor's degrees (with details of Park Slope), 1980, 1990, 2000, and 2010

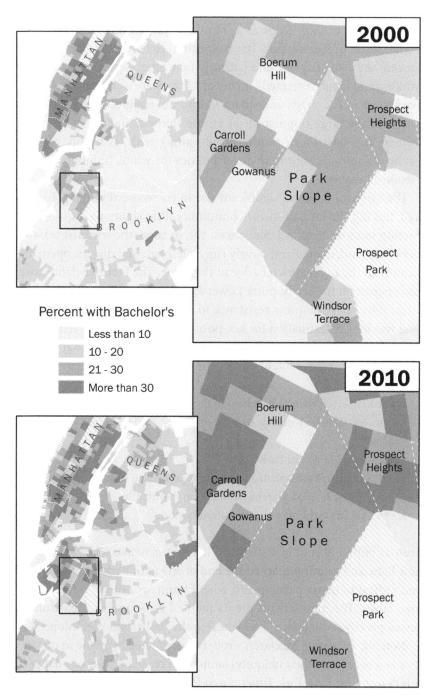

Figure 4.9. *Continued*

The notion of Park Slope as a "family neighborhood" also emerges from a series of stereotypes. The connection to family recalls the large concentration of Hispanic and Latinx people often stereotyped as hard-working and family-oriented—many of whom were working class—who lived there in the 1970s and 1980s. Corporate engines and politicians also read the large population of visible (lesbian and queer) (white) women as a bastion of motherhood—along with its highly ranked public schools—as shunning queer politics for white, homonormative pseudo-liberation.

The early 2000s saw a significant rise in commercial rental prices as well, leaving the lesbian-queer community little ability to acquire and develop long-term, affordable spaces. Yet, in 2008, the feminist sex-toy store Babeland, owned and mostly run by lesbians and queers, opened a location at the north, pricier edge of the Slope. The first Babeland store had opened on the seedy, punk Lower East Side in the late 1990s with a celebratory sense of queer resistance to dominant sexual mores. Babeland was long a destination for sex-positive dykes, as many participants attested, so that many also felt a jolt that Babeland would now appear in the lesbian stronghold intent on targeting the elite, white mom market:

ISABELLE '06: [There's] Babeland in the city and in Brooklyn now.
KATE '03: Which I just rode past the other day. And I was like, "Oh my God!"
SUSAN '92: But it's *not* Park Slope!
JACK '91 (ME): Participants in a previous group said it's all women with [expensive] Maclarens [strollers] in it evidently.
KATE: And it's right next to that maternity store.

Seen as both a homonormative and heteronormative retail space, the new Babeland location marked the end of an era of Park Slope as queer and radical to many participants, what Quinn '95 called "WASP-y lesbian land." The mainstream media painted Babeland as a bastion of sexual proclivity that gave "bad vibes" to the "baby-boomlet" Slope.[67]

Notably, expensive Maclaren strollers (mentioned by name in our interviews because of their ubiquity) launched a recall because of a dangerous defect. The *New York Times* posed Park Slope as the de facto home of elite parenting and the city's family neighborhood to the public with the article "Stroller Recall Stirs Unease in Park Slope."[68] In multiple interviews, participants also brought up "double-wide strollers," an allusion to the high multiple birth rate in Park Slope, which could be linked to "career women" having late-in-life births and—more obviously to my participants—lesbians using IVF treatment. What historian George Chauncey calls the 1980s "lesbian baby boom"—the large spike in the number of lesbian parents after IVF clinics began opening in 1979—still leaves an image of lesbian-as-mother in the public imaginary.[69] Historian Laura Briggs's research gets to the stressful crux of why many younger participants would be frustrated by the focus on traditional families. While the expensive IVF treatment "made lesbian and gay reproduction much more routine," Briggs writes that this normalization ignored those "creative family forms" that "receded as the norm in queer family life."[70]

My findings indicate it was not a coincidence that the lesbian-queer markers of the neighborhood began to physically disappear just as essentialized lesbian identities defined by an assumed cisgender "woman" identity began to unravel. The proliferation of feminist and queer theory, feminist and queer activism, trans activism, and queer identities in the 1990s unhinged fixed notions of gender and sexual identities. On (and in) the heels of these linguistic, cultural, political, and intellectual shifts—with particular interventions from the burgeoning transgender movement—the city's lgbtq health clinic, Callen-Lorde Community Health Center, began to distribute hormones without the traditional year-long wait. What I call the female-to-male (FtM) trans-surge is the drastic increase in the number of and positive or somewhat neutral attention paid to transgender-identified and, at times, transitioning bodies that began around the turn of the century in New York City. Trans men were able to flourish or, at times, at least survive in greater numbers and with increasing support.

Magdalene '04 even waited until after our interview, when we were on the F train back to Brooklyn, to speak openly about trans people during the FtM trans-surge. As a cisgender femme, she worried other participants may find her pro-trans stance to be anti-lesbian, and/or her transphobia, which she had recently begun to confront, may still offend: "I didn't know if my friends' ex-girlfriends were now their ex-boyfriends, and I didn't know if [he, a friend's FtM ex-boyfriend] belonged in the [lesbian] bar we all used to go to. And then, because I thought [he] was cute, I didn't know if I should go there either." Magdalene brings to life the agony and energy required to reinterpret the basis of lesbian-queer identities and spaces, not to mention the turmoil that trans people were experiencing when denied these spaces and communities when they sought them. This queer failure of essentialized lesbian identity was a radical turn at the new century, with violent, painful, and harmful stops and starts.

I want to be clear that placing the burden for the disappearance of a lesbian neighborhood, and lesbian-queer spaces on the shoulders of trans people would be a (transphobic) errand. And these changes are not specific to New York City. They are another generational step toward our best understanding of ourselves, another radical step forward to embrace queer/feminist/lesbian/trans life at its fullest—all of which is bound to and restricted by white settler cis-heteropatriarchal capitalism. My participants experienced similar shifts in New York City to those Podmore found in her research on Montréal lesbian spaces: "the loss of lesbian territory signified . . . a transformation and multiplication of lesbian identities . . . brought by the mixed [lgbtq] bars and the increased visibility of lesbians in society."[71] Extending Podmore's arguments to Park Slope's "disappearing" identity as a lesbian stronghold, Magdalene and other participants pointed out that frequenting lesbian spaces became a fraught endeavor in the FtM trans-surge. I remember a once-packed weekly party on the Lower East Side emptying out over a series of months in 2001 over these concerns.

Identity redefinitions necessarily required redefinitions of space. In the midst of intense gentrification and skyrocketing property values, the seismic shifts in gender and sexual identities rewrote the lesbian-queer geographies of the entire city. It became even more difficult to hold on to lesbian-queer claims to spatial community. Prominent clusters of lesbian-queer spaces were forced to dim their lights as fewer stars remained. Prominent non-profits became part of the nonprofit industrial complex so that participants recalled do-it-yourself top surgery fundraisers in and beyond Park Slope to support transitioning friends through informal economies.[72] White, working middle-class Sudie '99 hung out in hipster Williamsburg instead which she found to be "super, super dykey at that time." She added, "I moved to the new Park Slope." Of note, Transy House, a collective shelter and site of activism for transgender people and tgncp, went unmentioned; it ran from 1995 until 2008 on the less moneyed, southern side of Park Slope, with its more Hispanic population.

With fewer visible lesbian-queer bodies on streets of the Slope, the lines between the stars of their constellations became less clear to spot over time. Place-based stars became more important than ever to mark and find queer life, just as many of these locales and events, and always the lines between them, also receded from view across the city. The invisibility of older lesbians and queers and women more generally—fueled by cis-heteropatriarchal definitions of women's beauty—has ramifications for cross-generation community and understanding. The popular short haircut of US middle-aged mothers erased much of the middle-aged, public queerness evoked by popular dyke short haircuts. In a 1980s-generation interview, feminine Jackie '85 argued that lesbian invisibility was "also a product of age. My mother has super, super short hair now, and she's straight as a die." Then, palling around with butch Chris '86, Jackie turned to her and said, "And you could look like a Midwestern farm wife." And we all laughed. But younger generations may lack the ability to even spot let alone get to know older dykes. As Isabelle '06 said in regard to her gaydar, "Whereas if you're just walking around Park Slope you might say, 'Well, I don't know!'"

At the same time, often recently out, younger, less-moneyed, queer-looking (cisgender or tgncp) bodies could not afford Park Slope rents in the 2000s. As many trans people began to pass, (visibly) butch dykes were also fewer in number, as I increasingly experienced over the decade. Participants described how some predominantly white, femme fashions turned from 1990s punk to 2000s high femme, *L Word*–influenced or 1950s pinup and vintage styles that masked or reworked much of the visible, androgynous queerness in decades past. Further, the appropriation of white lesbian-queer styles by white mainstream stars like Justin Bieber erased queer difference.[73] To the public, the mass of aging women and tgncp in a place and displacement of younger women and tgncp was simplified to a narrative of safety, family, and the exclusion of pathologized youth.

Still, a set of key locales in Park Slope remained bright and beckoning. Thus, the sense of Park Slope as home was fueled by those stars by which all of my participants navigated and drew the lines of their constellations.

Much like the lesbian-queer North Star of the LGBT Center (discussed in chapter 2), Park Slope had its own bright double stars (like the double Alpha star in Ursa Major): Ginger's bar, and the bar and club Cattyshack. To some a lesbian bar and to others a lesbian-owned neighborhood bar, Ginger's became the central star of Sally's world (figure 2.7 in chapter 2):

> Ginger's is sort of at the center . . . and then I have like two little lines to indicate the passage of time where I have Cattyshack and so on, all after the post–*L Word* dawn. And I have lesbians radiating out from Ginger's [*makes starburst motions with hands*] 'cause, you know, like that's kind of how I saw Brooklyn. And then I have little things . . . that are in hearts, like softball and tea in Brooklyn.

Ginger's was still open in 2019 when I finished writing this book, continuing to serve as an orienting locale to the constellations of queer Brooklyn for many lesbians and queers.

Both bars were important in the 2000s because they were one of the few places afforded a space where participants could mix across races and classes—in the same large building if not on the same dance floor, as many participants remarked. As mixed-race/Black, working middle-class Bailey '95 recalled, "I really love Cattyshack, because it can be like a place where you have hotdogs and hamburgers on Saturday afternoon and watch the Mets. Or it can be like a Saturday night dance party, because Black women and white women and Latin women *all* go." Cattyshack emerged in 2004 on the literal, working-class, and still Latinx "fringe" of Park Slope's Fourth Avenue, which has since been gentrified into a boulevard of look-alike, pricey condominiums and box stores. It was also likely the largest lesbian-queer bar in the history of New York City, with two dance floors, a pool table, and outdoor patio—and it too closed in 2009. Parties were and continue to be thrown in lesbian-queer-friendly spaces like music venues Southpaw (until it also closed) and Bell House. The loss of more affordable social spaces open both day and night, and warm in the winter (unlike public parks), were sorely noted. Yet these closing places, namely the absence of cafés, were almost always at a middle-class price point.

Amusingly, participants frequently preferred to gossip about goings-on at the Park Slope Food Co-op rather than bars in our conversations.

Jess '96 said, while laughing, *"That* is a lesbian space! I go in there with my partner and we compete in this game [we made up] of Who Knows the Most People in the Co-op." The Co-op requires partaking in dyke politics of anticapitalism and volunteerism all the while running into people you know, once knew, or wanted to know; more than one participant described how common it was to run into an ex-girlfriend there. I joined the Co-op in the 2000s, hoping to meet someone. A cute seventy-ish-year old femme once complimented my "butch box-lifting talents." I never told her they were nacho chips I lifted so easily. In all of these interactions, the sense of landed community feels like it spreads on to the streets like the familiarity found in the aisles, reflecting the clustered stars of participants' constellations nestled in the Slope.

Much lesbian history remains ignored and unrecorded. It then makes sense that participants who arrived in Park Slope in the late 2000s had never heard of the rapes, draggings, harassment, and violence that made 1990s headlines. Yet lesbian bashings continued more occasionally and unsystematically, now without media attention or activist response. White, working-class Donna '05 recalled, "My friend . . . in Park Slope, she was coming out of a bar . . . I guess she looked like a lesbian and this guy came up, and he's like, 'Dyke!' and he punches her in the face." Her white co-interviewees were shocked, again repeating the exception to violence against white women that Bailey defined earlier. I nodded, remembering the long, overly cold or overly hot, twenty-block walk along Fifth Avenue between the Rising, Ginger's, and my apartment in the early 2000s. While I was never hit, I was twice verbally harassed and threatened. My straight, cisgender, Black male roommate would be out late as well and we would time our walks home, often drunkenly discussing who was protecting whom in such a white, cis-heteronormative space.

All along, my participants (and I too) kept talking about Dyke Slope as (if?) it still persists, caught between a strong lesbian-queer geographical imagination and the violent processes of gentrification that persistently unwind the arms and legs that lesbians and queers had wrapped around their promised (urban) lesbian land. Working middle-class, white Linda '96's adoration of Dyke Slope especially struck me. She and her partner could never afford Park Slope. They had moved farther south to the Sunset Park neighborhood, but they dreamed of living in the Slope: "We're a very affectionate couple . . . [but] we don't really feel comfortable even holding hands or even expressing outward affection. Well, [in] Park Slope we definitely do. We get off the subway and we're like, 'We're in Park Slope!' [*smiles and dances*]." All of my middle-class, college-educated, and/or white participants saw an idyllic homeland they could only imagine coming home to. Many of my working-class, less-educated participants and/or participants of color saw and experienced an area they did not speak to except for to visit or pass through in the 2000s, much like Greenwich Village always had been and would be.

## "By Dint of Their Believing It, It Is"

My arguments in this book dwell on the scale of the neighborhood even though it is not the meaningful scale of relationality (dare I say community?) for many women and tgncp for many paradoxical reasons. First, my participants began their stories about the "neighborhood," and then immediately turned to lesbian Park Slope's disappearance. Second, white, middle-class, and/or college-educated participants saw the loss of the celebrated space of the neighborhood as the failure of their settler colonial fantasy, an affective undercurrent of blame and internalized homophobia and sexism that I seek to reveal and disrupt. Third, how the myth of neighborhood liberation takes shape for women and tgncp specifically requires attention, including its links to the lesbian land and back-to-the-city movement. Finally, lesbians cannot "keep" a neighborhood. This inability speaks to the limited power of non-heterosexual women and tgncp—white, middle-class, college-educated, or otherwise—in a propertied society. I concur with Halberstam that in queer failure—when it subverts racial capitalism rather than succumbs to it—"a new kind of optimism is born." He goes on,

> Not an optimism that relies on positive thinking as an explanatory engine for social order, nor one that insists upon the bright side at all costs; rather this is a little ray of sunshine that produces shade and light in equal measure and knows that the meaning of one always depends upon the meaning of the other.[74]

By instead illuminating the patterned light rays of constellations within and across Park Slope, lesbian-queer geographies can emerge foremost in constellations without acquiescing to terms and spaces built by, for, and about patriarchal, cis-heterosexual society. African American, middle-class Naomi '89 described her time with her queer, (then) teenage friends: "We just heard there were lesbians there [in Park Slope], so we'd walk around in circles . . . to see what [we] would look like when [we] grew up."

At the intersection of urban women's and tgncp's history, and lgbtq history, Park Slope afforded some lesbians and queer women a temporary space of personal recognition and many lesbians and queers the promise of recognition and homeland in New York City for decades. White, upper middle-class Jackie '85 points out how strong the geographical imaginary of Dyke Slope was over my period of study:

> [I]t's funny—I almost never go to Park Slope. I feel like it's not a lesbian neighborhood anymore [in 2008]. . . . My girlfriend's aunt lived there in the seventies and when we moved there in 1989 she was like, "Oh! It's not a lesbian neighborhood anymore! All of the Columbus Avenue [implying wealthy, predominantly white, elite] people have moved in." . . . It's interesting because we [lesbians and queer women] all talk about Park Slope as this sort of Shangri-La of lesbian safety . . . but all of the—I don't know like institutions, like, the Rising [Café and Bar]—they've disappeared. [*pauses*] But I guess it doesn't really matter, I suppose, because if people feel like something's a lesbian neighborhood then by dint of their believing it, *it is*.

Sitting across from Jackie, white, working middle-class Kathy '05 responded by saying:

> At least amongst the queers that I hang out with, lesbians don't U-haul as much as they get gay-married and move to Park Slope. So, it's the idea of being the lesbians with the double-wide stroller. . . . And your own brownstone in Park Slope. . . . But [also] the . . . [monthly sex] party.[75] Yes, it is a sex party . . . in undisclosed locations in Park Slope. . . . I went and it was pretty fucking fantastic. So I have a soft spot for Park Slope—but as the "Shangri-La"—to borrow your phase—of lesbian domesticity, *as well as* the Shangri-La of tawdry, anonymous sex.

At the intersection of "lesbian domesticity" and "tawdry, anonymous sex," Kathy defines Park Slope in a queer dialectic of desire. But the crux of the contradiction of Park Slope, or how it ever came to be a "lesbian neighborhood," can be read in Jackie's statement, between its fleeting physicality ("all of the . . . institutions . . . they've disappeared") and certitude of the lesbian-queer geographical imagination ("by dint of their believing it, *it is*"). Meanwhile, women and tgncp of color consistently described their attachment to as well as, at times, their marginalization in the space, particularly as young, not yet college-educated people.

In many conversations, participants debated whether practices of claiming space supported dyke politics. The very nature of propertied territorialization was politically and economically questionable to many, such as white, working middle-class Sally '96. She spoke to the dyke politics of feminism, antiracism, and anticapitalism in refusing to act on this colonial territorialization:

> I think there's something a little insidious about colonizing a patch of land and calling it your own and taking out everything else and owning everything. It's just not—it doesn't quite appeal to me, but on the other hand sometimes it does because you see what men have and . . . yeah. [*sighs*]

Ethnic studies scholar Jasbir Puar writes that recognition is long overdue that the claiming of space, "even the claiming of queer space . . . [is] a process informed by histories of colonization, these histories operating in tandem with the disruptive and potentially transgressive specifics at hand."[76] Other participants also likened territorialization to a practice of settler, patriarchal, urban colonization, especially in instances of the white middle class moving into poor and working-class neighborhoods of color.

Indeed, all of my participants painted Park Slope as both racist and yet all-welcoming. They saw long-term lesbian-queer territory as always possible and always out of reach of their wallets and dyke politics. What Halberstam calls "failure as a way of life" echoes the gendered pattern of lesbian-queer (urban and rural) neighborhood-making that has persisted for over forty years, at least for white, middle-class, and/or college-educated lesbians and queers.[77] My participants' stories reveal that queer failure is a broader practice of women's and tgncp's resistance of continuous appearance (let alone reappearance) that is a core value of urban dyke politics. Yet they also cannot fully escape from white capitalism, heteronormativity, patriarchy, and racism with these tactics, even as they seek to resist those forces for, in the words of Audre Lorde, "the master's tools cannot dismantle the master's house."[78] My participants have not fully achieved the sort of queer failure Halberstam extolls in evading "the punishing norms that discipline behavior and manage human development" that result in unpredictable adulthoods.[79] This antisocial, white, and privileged perspective fails to account for how the social geographic precarity of capitalism does not afford the pattern of predictable housing in adulthood that so many seek, particularly as dependable, safe, and affordable housing is so often denied queers.

Notably, participants from each generation felt like Park Slope was on a downswing as a lesbian neighborhood just as members of another generation found out it was *the* lesbian place to be; thus, participants continued to remark that Park Slope was the *most* lesbian-queer when they arrived and that it terminally gentrified shortly *after*. While many participants described nearly identical types of places in their constellations, they looked at the night sky, generation after generation, and saw Park Slope as if it was their generation's alone. The upscale *New York* magazine ranked Park Slope as the most "liveable" neighborhood in 2013.[80] In a striking comparison, white privilege similarly disavows the racism of policing and prisons to target, shape, sort, categorize, and limit Black and brown lives through vulnerability to "premature death," writes Black geographer Ruth Wilson Gilmore.[81]

In fact, as I argued in chapter 2, women's spaces are in fact often "paradoxical spaces" as urban geographer Gillian Rose suggests, spaces occupied simultaneously that "would be mutually exclusive if charted on a two-dimensional map."[82] In other words, Park Slope is a feminist paradox: the lesbian-queer everything and absence thereof, a lesbian-queer place attachment that emerges through specific sets of spatial relations and flows at a particular time. Altogether, the tendency for lesbian-queer spaces to be fleeting means the staying power of the Park Slope geographical imagination and the set of key locales (LHA, the Co-op, Ginger's, Prospect Park, Rising Café, and so on) heralds a homeland. The fantasy of lesbian-queer community is impossible to enact even in (queer) New York City precisely *because* it is the finance and media epicenter of the United Sates.

To many of my participants, Park Slope is also a site of revolution in which women and tgncp openly claimed a territory of their own in New York City. Into the new millennium, many of my participants extolled a territorial vision of LHA co-founder, activist, and writer Joan Nestle's description of creating lesbian and gay community in 1950s and 1960s New York:

> Surely the struggle between our public expression and societal control has not gone away, yet I think there is something deeper calling out from these places. . . . It was here that women transformed themselves, right under the fist of the state. It was here, on continuously shifting ground, that we created the semblance of communal permanence. It was here that we found a way to be real in places that were never our own, by deed or laws of property.[83]

Nestle's words continue to inspire me and many other dykes. But my research shows that transplanting the radical strategies of the past on to the present can reproduce the same injustices against which they were devised.

To say that the gender and sexual landscape of 1980s New York City, when my research begins, was a different time is true; yet the same white, middle-class mentality that fueled the occupation of land and displacement of poor and working-class people of color then continues decades later. Surely there are variations to whiteness, especially as my Jewish and Armenian participants expressed. Still, like the white and class privilege that has long fueled the production of gay men's neighborhoods, it is the combination of white, middle-class, and college-educated privileges that participants drew upon to lay claim to Dyke Slope. The absence or restriction of Puerto Rican, other Latinx, and Black queers, working-class and poor queers, and non-college-educated queers from a neighborhood that once was home to many members of these groups is palpable and painful to record. Lesbian-queer gentrification was and is analogous to the outgrowth of the settler mentality that combines the lesbian land movements with the back-to-the-city movement of antisuburban (and what they saw as anti-cis-heteropatriarchal) sentiment.

Is Park Slope a lesbian neighborhood? A lesbian spatial fantasy? (Or—to dream!—a tgncp neighborhood?)[84] To many of my participants, it is (or was)—but I add that it is not a traditional neighborhood. Rather, the spatial "concentration" of Park Slope is an "enacted neighborhood," a neighborhood that "has salience when acted upon—when residents seeks to protect or define neighborhoods for some political and social purpose," a space of possibilities for connection and self-understanding.[85] We can look at the list of commitments in local dyke politics mentioned by my participants and see that lesbians and queers act as producers of capital as well. A constellation perspective reveals that the "lesbian neighborhood" of Park Slope was really more a cluster of stars and lines between them in participants' constellations, created to navigate between, make sense of, and work against cis-heteropatriarchy. The "semblance of communal permanence" that Nestle referred to earlier need not take the form of a neighborhood to produce solidarities and connections.

And such spaces for women as well as tgncp are rare. Park Slope exists alongside the imaginary realms for women like that of the Amazons, *The City of Ladies*, and Sappho's Lesbos; physical domains of women such as the eternally besieged Umoja Village in Kenya; and the disappearing (or, now, also disappeared) "lesbian neighborhoods" of the Mission District and Andersonville, among others. The dyke project of producing urban space is best articulated in the words of performance studies scholar Tavia Nyong'o, who writes, "It is less a question of choosing failure than choosing what to do with the failure that has chosen us."[86] And, as (lesbian) poet Elizabeth Bishop wrote, "The art of losing isn't hard to master; / so many things seem filled with the intent / to be lost that their loss is no disaster." Through the lens of queer failure reacting to white cis-heteropatriarchal capitalism, one can see that the loss of these neighborhoods is no disaster—but the loss of home and community is tragic.

And so this chapter is part of the record of what must be a long apology to and call to action with lesbians and queers of color and working-class and poor lesbians and queers in order to produce new lesbian-queer geographical imaginations and spaces. It is also an admonishment and warning to the white, middle-class, and/or college-educated lesbians and queers—myself included—who made Dyke Slope and, worse, those who may seek to elsewhere re-create Park Slope (in Kathy's words) as the "Shangri-La of lesbian safety," again based upon the same white settler colonial mentality. (In fact, Shangri-La was a fictional utopian, exotic, and Orientalist creation of the British empire.) Given the current cost of property and everyday necessities, as well as the ongoing antiracist turn among white queer liberals, it would be impossible and even undesirable to make another Park Slope of the same scale or notoriety in a major urban center. This realization should urge us to revisit or form anew a notion of lesbian-queer urban justice that considers how an imagination and enactment of "settling a neighborhood" (Park Slope or elsewhere) should be refigured to resist gentrifying, capitalist forces and struggle for social justice for all.

# 5

## Constellating a Queer Map of the Lesbian City

When I shared the idea of constellations with my participants, most, like Eva '98, adored the concept:

> Path-making with bodies . . . yes, it makes sense! It's where I hold memory, lust, habit, visibility, secrets. It's what I use to touch women. It's where I am touched by them. Especially in NYC, my body is my car. It's my vehicle that moves me from star to star in my constellation. My tattoo tells a story. My voice does. My hair does. All of it.

Other participants agreed with the premise but pushed me to further unpack the idea of queer space, like Maral '02:

> The path-making between bodies to make up constellations makes sense. However, I still do not see [queer spaces] as set places such as bars or clubs, because these [places] are so intangible. . . . it would be hard to point it out to someone when talking about where I go that is a queer space. What do I say? It's on my body? . . . My identity is queer in more than the sense of sexuality. . . . Even if I called my navigation with and to other queers, street corners, the steps in Union Square, Bluestockings—is that [queer] space? Yes, I guess it is something that is written on my body, but it is not set in stone. More like set in flesh and skin that sheds, renews, changes color, shape.

Eva and Maral articulate how lesbians and queers embrace a practice of queering space in constellations that, indeed, is at times "so intangible." How then can reading the city through the components of constellations help us theorize urban space on behalf of (queering) liberation? In geographically rendering a queer New York, this final chapter goes beyond the examination of generational change that I structured into my previous chapters around the change in Greenwich Village, Bed-Stuy, Crown

Heights, and Park Slope neighborhoods. Here, I also turn to the practices of lesbian-queer life that remain consistent or similar over time, in and beyond neighborhoods.

I theorize constellations as a queer feminist geographical imagination of urban pasts, presents, and futures that dislodges lesbians and queers (sexual and "other"-wise) from the lgbtq fixation on neighborhood liberation. Applying an "ethnic enclave" model to city life that (supposedly) worked as a project of claiming rights for certain marginalized groups before them, white, middle-class, and/or college-educated people with the resources to produce these neighborhoods were disappointed to find them untenable. Many lgbtq people across races and classes have long clung to the American Dream–saturated belief that producing lgbtq and/or lesbian neighborhoods would afford their liberation.

Constellations, instead, realize the lesbian-queer ways of producing urban space that do not and often cannot rely on neighborhood exclusion as bound to property ownership, which, in turn, invoke politics of resistance as well as resilience and reworking. The model of constellations accounts for the fluidity and flux of queer life that is more fragmented and fleeting, but still connected and devoted to the tenets of social justice inherent to feminist, antiracist, and anticapitalist dyke politics. In other words, constellations afford a way of queering the production of urban space as it relates to and works against capital to radically make sense of, more aptly describe, and take action in radically shaping the lesbian-queer role in the city. Thus, the political insight of constellations is that lesbians and queers resist cis-heteropatriarchy in claiming and making spaces (for however long), and by finding one another (however few or multiple) in and beyond neighborhoods. Constellations speak to how lesbians and queers make sense of their direction in life, their irregular temporalities, and the tropes and myths of their world-making. Queer, feminist, trans, antiracist, and anticapitalist practices of urban survival can offer profound insights in support of organizing against white cis-heteropatriarchal capitalism—constellations reveal workarounds and tactics to work for social justice.

Since the early 2000s, many queer theorists have focused on theorizing queer time on behalf of cultural and political interventions,[1] but often at the cost of splitting (fabulous, delightfully promiscuous) queer time from (vague, static) queer space. A partial list of prominent queer theories (all emerging from the humanities disciplines) speaks to this range of temporal-focused work: a queer death drive toward "no future" (Edelman 2004), "queer futurity" derived by, for, and about minoritarian subjects (Muñoz 2009), "feeling backward" to find community through discontinuity (Love 2009), "temporal drag," which describes the fuzzy understanding of lesbian generations and the difficulty of knowing what practices actually belong to the past (Freeman 2010), and "queer temporality" to name dimensions of time that produce risk (Keeling 2019).[2] Most notably, Jack Halberstam coined "queer time" to describe how the rhythms of the everyday are derived from what media and governmentality deem to be heteronormative sociobiological patterns that make a "life"—marriage, house-purchasing, and childbirth at certain life stages and in certain family structures—which are passed on as American values and norms.[3] I read the multiple projects of exploring queer time as reflecting how lgbtq people are so deeply cut off from their history and one another that they have created their own temporalities to negotiate heteronormativity.

Drawing primarily on the work of queer feminist theorist Sara Ahmed along with geographer Doreen Massey, my arguments here contribute to and draw upon queer theory, and vice versa—particularly as queer theory rarely draws on geography, and most geographers (and social scientists) rarely apply queer theory.[4] Massey argues that scholars across disciplines must intervene in this space-time split. Space, like time, she writes, must be "never finished; never closed. . . . In this open interactional space there are always connections yet to be made . . . to pursue an alternative imagination."[5] Geographical imaginations remain flat if only time is always innovative, liberatory, and mysterious, while space remains fixed, assumed, and merely a surface upon which to record time, a two-dimensional map. To embrace acts of liberation and justice, we must reenvision time and space, because, as Massey notes, a "spatialisation of social theory and political thinking can force into the imagination a fuller recognition of the simultaneous coexistence of others with their own trajectories and their own stories to tell."[6]

Halberstam also frames "queer space" as the "place-making practices . . . in which queer people engage and it also describes the new understandings of space enabled by the production of queer counterpublics."[7] Literary scholar Michael Warner uses the term "counterpublics" to describe the ways marginalized groups produce their own discursive and social publics against the dominant public, still maintaining awareness of their marginalized status.[8] I read Halberstam and Warner to mean that queer people and practices make queer space, both outside of and against dominant values and ways of being.

Like other queer and feminist geographers before me, I ask, Beyond queer bodies producing queer space, what of the queer practice of producing space itself?[9] I rely heavily on the work of queer, feminist, trans, and sexual geographers who, in the last decade or so, have produced work that does not presume that queer identities and spaces equate with a radical way of being, at all times, "beyond normativity."[10] I too do not suggest that constellations are always radical or "alternative." Rather, they show how practices of queering sometimes necessitate sitting in and dwelling alongside white cis-heteropatriarchy, inasmuch as they require navigating through, around, and against the same systems of oppression.

Further, the practice of queering space requires looking beyond the hetero/homo binary for, as queer geographer Natalie Oswin writes, queer space is "productive rather than simply oppressive."[11] Drawing on prior scholarship, I take a queer feminist approach that seeks to destabilize privileges, assumptions, and normative models of "secure" white supremacist cis-heteropatriarchy. I relate constellations to a range of other spatial models that have been used to describe the lgbtq production of space, because, as shown in my study of lesbians and queers in New York City, they have relied on models of places, mobilities, lines, and networks for their survival over generations. Constellations are both a critical amalgamation and rethinking of these models that offers lesbians and queers their own term inspired by their own world-making.

Most importantly for my project, the task of queer critique in the words of Oswin is to "do the work of understanding how norms and categories are deployed"; to accomplish this, we also need to critique the norms and categories of spaces.[12] While other research has called for accounts of the rural and suburban to upset the equation of the urban and the queer, I am pushing back against the same old narratives of the urban that fixate on the lgbtq, gay, and lesbian neighborhood as the only or even primary path toward lgbtq liberation. Oswin also writes that queer geographers challenge simplified "conceptualizations of queer space as dissident space, resistant space, progressive space, colonized space or claimed space."[13] I concur and add that the notion of queer space is useful exactly *because* it inspires thinking about and acting on behalf of dissident, resistant, progressive, colonized, and claimed spaces. We must attend to space along with time, because if space is foreclosed, unattended to, and ill-defined in the words of others, then queers are too.

## A Star Is Born: The Queer Practice of Making Space

The metaphor of the star, in all of its varying brightness, is the best means I have to convey the magnitude of import that my participants attributed to the lesbian and queer places they described. I define a star as a space that holds meaning for lesbians and queers, a spatial iteration of dyke life. Stars are our guides: experiences, ideas, and memories that accumulate in place, and in bodies and memories.[14] Stars are how we find our way when the physical landscape fails us. Sudie '99 had become accustomed to surviving the absence or loss of support from heteronormative spaces by making her own stars: "When I need or want to fill the queer void I feel, I create my own party. I don't know if I need to imagine community anymore in the same way I used to. I can have it, create it, find it, and it's okay for it to be fleeting." When we are lost in the dark, stuck on the subway, or wake up at some new lover's house in the middle of the night, we look for light and direction. Even when stars fall out of view (due to pollution, racism, isolation, violence, aging, cis-heteropatriarchy), they burn bright.

And even long after stars eventually burn out or implode, the light still reaches us. As Ahmed writes about the queer phenomenology derived from lesbian experience, that which is "queer unfolds from specific points, from the life-world of those who do not or cannot inhabit the contours of heterosexual space."[15] The stars or nodes of lesbian-queer life change over time, and often are only found by those who know where and when to look. Even accounting for the range of class positions of my participants, the fleeting and fragmented qualities of these stars derive from these women's and transgender and gender non-conforming people's (tgncp's) diminished economic and political power that they described in their stories, which leaves many spaces vulnerable to (materially) closing.[16]

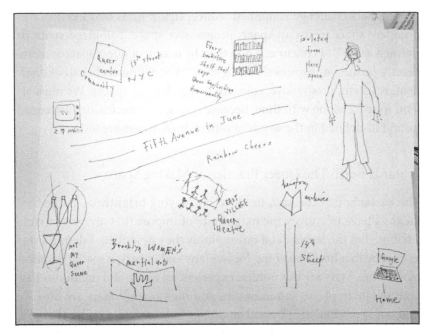

Figure 5.1. Eva '98's mental map (white, middle-class)

I share a series of participants' stories so that you too can read their star charts (see jgieseking.org/AQNY). White, middle-class Eva '98 arrived in New York City in the early 2000s. She described and also drew a sense of isolation and dispersal in her stories and her map (figure 5.1):

> I just felt like [my lesbian spaces were] every bookstore shelf that says Queer/Gay/Lesbian/Homosexuality. The [LGBT] Center, I've gone to things there. I don't think I've ever gone with another person, except [a friend]. So I heart Netflix. [*Jack '91 (me) and Alex '98 laugh*] Googling. Herstory Archives on 14th Street. Fifth Avenue in June, Pride, and East Village queer theater. I've seen some great lesbo plays in the East Village. They've all been in the East Village. [*pauses*] I was thinking about that, [*sarcastically*] "Wow, they've *all* been in the *East Village*! Wow! That can go on a map!" So that's mine. And it's always fragmented.

Her mapped spaces—translated from fluent New Yorker—include Brooklyn Pride, which is held on Park Slope's "Fifth Avenue in June," while "Pride" is in Manhattan. "East Village queer theater" includes the feminist WOW Café Theatre and La Mama, among others. Eva's "always fragmented" constellations include similar types of places (book-stores, bars, archives, co-ops, cafés, art spaces) or even the same places (Cattyshack, Lesbian Herstory Archives, Park Slope Food Co-op, etc.) as the constellations of other participants, places that convey a shared urban geography of belonging as much as exclusion and emptiness. Eva includes herself in her constellation in a way that recalls Ahmed's description of how lesbian experience begins in and grows from the body: "the starting point for orientation is the point from which the world unfolds: the here of the body and the where of its dwelling."[17] Similarly, the smallest stars make up the majority of the sky, yet we can-not see them with the naked eye and they fizzle out without the mass necessary to maintain fusion.

While digital geographies, like Eva's mention of Googling and Net-flix, increasingly appeared in 2000s-generation participants' stories, my participants, who ranged in age from nineteen to fifty-six in 2008, still depended on and described a world always comprising physi-cal places at a time when the internet was a part of everyday life but smart phones were still new. Throughout my period of study, my par-ticipants also revealed an attachment to virtual places long before the digital era.

The history of lesbians and queers is always fragmented, so it makes sense that their spaces would be as well. In queer life, there are neces-sarily fuzzy boundaries between material, physical, discursive, imag-ined, virtual, and metaphorical spaces to survive if not thrive. White, working-class Chris '86 recalled that

> I couldn't afford to go to the city, so the only way that I had any kind of community at all was those [lesbian folk] albums [like those of Holly Near and Chris Williamson]. I played them in my Walkman. . . . on a cellular level, that music kept me from [committing] suicide. [*collective nods*] . . . I thought, "Okay, these people are finding this, then it's possible for me to find it somewhere."

Just as Chris described existing in the space of music as refuge, white, Armenian, working middle-class, feminine-presenting Maral '02 said she did not see queer spaces "as set places such as bars and clubs because these [places] are so intangible." These women's and tgncp's everyday geographies reveal that the stars that populate lesbian-queer lives illuminate the wide range of what queer space is and could be. Participants produce their stars with others (first kiss, proposal, hot one-night stand, tragic breakup, activist zap, friendships, popular bars, drag queen bingo at the LGBT Center, chat rooms) or on their own (reading, listening to music, a realization of one's sexuality, first-time binding, reading lgbtq history in a library, crying over a tragic breakup, bookstore, or online). Like other marginalized groups the world over, along with constellations of physical and virtual places, they also use people as infrastructure, often referring to ex-girlfriends, lovers, and friends as guiding beacons.[18] Many stars are shared, but many are unique, much like the constellations of different cultures who projected myths onto similar but not always identical groups of stars. Annabelle '97 told the online discussion group, "We are like stardust—passing by each other sometimes alone, other times in big clumps and in formation."

Dating, for many participants, had long blended virtual and physical spaces. Noelle '83, who was recently single again after a long relationship, mentioned "sitting home alone cruising the personals" just like she had done in the 1980s, spending nights scanning the *Village Voice* or listening to phone personals. As Rachel '00 said, "I didn't need to go to a bar . . . you know, I never really truly *loved* the bar scenes. . . . Which is important, actually, to be in a girl-positive space, you know? But then for actually meeting people that I really wanted to date, that's a whole different thing." Those looking to meet people to date had already been driven to sites like PlanetOut, Nerve, OkCupid, and Match, and unlike the use of newspapers or phone personals in years past, digital geographies threw the seemingly ultra-bright stars of traditional lesbian-queer life like bars into question. Some participants remarked that, even though online dating often did not afford the connections they sought, it sometimes blunted the actual need and even the ability to connect in person.[19]

Phrases like "It's closed now" or "It's just gone" were spoken by participants across races and classes, sometimes in mourning, sometimes in anger, sometimes with a sense of inevitability about the shooting-star-like quality of many lesbian-queer places. White, working middle-class

Quinn '95 discussed the mass of bodies of often younger, more easily queer-identified people who were now missing from the city because they could not afford the rent (figure 5.2a-b). The visibly queer bodies that once marked spaces were now a rarity:

> Things had started to go away. . . . I moved right near Atlantic [Avenue in Park Slope], seven years ago . . . it was definitely not as fancy as it is now. And even then it seemed dykeier, and I remember walking by and seeing DYKE TV and I was like, "Holy crap! Here I am in New York City, and there's DYKE TV." And so it was kind of cool. . . . The next thing you know, it was just *gone*, you know what I mean? [*collective nods*]

When Quinn remarked, "It was just *gone*, you know what I mean?," all of the participants in her group understood. Similarly, most of the brighter stars that made up the constellations of 1980s- and 1990s-generation participants were long gone by 2008, like bars, nonprofits, bookstores, social groups, and less regularly policed parks and other public spaces. While amplified by the extreme property financialization of the 2000s, the phenomenon of closure and sense of cultural and political abandonment was common to every generation.

Ahmed, discussing the fleeting quality of lesbian spaces, argues that it is "as much a sign of how heterosexuality shapes the contours of inhabitable or livable space as it is about the promise of queer. It is because this world is already in place that queer moments, where things come out of line, are fleeting."[20] I understand Ahmed to be asking lesbians and queers—as I do as well—to approach understanding lesbian-queer spacetime differently, for the "unknowable length of its duration" under late capitalism.[21] The other prominent option is to attach one's self (again) to the myth of neighborhood liberation, but the path to justice is revealed as lesbians and queers still "come out of line" to enact the world they desire. As racial capitalism structures cities as it structures constellations, I take heed when Ahmed writes, "It is important that we do not idealize queer worlds or simply locate them in an alternative space."[22]

Further, Quinn's and all of my participants' shock articulates what they experienced as a sudden loss of seemingly timeless, recognizable geographies. In the words of Ahmed, "To make things queer is certainly to disturb the order of things."[23] Thus, the queer spatiotemporality of

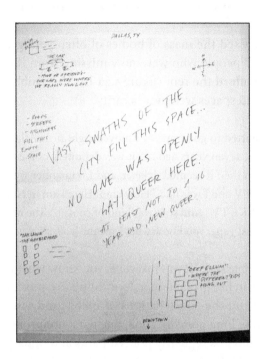

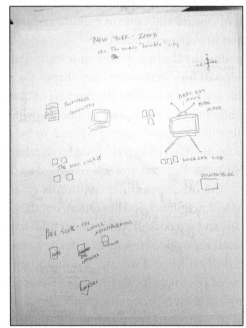

Figure 5.2a-b. Quinn '95's mental map (white, working middle-class)

fragmented and fleeting lesbian-queer space also shapes these women's and tgncp's ideas of themselves and their culture. The stars of astronomy seem close and proximate at a distance, much like the idealized lgbtq neighborhood. Only when we come close do we realize how far apart they are. The actual stars of the sky remain for long periods of time but their departure from the sky can be equally abrupt, even when we carry their light with us.

I chose "constellations" for its metaphorical fit as well as lesbians' and queers' dedication to astrology, which speaks to their ways of making worlds both imaginary and physical. In so doing, I reveal the dyke stars that dazzle and inspire us out of our expectations that any sort of neighborhood-based normalcy will liberate us. Some scholars use variations of "archipelagos," which is also appropriate to the fragmentation of my participants' places.[24] However, while astronomical stars have more staying power, the come-and-go quality of lesbian-queer stars and lines between them makes "constellations" more fitting.

In the early 1990s, queer geographer Gill Valentine found that lesbian spaces, more than gay men's, were "time specific, that is they are only gay on one night a week or one night a month."[25] Participants often conflated bars and parties—i.e., open-daily bars versus those "time-specific" events. Of the ten most often mentioned bars and parties, only Clit Club, a popular party that ran from the mid-1990s through the early 2000s, had such staying power in participants' memories that it was sometimes misremembered as a seven-day-a-week bar. Participants described and I too recall its great music and clublike atmosphere. Lesbian porn played on TVs, and there were hookups after hookups in corners or even the middle of a packed dance floor. As Naomi '89 put it, "Clit Club was off the chain."

Clit Club was perhaps most well-known for being the most mixed-race, welcoming party, as well as the most pro-sex: it was the first lesbian place to host go-go girls in New York City—who danced only for other women.[26] Wanda '85 vividly recalled that dancer "Cinnamon was bank!" Giuliani's anti-sex zoning policies that severely limited "adult establishments" also helped to thwart what Warner described as late-1990s New York City's "nascent lesbian sex culture," leading, for example, to the closing of the Angels strip club "farther downtown" which "used to have a lesbian night."[27] The feminist sex toy store Babeland was unable to sell video pornography for fear of being closed; Warner described how their "display windows [stood] empty, with nothing but discreetly drawn curtains. From the street, it looks like a podiatrist's office."[28]

The Meatpacking District, where the party was long hosted, gentrified into a bastion of highest-end boutiques and high-priced condo developments in the early 2000s. In the face of financial and political challenges, the Clit Club party moved around until it disappeared entirely from New York City. Alex '98's description of her brief experience of the Clit Club party was echoed by participants about other spaces: "Yeah, I went once. A few times. Then it just closed down. . . . They were [*imitates closing door*]. [*pauses*] 'Bye!!' [*waving*]. And I'm like, 'Oh. What just happened?'" Like a shooting star, Clit Club burned bright across participants' memories.

Correspondingly, there are absences that fill the space between these fragmented stars of lesbian-queer urban geographies. Seemingly banal backgrounds of empty darkness, these can be structures of oppression that participants learned to resist or at least pay less attention to. I often imagine this interstellar medium in the terms of queer activist and scholar Amber Hollibaugh, who writes, "What cannot be named, admitted to, or claimed delineates the geography of our risks, becomes the slippery slope of our needs and desires. The end result of keeping the secret . . . will be the crisis this movement needs to break through."[29] The darkness often held haunting exclusions, disconnections, missed connections, and silences, as participants navigated to, from, and around white cis-heteropatriarchy and the violence it imposed on their world-making. It included not only the violence and harassment my participants faced but also what is obliterated from their experience, and what is erased when lesbian and queer histories go unrecorded.

White, working middle-class Holly '03 still felt how the lgbtq community was attacked from both without and within—a feeling shared by other participants, lgbtq people more broadly, and the lgbtq media—regarding the treatment of Black, butch-identified Khadijah Farmer. Farmer had been forced to leave a local chain restaurant in Greenwich Village during Pride 2007 by an employee for using the women's restroom.[30] Holly exclaimed:

They threw her out because . . . she was in the women's room and they were like, "You're a man!" And she's like, "Here's my ID." And they [said], "We don't want to see that." . . . I think that happened during Pride in the *West Village*! [*shakes her hands in the air*] That shit's *still* happening.

Farmer's story amplifies the import of the presence and absence of lesbian-queer places. Women (and, I add, tgncp and many other marginalized people), writes urban geographer Gillian Rose, bump up "against invisible barriers, of dead ends, of being jostled and bruised by sharp appraising glances [for this] is a language of a body being defined by powerful others who control the view.[31] But Holly, like all of my white participants, discussed the inequality Farmer faces because of her gender and sexuality, while failing to account for her Blackness. Holly assumes the Village was for all lgbtq people based on her white, cisgender experience.

I would be remiss not to amplify how the absences of places continued to permeate my participants' stories and maps. Recently out, white, working middle-class nineteen-year old, Victoria '04 produced a map that includes an enormous amount of blank space (figure 5.3). Quiet

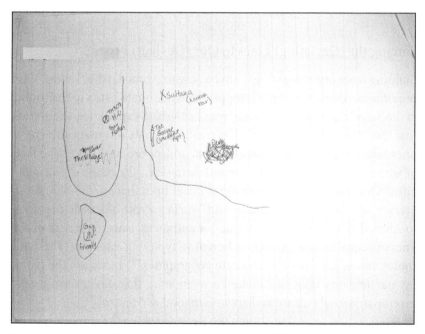

Figure 5.3. Victoria '04's mental map (white, working middle-class)

during our conversations to the point that she spoke only three times, she still found it imperative to share: "I came out in Staten Island and there's really nothing there, so I put gay *un*-friendly." The largely Christian, historically white ethnic, and primarily suburban borough of Staten Island rarely made participants' maps, and even those who included it felt unwelcome there. Some of my participants independently described different parts of the city as "no-go" areas where they felt threated or experienced harassment or violence, ranging from different blocks of business-focused Midtown to the entire very white and wealthy Upper East Side. Many participants, including most of the 2000s-generation participants and all of the participants of color, remarked on what queer geographer Lawrence Knopp refers to as a "sense of placelessness" or a lack of physical places, closely connected to the policing of their homes and hangouts.[32] Others, meanwhile, often white and/or middle-class participants, just saw the cumulative dispossession experienced by their community as indicative of the new, the cool, and the ever-changing idea of what queer is. From either perspective, the "un"-places of queer life render bodies and virtual and imagined places all the more valuable and essential.

## Finding the (Deviating) Lines to Our (Deviant) People

Building from our stargazing, I am back with Ahmed, who writes, "Our response need not be to search for permanence but to listen to the sound of the 'what' that flees."[33] Writing from her lesbian experience, she argues that there are "lines of desire" that create alternate orientations. These lines take directions that rework, resist, and/or are resilient in the face of white cis-heteropatriarchal colonialism—i.e., the paths of "straight lines." Queerness comes into being as queer lines that are out of line. As literary scholars Lauren Berlant and Warner wrote a decade previous to Ahmed: a "queer world is a space of entrances, exits, unsystematized lines of acquaintance, projecting horizons, typifying examples, alternate routes, blockages, incommensurate geographies."[34] Lines are the paths my participants take and make between stars that deviate from cis-heteropatriarchal culture and are understood as "deviant."

From rolling or walking down the street to taking the subway, bus, or taxi, from wandering online for Dyke March directions to wandering in one's memories of lesbian soccer games, from the emotional connections of relationships in the present, past, or merely hoped upon, the sum of the lines and stars of each participants' constellation is unique. Many of the lines and stars of participants' constellations overlap as New Yorkers take city subways and buses, or travel to the same well-known places or areas. Upon describing one place her group did not know about, Cullen '99 added, "It's pretty accessible to the community 'cause so many people live on the F line." Historian Finn Enke, who researched urban lesbian spaces in the 1970s Upper Midwest, found that lesbian archival projects never included why a meeting was in a certain neighborhood, or "what social and cultural boundaries they had to traverse to arrive there. In contrast, [their interviewees' like my participants'] narratives of their lives were 'travel stories.'"[35] In other words—and as I found as well—asking about lesbians' and queers' everyday geographies revealed that the dots on their maps and how they moved between them were equally important. Queers inherit and rework the paths of their ancestors as they inherit and rework their places and politics. Constellations are historical acts and promises of radical futures.

While Ahmed observes how "points accumulate, creating the impression of a straight line," I believe that rendering lines is a matter of scale: we can zoom in close on the social production of space to render lines' non-straightness.[36] Countless queers may have walked the same streets and visited the same clubs, basketball games, and knitting groups, and they may have dated, befriended, and/or slept with the same women and tgncp, but they may not have met or interacted. Rather than a linear progression of narratives, their constellations are comprised of rhizomatic lines that shoot off in various directions and grow back on to one another.[37] For those people who can't even "think straight," the lines they draw are not necessarily orderly or geometrically straight, but rather articulate what is "*artificial* about straightness . . . [revealing] a quality of things that are made, rather than of things that grow."[38]

Geographers have long noted the use of social networks in lesbian-queer spaces life but have accounted less for the network as a *spatial* form. Queer geographer Julie Podmore writes that "lesbian communities were constituted in space through fluid informal networks that linked a variety of public and private sites and, as a result, were quasi-underground in character and imperceptible to outside observers."[39]

Relatedly, in her study of Black queer women's spaces in 2010s DC, American studies scholar Nikki Lane relates these women's geographies as primarily network driven: "the Scene, as I have defined it—the collection of [social] networks and spaces those networks inhabit and produce—is comprised of a set of constantly shifting, constantly moving scene spaces."[40] Lane's insights also point again to the privilege of whiteness: even while all middle- and working-class lesbian-queer spaces are fleeting and fragmented, some white women and tgncp often possess an increased sense or presumption of remaining in place. Just as astronomical constellations can be seen only at a distance, we can see how the lines of lesbian-queer constellations can be accounted for only by looking beyond neighborhood bounds while critiquing the ways race, class, gender, sexuality, and generation shape the urban landscape.

The racist restrictions placed upon women and tgncp of color reconfigure any notion of the lines that participants could walk, roll, or ride through, just as it limited their choice of stars. A particular pattern of line-making arose across generations of women and tgncp of color as they crossed the border constituted by Grand Army Plaza, which includes a three-story archway and memorial to the Civil War dead in a small park above ground and a subway stop below. Grand Army Plaza and adjacent Prospect Park divide the predominantly white and wealthy as well as lesbian Park Slope from Crown Heights and nearby Bed-Stuy—working-class and, per my participants across races, outwardly heteronormative neighborhoods of color—and the gentrifying Prospect Heights neighborhood.

Grand Army Plaza is one of many interstellar mediums between stars, and I want to amplify how these large swaths of white cis-heteropatriarchal dominance appeared in many participants of color's constellations—even as they were generally invisible to those with white privilege. Mixed-race/Black Bailey '95 shared with the women and tgncp of color group how she would "talk" white in order to camouflage herself in her home neighborhood of Crown Heights:

> One of my girlfriends—I would not even let her put her hand on my leg in the car before we passed Grand Army Plaza. . . . It's Jamaican, West Indian . . . which for me is comforting in some ways because I'm West Indian and I like being around that. But in other ways, I don't want to be

around that. Because I have *to hide that*! And we *live together*! And the old men in the building, like everybody knew. . . . then the men would try and talk to me and I have to be, "I have a man" . . . or "My man's a cop." [*group laughter*] And it's like I haven't had *a man, ever*! You know what I mean? [*collective nods*] I have to walk around with that narrative in my head: "I have a man." . . . My [masculine-presenting] ex-girlfriend—she just *is* gay. And there's no question! And on the one hand she experiences different types of harassment that she doesn't have to pretend. But at the same time, it's more hostile.

Grand Army Plaza is one of the sociogeographical voids Black and brown women and tgncp must cross to be together—the same voids that drive them apart. Four of the six participants (Bailey, Wanda '85, Naomi '89, Tre '02) in the women and tgncp of color group interview alone mentioned breakups—Bailey had also just broken up with her now ex-girlfriend—caused (at least in part) by the fact that they or their girlfriends did not feel safe to hold hands in public. Later, in the same conversation, Naomi shared, "Even to this day my girlfriend deals with it. . . . Like if I go home to the projects, I go, "Oh! [*mimes dropping hand, whistles, and looks around like nothing happened*]."

Coming out nearly a decade after Bailey, Tre also included Grand Army Plaza in her mental map as an absolute border, marking the limit of where she grew up and resided in Crown Heights, and Park Slope (figure 5.4). Even though the story of her constellation includes her apartment, Tre's visual map portrays a smaller queer world: she left off Crown Heights but included Park Slope, which the subway passes through en route to Manhattan. In Park Slope, she felt she did not belong as a nonresident Black person, but she could deploy her masculine gender presentation to "play" and "fuck with" race, gender, and sexual norms. Tre shared:

But spaces in between there was—access? . . . you knew you weren't—it was just like—[*frustrated*] mmmm. You shouldn't belong here. Shouldn't belong here. . . . And that's not sexuality, that's Blackness. . . . I don't fuck around in my neighborhood. I don't hold my girlfriend's hand, like if you see that—I'm whatever—I don't play. I do after the Grand Army Plaza stop. Then I'm fucking with it. So Park Slope. [*sarcastically*] Yay.

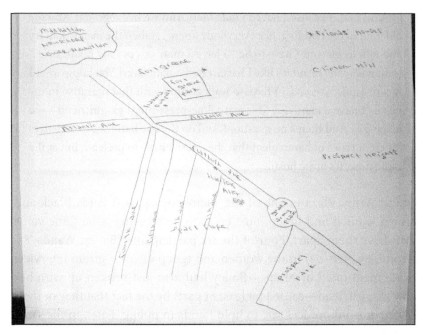

Figure 5.4. Tre '02's mental map (Afro-Caribbean, working middle-class)

Sharing this story in the women and tgncp of color group conversation, she added that at Grand Army Plaza "all the white people get on the train and now: 'Motherfucker, I have privilege.' . . . Because Black people don't say *shit* to white people!"

In response to Tre's story, Bailey '95 and Wanda '85 snapped and waved their arms, Naomi '89 and Mia '99 echoed their assent, and all the participants laughed with the joy of refusing injustice, as fleeting and fragmented as such acts may be. I take to heart what Ahmed writes of the importance of "what is repeated" to produce lines—here, the further labor required by Black and Latinx women and tgncp over generations to make, find, and sustain spaces. Such repetitions evolve in stories, barhopping nights, rainbow stickers, dating the wrong type of person, U-hauling, cruising, and fantasizing that shapes our directions, thoughts, "feeling . . . judgment, and . . . the sense of aims, aspirations, and objectives."[41] Tre's words clearly articulate Ahmed's theorization of lesbian lines: "one has to go to another side, perhaps even to what is behind, to reach points that do not accumulate as a straight line."[42]

While white, working middle-class Faith '03 does not record the race or gender of the lesbians she sees kissing on city streets, particularly at Grand Army Plaza, her whiteness obscures understanding of this racialized border marker: "There's a point of resurgence of lesbians in Brooklyn, like [*shocked*], *making out* on the street. . . . I was at Grand Army Plaza . . . last summer . . . all these women . . . necking on the street and I'm like [*mimics staring at them, appalled*], '*Come on!*' Like this is really not hot." In the women and tgncp of color group interview, most participants felt the exact opposite:

> BAILEY '95: But I worked as a bouncer in clubs so that was very empowering. But as soon as that was done, you know . . . you *just don't act gay* in certain places. And I see these *young women* [*slapping fist into palm once to each word*] on the train [implying making out]. [*gasps*]
>
> WANDA '85: Isn't is *beautiful*?! It's so beautiful!
>
> MIA '99: [*nods and smiles*] Um-hm.
>
> NAOMI '89: [*nods and smiles, wide-eyed*]
>
> BAILEY: It just [*grabs her heart*]. And I smile at them and they think I'm crazy!
>
> WANDA & MIA & NAOMI: [*laughter*]

Poignantly, Tre is the one participant who did not nod or laugh. As a twenty-year-old, she felt such behavior was dangerous as well as beautiful, and, as other scholars have noted, "contingent on the situation (i.e., to be Black in a lesbian community or to be lesbian in the Black community)."[43]

Above in the park or below in the subway at Grand Army Plaza and across a host of invisible borderlands across the city, there is no escaping the literal and figurative intersection of the oppressions lived in these women's and tgncp's bodies. Rather than be shut out at these borders or invoke separatism by excluding others, some women and tgncp cross lines invoked by identities to increase recognition across difference and amplify diversity. Chicana feminist theorist Gloria Anzaldúa calls this process "crossing over":

> At the confluence of two or more . . . streams . . . constantly "crossing over," this mixture . . . rather than resulting in an inferior being, provides . . .

racial, ideological, cultural and biological cross-pollenization, an "alien" consciousness is presently in the making . . . a consciousness of the Borderlands.[44]

In other words, Anzaldúa explains that we expand our minds by "crossing over" nation-state borders that fuel queer identities and, I add, the spaces and times of queer life in cities. I apply Anzaldúa's idea spatially by examining how Black and Latinx lesbians and queers cross over spatial boundaries that bear affective, emotional, social, political, and economic weight within cities to shift the meaning of spaces that lesbians and queer women occupy.

Mixed-race/Puerto Rican Olivia '03 shared "the first gay flag I ever got" in her interview. She went on, "I got it my sophomore year of high school at the AIDS Walk . . . That day me and my bi friend . . . went and bought the little gay flags and that's how we sort of came out to, like, our entire group of friends." Olivia was soon after thrown out of her home, and she was living on the street or with friends at the time of our interviews. Her story reveals how crossing over these spatial boundaries—much like how the lines and stars of constellations create relationality across an empty interstellar medium—are specific to the individual, but relatable among many dykes.

"Crossing over" queers the geographic imagination of cities whereby queer feminist urban territories ebb and flow and are not fixed to boundaries defined by the elite and/or propertied.[45] Ahmed might understand this as a "reorientation," by which "the queer effect is overcome and objects in the world no longer appear as if they were off-center or slantwise."[46] Many lesbians and queers, often white, college-educated, and/or middle-class, took part in these processes of gentrification as the bodies that could cross over into and reside in neighborhoods of color with impunity—even as the reverse was rarely possible. In reorienting our gaze to recognize constellations, the particular race, class, and gender formations of lesbian-queer spaces become all the more evident. At the same time, we see how lesbians and queers make connections across space and time that at times defy and at times bend around white cis-heteropatriarchal norms to account for fuller geographies of lesbian-queer life that are often hidden (to the public and even to one another) by such structural oppressions.

Participants of color often described overlapping yet distinct spaces with gay men of color in producing their constellations. Naomi '89 shared:

> I lived in Jackson Heights [Queens], and we started a Jackson Heights gay dinner. And even there, there would be three of us—three lesbians—we would sit there for three hours with the guys buzzing about, and we'd be like, "Well, I saw lesbians at the laundromat." "Me, too. Where are they?" We'd be like almost to the point where, "Well, let's go out on the street and just wait."

Naomi's humor is uplifting. But it also reveals the isolation she and her friends felt as Black and brown women in the largely Latinx and South Asian neighborhood—"three lesbians" could not lay claim to public space there as men do. This experience mirrors how they often felt in predominantly white neighborhoods.

Anthropologist Martin Manalansan described Jackson Heights as a key cruising ground for gay and queer men of color—"the guys buzzing about," as Naomi put it. But these men's claims are limited and cyclical, which recalls the fleeting nature of constellations:

> The seeming antipodal narratives of emergence and disappearance actually mutually constitute a form of structural violence. The rise of a vibrant exclusive real estate gay commodified businesses and other signs of the new gentrified New York are based on the very process of eradication and disappearance of the unsightly, the vagrant, the alien, the colored, and the queer.[47]

Manalansan is describing how these gay and queer men's and tgncp's bars and informal territories for cruising are intermittently dissolved *and* reconstituted. Due to their relative lack of economic and political power, it is much more difficult, if not impossible, for people of color, the poor and working-class, and/or women to sustain formal lgbtq neighborhoods and places. Black gay and queer men were also tied to, ostracized from, and/or invisible both in neighborhoods of color like Bed-Stuy and Crown Heights and in (white) gay neighborhoods as well.[48]

Lines are redrawn again and again between stars to make a place in the world that refuses you or accepts you only when and how it sees fit. I found that the racism that women of color and tgncp face makes their claims to the city even more fleeting and fragmented. Manalansan writes of gay immigrant Filipino men "who with the wildness of their lips, tongues, and bodies are able to lay claim to a space no matter how fleeting or limited in the transnational setting of New York City."[49] It is clear that queers are indeed "not yet here" in the radical "queer futurity" that performance studies scholar José Esteban Muñoz proposes for queer of color subjects until we imagine and enact a world otherwise.[50]

Queers seek escape from or even through cis-heteropatriarchy, which means trudging through the interstellar medium between stars like the "lesbian flâneur" who wanders city streets, a paradoxical site of freedom/ violence for women and tgncp.[51] Queer geographers Catherine J. Nash and Andrew Gorman-Murray focus on mobilities "to avoid the somewhat binary deterritorialising/reterritorialising arguments about the decline of the gay village and the rise of alternative spaces."[52] Constellations do similar work of describing the "rise of alternative spaces." Yet over a prolonged period of time and across many women's and tgncp's experiences in the city, constellations also do the work of showing the resonance of places no longer physically present but still mentally and emotionally substantial—they do not just note mobilities but catalogue their traces as well.

The ability to determine one's lines has changed vastly over my period of study, and race and class largely defined my participants' mobilities and immobilities. Nash and Gorman-Murray found that "queer people are experiencing greater urban mobilities because of ameliorative human rights and social-political gains that both foster and shape these new mobilities."[53] Yet, as queer of color theorists Fatima El-Tayeb, Jin Haritaworn, and Paola Bacchetta write, "neoliberal economies fetishize the mobile worker," while discussions "about migration simultaneously demonize the movement of racialized bodies, justifying constant policing and containments."[54] The lines that lesbians and queers make range from migrations across continents to commutes across the city, and each are as racialized, gendered, sexualized, and classed as the borders they cross over in making them. These lines proceed forward, sideways, and sometimes backward when queers make a way out of no way. Lines are the unwritten, invisible records of how we survived to get here, to get anywhere.

## Together Now and Then and Again: Piecing Together Constellations

How do constellations come together? Many of the lines and stars of my participants are shaped by and shape the paths of gentrification throughout the city. Constellations speak to the complicit nature of lesbian-queer gentrification, as much as they relate to the material, social, virtual, imagined, and physical elements that make up the stars and lines of constellations. Forms, like people, change over time, and the constellations of participants accumulate, but memories also fade as stars get lost from view due to pollution or fading eyesight.

A component star or line may change (say, the series of stars you visit most, who you're friends with or dating) while the core quality of the constellation, the lesbianness and/or the queerness formed through the relationality of the constellation, is maintained. Literary theorist Walter Benjamin's theorization of constellations speaks to the philosophy of ideas that have, in the words of literary theorist Frederic Jameson, "no centers, no 'ultimately determining instances' or bottom lines, except for the relationship of all these [aspects] to each other."[55] With their fleeting and fragmentary quality, constellations are filled with kinds of interchangeable parts of queer life and the paths between them: ex-girlfriends, subway lines, walking or rolling from the same few dyke bars to the same handful of feminist landmarks to a range of pizza places, and so on. Consider the description of the way lesbian-queer life develops as offered by white, working middle-class Kate '03:

> There were a series of moments of gut-pulling potential where I realized that for every off-hand mention of something going on, there must be worlds upon worlds more that I'd never really . . . been able to dig into. And if I started to follow one of them and pick up a thread, any thread, I'd find another, and another, and instead of just sort of auditing the places and happenings, I could build a whole different life.

Just as Kate describes following the threads of possibility to form a queer life, Ahmed writes, "A queer politics does involve a commitment to a certain way of inhabiting the world, even if it is not grounded in a commitment to deviation."[56] Kate's quote also speaks to the changing relationships of the moment that persevere into a greater sense of being in repeated forms that hold. Such are constellations.

Which brings me to lesbian-queer geographies and practices that at times resist and at times are complicit with the myth of neighborhood liberation in producing gayborhoods: cruising and U-hauling. Cruising can be understood as searching for a sex partner(s) and having sex with that person or those people—usually casual and anonymous—in public space. Cruising is often a spotlighted practice in the literature on queer spaces, which describes radical sex publics as typical of the queer or lgbtq claim to space.[57] Throughout urban history, cruising spaces have been highly regulated across races and classes.[58] In his critical analysis of Times Square's "revitalization" at the turn of the century, novelist and essayist Samuel Delany describes how the elimination of many gay male cruising hubs is in fact a refusal of queer bodies, practices, and livelihoods—especially those of working-class people and people of color—by the city itself.[59]

Cruising is also a popular topic among and associated with lgbtq people, namely gay and queer men. Notably, no one brought it up in our conversations before I asked, even though participants often brought up sex as a topic without hesitation. For all that it is regarded as a signature "queer" act, significantly less attention is paid to lesbian-queer cruising—indeed, per my participants, lesbian-queer cruising may just be significantly less common than gay-queer male crusing. The attention paid to cruising also shaped my participants' ideas of themselves, as more than one wondered, If lesbians didn't cruise, were they still radically spatially queer?

Across races, classes, and generations, most of my participants, like Rachel '00, described their use of the term "cruising" as "tongue-in-cheek." In the lesbian-queer geographical imagination, participants asserted it is common to envision that lesbians do not have "that public cruising thing" per Bailey '95, or what Noelle '83 called "the Shane thing" referring to the hook-up queen of L Word fame. In another interview, Gloria '83 shared that lesbians "would use [the word 'cruising'] for ourselves but it wasn't the same thing [as gay men]. It wasn't going to a park and having anonymous sex in the bushes." After everyone laughed, I asked her why lesbians don't seem to do that. She replied, "Well, we'd at least try to get their first name before we had sex." Gloria alludes to an expectation of getting to know one another, which some participants associated with fostering intimacy or safety.

Vanessa '93 expressed a sentiment that many women and tgncp share: that both cruising as well as the hanky code—using handkerchief placements and other codes to signal desires, intrigues, and fetishes— were both "a gay male thing." While the pro-sex magazine *On Our Backs* published a hanky code for lesbians as early as 1984 (figure 5.5), hanky codes, like cruising, usually came across as matters of speculation— often accompanied by longing or dread—rather than experience and practice.[60] Relatedly, sex was often projected onto private spaces, especially when participants discussed pornography. Most of the sexual media participants described was largely crafted for individual or small group viewer/readership. Looking back to decades before what Magdalene described as the "queer porn revolution" taking place around the time of my 2008–2009 interviews, Noelle recalled how the works of Carol Queen and Pat Califia presented radical lesbian-queer sex on the page in the 1980s and 1990s.[61]

However, the fleeting and fragmented quality of lesbian-queer spaces, as well as their knowledge, means that claims about the frequency of practices like cruising are based on little more than stereotypes and word-of-mouth anecdotes. Three participants asserted that they did cruise for casual sex, and a handful more each had a friend or two that cruised. Alex shared: "That's what the [lesbian] bars are for." Alex added that she had sex with people she just met after dancing with them, and other participants expressed jealousy or said they felt inspired. Kathy '05 shared that she often did the same with women she met randomly at lesbian or lgbtq bars and parties. But the bars also intimidated many. As Rachel '00 experienced it, "Making eye contact was a big deal."

But *why* do lesbians and queers assigned female at birth presume they do not/choose not to cruise? When I asked participants if they would ever have sex in the Ramble, a well-known gay male cruising territory in Central Park, Alex said, "That's gross. It's unsanitary." To which I added, joking at the time, "It's also outside and it's cold!"

Figure 5.5. "Whatever Color is Your Hankie . . . ," *On Our Backs*, 1984

And this is when the geographies of lesbian-queer sex changed every-thing I was writing and thinking. At the intersection of the history and socialization of gender, design, and issues of "women's safety," I realized that the actual geography and physiology of people assigned male and female at birth and the temporality of their sex and orgasms both tend to afford very different sexual practices. Historian George Chauncey writes in *Gay New York* that, for gay men in the city from 1890 to 1930, "pri-vacy could only be had in public," because working- and middle-class gay men could not share private spaces.[62] Yet, women and tgncp are more associated with private or semi-public spaces, and largely lack the economic capital to make spaces of their own, let alone neighborhoods. Bailey pointed out that there are fewer and fewer lesbian bars and, again compared to some gay men's bars that allot literal backroom spaces for casual hookups, "There's no [back] room there!" Cruising often requires or is imagined to require public territory such as streets and parks or semi-public spaces that can be claimed for undisturbed sex.

A few participants even mentioned being excluded from gay male spaces because the focus was on sex foremost rather than camaraderie or sociality. A handful of my participants preferred to spend their time among gay and queer men. Phyllis '88 said that "for a while I identified as a gay man" because "they had the best [techno] music." Annabelle '97 shared how her coming out in London was bound to the gay male club scene: "I was the only girl in a sea of sweaty Muscle Marys and I *loved it*. I felt so accepted and so loved." Framed through the lens of those assigned female at birth—as well as trans women who are already policed, denigrated, and harassed—my findings suggest that the radical production of queer space needs to herald the geographies of queer sex and sexuality as evidence of more multiple and varied ways of queering space. This queering of space is more than a project of merely claiming public space, especially when recognizing that it is cis- and passing men who have a greater ability to claim public space.

Seemingly antithetical to cruising and central to the lesbian mythos is a practice I originally encountered in joke I first heard in the early 1990s: "What does a lesbian take on a second date?" Answer: "A U-Haul." The practice of what lgbtq people—most especially lesbians and queers—colloquially term "U-hauling" involves moving in with someone shortly after you start dating. My participants often proffered an explanation for dyke tendencies toward quick-start serial monogamy: those assigned female at birth are socialized to nest. I knew this explanation was reductionist at best, and even used as a way to legitimate why lesbians are not seen as central to urban culture—as Sally '96 pointed out, they were said to "drop out of the culture."

With queer theory's fixation on cruising, I had not given the practice of U-hauling much thought until Eileen '96 said she found that same old joke frustrating. After I shared the joke in one group interview, she laughed but then shook her head. Then she began to talk quickly and with great passion, waving her arms:

> It's so much fuckin' work just to live here [in New York City] that it makes sense to me. [*laughs*] . . . This is coming from the experience of someone who has dealt with this shit for my whole life . . . you're on guard all the time, and you're kind of dealing with . . . millions of people that don't give a shit about you . . . And to find someone who gives a shit about you and wants to make a safe space with you is a pretty big deal. . . . it makes sense to me that people do that. . . . So it's like having some stability when there's not a lot of room for movement because of your economic constraints.

I was floored as I realized the white cis-heteropatriarchal fog I had succumbed to. I had missed why our fragmented and fleeting stars in the context of New York City often came together with a gravity I could not previously discern. In my focus on people's inability to afford housing, I had forgotten to account for the urban political economy of affording queer life, which often requires splitting rent in relationships—or with (many) roommates—a practice induced by racial capitalism as much as the gender pay gap.

Then there were Afro-Caribbean, working middle-class Alex '98's keys. In one interview, she shared her artifact of two sets of keys, totaling over twenty:

> The reason why I keep these keys is because . . . I moved out of my mother's house after I came out. She didn't kick me out but it was sort of, like, respectful. I didn't want to be there taking girls. . . . And so ever since then, at seventeen, I always was living with a girlfriend. I have never *not* lived with a girlfriend. . . . I just moved from my last place—where

these keys are [*holds up one set of keys*]—to my new place [*holds up the other set*] where these are. [*laughs*] And I still go back and forth to get my mail. . . . My keys say it all. And, you know [*holds up a couple of keys*], the keys [for the place where I volunteer], [*holds up another couple of keys*] and the keys [for the place where I work]. Which is why I still have these.

While her "keys say it all," Alex implies that her experience as a Black woman only amplifies the stress and violence of precarious housing, which she negotiates with relationships and different forms of kinship over the years. Only through an analysis of gender, sexuality, race, class, and so on can we make sense of constellations.

Each of Alex's keys represents a star in her own queer constellation of relationships and places that, at times, navigate white cis-heteropatriarchal property ownership. In our online group conversation, Alex shared that "the queer community existed around [a friend or date], not the location. . . . Nomadic in action, we were coupled and free." For Alex, constellations are more social than spatial. Yet in the materiality of her keys, apartments, and ex-lovers, Alex's constellation endures as a sociospatial network of new forms of kinship, as well as a practice that accumulates each star of a home and the partner within it and the lines between them into constellations that *are* Alex.

Every constellation is equally produced in the deficit of social, economic, and political supports lesbians and queers must navigate. In her history of feminist bookstores, library studies scholar Kristen Hogan writes, "As spaces run by lovers, the bookstores were also sites of contentious break-ups and just plain bad days."[63] As Alex jangled her keys in front of us, I realized that she was also expressing the need to carry a representation of important spaces and relationships with her—on or near her body wherever she wanders—to show a queer space that remains open to her even amid the personal and collective lesbian-queer history of breakdowns and breakups in activism, work, businesses, and home life.[64]

Reader, I was one of those dykes who had previously mocked U-hauled relationships. I never thought I'd write this, but I contend that we must address the political economies of relational spaces in constellations—and to do so we must place U-hauling alongside cruising as a radical queer practice. Issues that lgbtq people are likely to face include lack of access to secure housing, abuse, domestic violence, lower incomes, longer commutes, and longer work hours, all of which in turn lead to more breakups and more frequent relocations.[65] All of my participants mentioned facing at least some of these agonies. U-hauling helps to articulate the spatialized networks of lesbian-queer constellations that have, again as Jameson framed Benjamin's relational understanding of constellations, "no centers . . . except for the relationship of all these [dykes] to each other."[66] Lesbians' and queers' lack of social, legal, policy, and economic supports place other strains on their relationships, which in turn lessens their ability to stay put and produce long-term spaces.

When we read the housing practices of many lesbians and queers in the late twentieth century, Hollibaugh's description of queer life makes all the more sense:

> We tried to make the world . . . predictable. Mostly, that meant being alone together, creating a little home somewhere that might provide a haven . . . We also tried to create a smaller world that included others like ourselves, a world we could relax and function in. We were scared all the time about who we loved. We were often afraid about who we were. We live each day in a hostile and volatile universe.[67]

The stories and maps of participants suggest that many lesbians and queers succumbed to the myth of neighborhood liberation by partaking in gentrification as a tactic of community-building for at least two significant reasons, even as they sought to enact a world based on the feminism, antiracism, and anticapitalism of dyke politics. It is well known that gentrification primarily displaces people of color and working-class and poor people, especially women and tgncp. My research also shows that many white, working- and middle-class lesbians and queers are eventually displaced as well when those spaces they occupy increase in value. My participants took part in processes of gentrification, while pro-gentrification policies and corporations took advantage of their instability, which was also bound to the lack of affordable housing, extreme property development, and the cis-heteropatriarchal policies, laws, and zoning of racial capitalism and settler colonialism.[68]

All of my participants shared the agony of facing intensified precarity through their stories. Yet the stories of lesbians and queers of color and working-class and poor lesbians and queers evidenced even greater instability. The intersectional composition of constellations reveals many shared spaces specific to generations (say, various cafés or bars) or across generations (Park Slope Food Co-op, LGBT Community Center), yet it is also and always racial and class identities that define the sprawl or clustering of constellations across the city.[69] Relative lack of capital (amplified when one or both parties relocate after a breakup) forces lesbian-queer spaces further from sought-after areas like city centers. The result is the ever-the-more fragmented and fleeting stars of lesbian-queer life across the city, as well as the sprawl induced by (and surely unintentionally furthering) processes of gentrification. With less capital, homebuying by lesbians and queers, whether single or partnered, must come later in life, if at all. For many lesbians and queers, this adds up to cycles of displacement and a lasting sense of place not bound to the physical world alone.

U-hauling is a spatialized pattern of what Halberstam calls "queer . . . failure as a way of life."[70] Halberstam also writes, "Like many others before me, I propose that . . . the goal is to lose one's way, and indeed to be prepared to lose more than one's way." But I hesitate to agree in this instance.[71] I want to embrace Halberstam's position, but my interviews tell me all loss and failure is not always celebratory: if we replace "to lose one's way" with "to lose one's home," we can see that there must be limits to embracing queer failure. The very promise/violence of capitalism must be confronted fully with dyke politics of feminist antiracism and anticapitalism to reimagine and enact new queer worlds and futures. In moving away from notions of default "lgbtq spaces" of neighborhoods, bars, and cities, I make the mutually material, virtual, and social qualities of lesbian-queer urban lives apparent. Constellations are evidence of lesbian-queer failure *and* resistance.

Seen through the lens of structural oppressions rather than failed relationships or personal preferences, U-hauling is not merely a pattern of women's socialization to "nesting," but rather an outcome of the precarity of lesbian-queer life. U-hauling and cruising can also be seen as queered responses to the hypermobility enforced by heteronormative state logics. U-hauling and cruising exemplify what queer geographer Gavin Brown coined as the "queer commons," what art historian Nadja Millner-Larsen and performance studies scholar Gavin Butt described as the "varied

ameliorative responses not only to the failures of mainstream LGBT politics but also to twenty-first-century austerity and gentrification."[72]

Millner-Larsen and Butt add that "queer activism—not to mention
queer life—is a particularly rich resource for imagining, experiment-
ing with, and enacting the improvisational infrastructures necessary for
managing the unevenness of contemporary existence."[73] That the term
"U-hauling" is a central action verb in the vernacular of lesbians and
queers speaks to their resilience to and reworking of their urban political economic situation. That U-hauling is also often considered a joke
rather than a tactic of political economic survival speaks to the fragmented nature of lesbian-queer spaces and experiences that I show are
tied together in the relationality of constellations.

## Constellations across the Urban Universe

It requires determination to make rooms of one's own under the structures of white cis-heteropatriarchy as women and tgncp. Indigenous
studies scholar Leanne Betasamosake Simpson (Nishnaabeg) writes
that constellations are places where spirits and knowledge live, which
are "visible to everyone all night and unreadable theory and imagery to
the colonizer or those who aren't embedded in grounded normativity."[74]
In lesbians' and queers' refusal to succumb to injustice, they also make
their own worlds that are both unseen by and work to unravel heteropatriarchal society, which are distinct from, and indebted and related
to Simpson's constellations as a project of decolonization. A visual construct of positionality, constellations represent lesbian-queer geographies
in a new light, to bring lesbian-queer politics to the world. Constellations
have the capacity to disrupt the promise of neighborhood liberation in
the form of a lgbtq or lesbian neighborhood and, perhaps, chip away at
and even dismantle the processes of gentrification, and the falsehood of
the American Dream and the racism, colonialism, sexism, and heteronormativity attached to it. That constellations are derived not only from
the patterns of lesbian-queer geographies but the fact that lesbians and
queers often reference astrology if not assert their downright dependence
on it makes the term especially appropriate in lesbian-queer words and
worlds in expressing a radical queer feminist geographical imagination.

Black geographer Katherine McKittrick summarizes the uneven geographies of the marginalized: "The production of space is caught up in, but does not guarantee, longstanding geographic frameworks that materially and philosophically arrange the planet according to a seemingly stable white, heterosexual, classed vantage point."[75] The place-making practices in constellations persisted—racialized, classed, generational, and gendered as they always are—over twenty-five years in New York City. This period included the HIV/AIDS crisis, the highest recorded antihomosexual attitudes in US history,[76] the rise of queer and transgender identities, 9/11, financial booms and busts, and, all along, increasingly austere neoliberal politics and increasingly precarious conditions of everyday (patriarchal, cis-heteronormative) life.

Constellations are already relevant to other marginalized groups. I make this suggestion of queer feminist constellations' generalizability with great caution, and through what critical social psychologist Michelle Fine refers to as theoretical generalizability: "the extent to which theoretical notions or dynamics move from one context to another."[77] Even more, work toward social justice also requires what Fine calls provocative generalizability: "researchers' attempts to move their findings toward that which is not yet imagined, not yet in practice, not yet in sight."[78] Constellations may be generalizable if only to encourage radical geographical imaginations determined from and by marginalized groups. Thus and foremost, I offer constellations as a theorization of the lesbian-queer production of space to strengthen and reflect the politics and purpose that my participants desire, thereby producing queer feminist spatial theory in their own words.

Constellations are a geographical imagination that can read and enact the antiracist, anticapitalist, feminist dyke politics my participants hold dear—and reveals the long overdue need to take up an anticolonial project as well. In this queer feminist call, I echo Simpson's Indigenous theorization of constellations when she writes, "This organizational structure seems to have relevance to radical resurgent organizing."[79] I do not idealize these group interviews or even the archival materials that are the evidence for my claims—they were, at times, awkward, discordant, confusing, and unclear, at other times, openly transphobic, racist, classist, imperialist, and almost always marked by some evidence of internalized homophobia, sexism, racism, and transphobia. But what came of these interactions and documents was evidence not only of community suffering and confusion, but also the resistance, reworking, and resilience enacted through the lesbian-queer body moving through space.

If they have been there all along, why am I arguing that we can see constellations now? I believe the obfuscation of constellations is due to three forces in particular. First, the pull of the American Dream and the promises of neighborhood liberation seemed to be reaping rewards for some (white, middle-class, college-educated) lgbtq people until the recent claims about and experiences of the end of the gayborhood. Surely all along, the political concerns of women and tgncp were never central (if not antithetical) to the project of the white cis-heteropatriarchal state. Constellations matter because they can extend these ideas and fuel new geographical imaginations on behalf of social and spatial justice.

Second, much of my argument about queerness has to do with time. Returning to Massey's insights, it may be that in the very act of gathering so many participants' stories, maps, and artifacts over time about one city, there emerges, in addressing the complexity of that time, a richer complexity of space. The blend of virtual-physical spaces that has heightened in the digital era was, as I have shown in my multigenerational study, always a key element of queer life; to the extent that devices, apps, and sites often inspire a sense of connection among marginalized groups, however, this virtual community rarely holds in the same way.[80] The range of places and place types in lesbians' and queers' geographies attests to their ability to make space when there was none to claim or share physically.

Finally, without many queer histories to turn to, we are prone to repeat the same mistakes again and again, and expect a different result. It is my most significant hope, my most profound queer feminist assertion, and my raging gay agenda that the urban production of space in constellations offer a practice of queering space itself, in the way that Muñoz describes "queer practice" as a "mode of being in the world that is also inventing the world."[81] By turning our geographical imagination to constellations that invent as much as they attach to preexisting spaces and practices, I provide an alternative account of lesbian-queer spaces that often are hidden by and disturb the order of structural oppressions.

My intervention here is an effort to write against the reduction of the lesbian-queer experience, revealing why neighborhoods do and will always hold power for my participants and other marginalized groups while offering another way forward to embrace practices of spatial connection and resistance. By using the metaphor of constellations to speak between queer, feminist, and critical urban theories, I do not claim constellations are the only or even the best theorization of the lesbian-queer production of urban space. Constellations are merely one way to imagine and enact space differently from and, at times, against the practices of cis-heteropatriarchal capitalism.

My research shows how lesbians and queer women produce and sustain their spaces and the city—at times, against their own long-term aspirations of community-building—in the face of intense oppression and inequality spanning generations. In constellations, I hope to have relinquished some of the white settler, middle-class cis-heteropatriarchal "stability" and promise of neighborhood liberation in the American Dream in exchange for a life on Earth among the stars. The production of lesbian-queer space tends to fixate on the bright clusters of star-like places and experiences, but it is the well-known places and the line-like paths between them repeated into the most recognizable constellations across participants' stories to create their own Queer Orionx, Lesbo Ursa Major, and Dyke Ursa Minor. In the words of queer astrologer Chani Nicholas, "Capitalism and patriarchy want to keep us separate, compartmentalized, afraid, and alone, and unconscious to our collective power. Astrology helps us to feel connected to something larger."[82] And as Ahmed writes, a queer politics has hope "because what is behind us is also what allows other ways of gathering in time and space, of making lines that do not reproduce what we follow, but instead create new textures on the ground."[83] In reorienting the queer gaze away from neighborhoods alone or foremost, we see how lesbians and queers make connections across space and time that critical urban theory has not accounted for previously.

Radical interventions and imaginations are required to pursue queering spacetime, which could be rendered through constellations and by any other metaphor or means possible to make worlds "not yet here," "not yet imagined, not yet in practice, not yet in sight." Political scientist Cathy Cohen declared over twenty years ago that "a truly radical or transformative politics has not resulted from queer activism," which is still the case.[84] She and many others have insisted and still insist on forming coalitions that organize for, by, and about the "nonnormative."[85] While the issues range far and wide that cruelly touch and unfairly shape the lives of lgbtq people, including my own research participants, my findings in this book make clear that antigentrification organizing is a central political issue requiring the activism of lesbians and queers. Constellations also reveal how nonnormative approaches to surviving and thriving in New York City have persisted for decades in the face of injustice. What other way forward is there but to take action on behalf of connection and change?

# Epilogue

## *What We Cannot Not Want*

It's August 2019 as I write this epilogue, and Google *just* changed its algorithms so that a search for "lesbian" finally no longer yields a majority of pornographic results. This long-time-coming fact doesn't surprise me and I doubt it would surprise my participants. Communication studies scholar Cait McKinney writes that there has long been a lesbian (and queer) practice of "finding lines to my people": women and transgender and gender non-conforming people (tgncp) read lesbian and queer and trans magazines, websites, bibliographies, anthologies, newspapers, blogs, social media, and so on to trace the lives of other lesbians and queers on the page and, in so doing, carve "out a textual community."[1] Most lesbians and queers have always had to find the lines and stars of their constellations first through the way the world sees them, rather than primarily in their own words, images, and stories. And we will never be able to leave these star-like places—virtual and physical, imagined and material—and their constellations behind because, in the words of queer geographer Natalie Oswin, "for as long as non-heterosexuals are discriminated against, queer spaces will remain something that . . . queers cannot not want."[2]

Queer theory now often focuses on digital, rural, suburban, migrant, global, and national geographies, and it felt a bit anachronistic to bring it back to the urban. Yet my research findings also encouraged me that it was (queer) time and (queer) space to take the theoretical insights gleaned across scales and temporalities and bring them back to well-known urban geographies—in order to read the city anew. Much of my book is a geographical tracing of gentrification on and by lesbians and queers through southern Manhattan and Brooklyn. I trail the stardust of queer places and experiences through prominent trajectories in now prominent neighborhoods: from Greenwich Village into the Lower

East Side; and then from northwest Brooklyn neighborhoods like Boerum Hill, Cobble Hill, and Carroll Gardens, into the northeast areas of Prospect Heights, Clinton Hill, and Fort Greene, and farther south via Park Slope, Windsor Terrace, and Greenwood Heights, into the central Brooklyn neighborhoods of Kensington, and, finally (for now), Ditmas Park. Many participants noted these trajectories:

> NAOMI '89: But [lesbians and queers are] not [in Park Slope] anymore. My friend was like, "Yeah, they were chased out. We're in Kensington." But now Kensington is . . .
> JACK '91 (ME): Into Ditmas.
> WANDA '83: We're in the water!

Wanda jokes that lesbians and queers may be forced to make community in Jamaica Bay and the Atlantic Ocean.[3] This jest also reveals that lesbians and queers feel unable to gentrify further into the white ethnic, middle-class, sometimes suburban-esque neighborhoods of south Brooklyn that many of my participants deemed unwelcoming to queer bodies.

I long worried about sharing the patterns of lesbian-queer gentrification I discovered during my research in 2008 and 2009, certain that developers would just follow patches of lesbian and queer residential clusters to raise rents. However, by the mid-2010s, it became clear to the me that, to put it bluntly, condos now outpaced queers. The mythical lgbtq or lesbian neighborhoods that promised neighborhood liberation were more clearly a fantasy than ever before. Queer residential and commercial dispersion intensifies and the pace of loss continues to quicken, but the possibility for a strong sense of community, organizing, and networks is not truly lost. I argue that liberation languishes precisely because it depends on a neighborhood-focused geographical imagination. The affordances of proximal living such as chance meetings, local networks, and shared sense of space and purpose must be recrafted through other means—and social media and online networking alone do not bring about the physical world we desire. Through the lens of constellations, core dyke politics of antiracism, anticapitalism, and feminism are given another way of shining through the clouds of oppression.

In fact, many things have not changed since 1983. There is no evidence that the number of lgbtq suicides, murders, attacks, or "micro-aggressions" *ever* decreased. There is still no federal law prohibiting discrimination against lgbtq people on the basis of sexual orientation or gender identity, and while some states and cities have enacted laws prohibiting it, the Trump administration increasingly supports policies against such protections. Conversion therapies are still practiced. The disproportionately high rates of intimate partner violence, cancer, illness, alcoholism, mental illness, and drug addiction among lgbtq people are still with us.[4] My arguments in this book then call out for coalition building, which, of course, includes antigentrification, antiracist, anticolonial, and trans feminist organizing.

Yet my book also makes clear that neighborhood-level gentrification, like all processes of injustice, is bound to and dependent upon racism, classism, sexism, and cis-heteropatriarchy writ large. My participants' production of urban space in constellations also speaks to the broader claim to the queer body and the sense of being in (queer) space and time. The preceding chapters don't include the terms "climate change," "AI," "data privacy," "algorithmic bias," or "facial recognition," and I was barely able to touch on the prison, military, and medical industrial complexes, or how disability shaped my participants' spaces. However, I think of little else these days than how these injustices shape lesbian, queer, and tgncp lives.[5] Trump administration policies proliferate that encourage or enact the exclusion and harassment of and violence against lgbtq people, people of color, Indigenous people, Two-Spirits, immigrants, refugees, Muslims, Jews, disabled people, prisoners, children, women, and/or working-class and poor people, and on and on. It is imperative for lesbians and queers to embrace "forms of queer life and relation that might come after the Internet"—an internet that increasingly does not work for them—as much as it is time to work across differences against those who oppose justice.[6] As large cities become tech hubs and the playgrounds of ultra-masculinist coder and finance regimes, I wonder what many lesbians and queers may yet afford and create in and across small cities, suburban, and rural environments, while working to upend settler colonial models of spatial community in coalition with other marginalized groups. What should and will the lesbian-queer relationship to the land be in the future? How will dykes be part of the work of environmental, data, algorithmic, and community sustainability and repair?

By the time I finished writing this book, the geographies of Black and Latinx New York City and spaces for working-class and poor people had been even more vastly diminished by government and corporate intervention. What Mayor Michael Bloomberg began in his corporatization of the city, Mayor Bill de Blasio continued, despite his campaign promises to act otherwise. It was then unsurprising but hard to accept when Bum Bum Bar, the only lesbian bar primarily serving working-class, Latinx lesbians and queers, closed just before the touristified fiftieth anniversary of Stonewall in the summer of 2019. Jackie '85 pointed out how injustices persist in playing out against those with the least among us, namely working-class and poor queer youth of color: "I was walking by the [Village's LGBT] Center *yesterday*, and there were half a dozen queer Black and Latino kids. And I was like, 'Didn't I see you—*for the last few decades*?'" Whatever "better" that certain lgbtq people now experience, the lives of lgbtq people of color, the poor, youth, homeless, sex workers, tgncp, and other marginalized groups remain policed, disinvested, displaced, and/or itinerant. My participants' stories and maps reveal how racialized, classed, and gendered constellations of lesbians and queers are bound to one another, as lesbians and queers come together and apart, again and again.

Which brings me to the question many people ask me: why are the people this book is about—lesbians and queers—divided and disorganized? We are a people who literally live on our own terms, so part of the answer is that these terms (like all terms) create exclusions and boundaries, setting gay against queer, trans against lesbian, and so on. Many of these breakdowns are framed as generational, suggesting the kind of steps we need to take to develop coalitions across generations of lesbians, queers, and tgncp. Indeed, as much as my participants shared experiences of marginalization and oppression, a lack of generational understanding or a presumption thereof arose again and again. In one cross-generational group, Heather '95 and Donna '05 were both shocked to discover that Gloria '83 could be and was "evicted from an apartment for being gay" in the early 1980s. Gloria told her 1980s-generation co-participants about this experience in anger and frustration, shaking a fist in the air as she said, "These kids today think it's all like *The L Word*!" But Heather and Donna were embarrassed about not knowing their history, and regretted that they had disrespected Gloria. I had to remind each of them that in sharing their stories—as I too came to understand during the interviews—we were writing lesbian-queer history for ourselves and others. Lesbians and queers can take to heart what the Lesbian History Group wrote in 1989: "Lesbians have been deprived of virtually all knowledge of our past. This is deliberate since it keeps us invisible, isolated and powerless."[7] Or as Ani DiFranco puts it, "I'm recording our history now up on the bedroom wall / And when we leave, the landlord will come and paint over it all. / . . . I am writing the story of how hard we tried."[8]

If you are a lesbian or queer or other marginalized human reading this, do not think I expect you to all get along or that I am frustrated with you inasmuch as I am livid at the systems and structures that leave us unable to communicate or congregate in a city that so clearly relies on our bodies, labor, and volunteerism to promote itself. Popular media stories posit that dating apps have replaced bars—and these narratives assume lesbian-queer community still persists in its depth and breadth, only online. When we use "free" sites and apps, we give away our data, and, in many ways, we give away our rights as that data is analyzed and patterned to manipulate our emotions, relationality, and sense of self—a process of "digital dispossession."[9] Algorithms behind search engines and "news" feeds only ever reveal some information and some accounts to some users, and are controlled by governments, hackers, trolls, and corporations—notably, the same sort of corporations that represented lesbianism as pornography produced for and by primarily white, cisgender, heterosexual men for nearly twenty years.

There is much to learn from the generations that went before us, about knowing when to act and when not acting did not serve our purpose—and also about knowing when to love and desire. I want to encourage many lesbians, queers, and other oppressed people to stop blaming themselves and to end the project of framing beautiful, radical lesbian-queer lives and spaces only through the lens of failure and loss. At the same time, I also seek to embolden the same groups, in the words of education studies scholar Eve Tuck and K. Wayne Yang, to enact practices, discourses, and worlds of decolonialization, to "be more impatient with each other, less likely to accept gestures and half-steps, and more willing to press for acts which unsettle innocence."[10]

Like the blue stars with which I begin this book, our renderings of queer New York are only partial knowledges that must be re-created, generation after generation. We re-create these spaces because, as José Esteban Muñoz writes, "The present is not enough. It is impoverished and toxic for queers and other people who do not feel the privilege of majoritarian belonging, normative tastes, and 'rational' expectations."[11] While Muñoz posits queer futurity—the "not yet here"—as a spacetime of recuperation, I also believe the project of recording lesbian and queer histories recuperates stolen queer pasts to rework and resist the toxic present. Perhaps that is why I find it so hard to stop telling my participants' stories. My hope is that writing about these women's and tgncp's lives and spaces helps lgbtq people renarrate the stories of their lives on behalf of social change. Noelle '83 wrote in her online group conversation: "Revolution is an abstract concept, though many lesbians . . . cite it as a goal or want or need as an end point for freedom in our society as well as a means to economic and social justice. This is yet another constellation that is imagined, but not yet real." It is written in the stars and on our bodies that in order to make revolution a reality, one must first imagine new queer worlds, past, present, and future.

# ACKNOWLEDGMENTS

I am indebted to many for their stories, teachings, advice, collegiality, and support. I am foremost and forever grateful to those forty-seven self-identified lesbians and queers I interviewed for this project who shared your lives, stories, and ideas. You continue to inspire me. I am equally thankful to the Archivettes who run the Lesbian Herstory Archives of Brooklyn, New York, and who shared tea with me, opened the door for me and locked the door behind me, and asked me how I was doing after another long day reading and typing at the back table on the second floor. I send gratitude to those who collected and donated materials; the thousands(+!) of women who made, attended, and/or even thought about attending lesbian-queer organizations and zaps; and those who wrote, published, distributed, and read lesbian-queer periodicals, texts, zines, and books. Together, you constellated the reasons I did this project: to record, to remember, to break apart and piece together, to galvanize, to record the heck out of our lives, and to choose connection over fear.

There is not enough spacetime in the universe to explain how much the community of the Environmental Psychology Program of the Graduate Center of the City University of New York (CUNY GC) helped me to bring to life my ideas. I am forever grateful for my EP home, as I am equally honored to have worked and continue to work alongside the members of the CUNY GC SpaceTime Research Collective (STReaC), Macaulay ITFs, and the radical feminist scholars who build a community for critical research across disciplines and theoretical perspectives. My ideas, scholarship, and everyday life are better for the collegial support, inspirational friendship, and ceaseless letter writing of Cindi Katz, Michelle Fine, and Melissa Wright. The three of you are my rocks and my eternal committee of joy who made this book possible while offering me support, edits, wisdom, and education to make me possible. I can only dream some day of weaving Marxism and ethnography like Melissa, who counseled me through job interviews and dilemmas, and had her hot tub ready for my knee. Michelle taught me how to not stop writing, to face the agonies of injustice in my participants' stories (in her words: "just keep writing"), and whose work puts a bounce in my step to keep going. Cindi's gracious line edits, generous insights, home away from home in catsitting for dear Pip, and wisdom changed me so much. I am sure many of her words lie in this text, shaping me still. I am forever your friend and colleague.

My own well-being and the book that came out of it would never have flourished without my GC+ community: the advice, listening ear, and stack of lezqueer astrology books offered by Jude Kubran, the friendship of my peers, and the mentorship of my utterly stunning faculty and mentors, including Susan Saegert, Setha Low, Roger Hart, David Chapin, Barbara Katz-Rothman, Caitlin Cahill, María Elena Torre, Joan Greenbaum, Leanne Rivlin, Wendy Luttrell, Gerry Pratt, Victoria Rosner, Dagmar Herzog, Do Hogson, Lynda Klich, Ida Susser, Joe Ugoretz, and Susan Opotow. A special shout goes to Don Mitchell, who helped me revise my focus on lesbian-queer urban political economy—may the political economy of midcentury braceros and urban lesbians find their way into conversation someday, my friend. I also send gratitude to Mary L. Gray, a mentor, friend, and social scientist who gave me support when I too wanted to write queer theory.

My colleagues in feminist geography and geographies of sexualities have stimulated me with their work and devotion to critical geographic work; my colleagues in American studies and digital studies have helped to make this project more rigorous, complex, and, I hope, necessary. The research assistantship, transcription, and collaboration of Julie Bolcer, Samantha Fischer, Allyson Foster, Ashley Hamelin, Erin Siodmak, Julia Gorka, Gina Stalica, Jennifer Edwards, Martie Janeway, Lindsey Funke, and Teresa Theophano was invaluable. I send special thanks to Jeffrey Levy, Nick Lally, and Kallista Bley who made the maps for this book, and Ilene Kalish, Adam Bohannon, Sonia Tsuruoka, Dan Geist, Martin Coleman, and NYU Press for their editorial work and support of this book. I am equally thankful to my students who have joined me in engaging in these ideas and constantly reinvigorating my passion for this work, especially the students of my Queer America classes at Trinity and Queer Geographies seminar at the University of Kentucky.

The financial and collegial support I sustained through fellowships and grants remind me how much this work means, and I hope it speaks to lesbians and queers everywhere of how much our lives mean to the world. Trinity College generously supported me with multiple Junior Faculty Research Fellowships, and the Five College Women's Studies Research Center Fellowship allowed me space and time to write among new friends. I remain grateful for the Woodrow Wilson Dissertation Fellowship in Women's Studies, Alexander von Humboldt German Chancellor Fellowship, Center for Lesbian and Gay Studies Diane Heller-Joan Barnard Fellowship in Lesbian and Gay Studies, and my scholarship to the Antipode Summer Institute for Geographers of Justice. I also continue to be thankful for the funding and awards I received from the CUNY GC that contributed to this book's production: Proshansky Dissertation Fellowship, Writing Across the Curriculum Fellowship, Instructional Technology Fellowship, Center for Place, Culture, and Politics Fellowship, Doctoral Students Research Grant, and Leanne Rivlin Environmental Psychology Student Award, as well as the Carolyn G. Heilbrun Dissertation Prize and the Honorable Mention for the Paul Monette–Roger Horwitz Dissertation Prize from the Center for Lesbian and Gay Studies.

Versions of this manuscript were made stronger and much more clever—and the same happened to me too, I am certain—by the insightful minds and collegial hearts of many readers, the likes of which include Wanda Acosta, Christian Anderson, Nicole Avallone, Judy Bankman, Kath Browne, Lisa Brundage, Hillary Caldwell, Caitlin Conyngham, Megan L. Cook, Joana Coppi, Rachel Cylus, Jessie Daniels, Casey Detrow, Gregory T. Donovan, Martin J. Downing, Desiree J. Fields, Allyson Foster, Scott Gac, Margaret Galvan, Erin Glass, Kate Gordon, Mary L. Gray, Kiersten Greene, Crystal Hall, Tina Harris, Roger Hart, David Harvey, Amanda Huron, Catherine Jett, Lynda Johnston, Erica Kaufman, Elizabeth Lapovsky Kennedy, Larry Knopp, Sara Koopman, Greta LaFleur, Nick Lally, Amanda Licastro, Jessa Lingel, Setha Low, William Mangold, Muira McCammon, Sarah J. Montross, April Morris, Tiffany Muller Myrdahl, Rae Rosenberg, Susan Saegert, Johanna Schuster-Craig, Nari Senanyake, Aga Skorupka, Collette Sosnowy, Megan Springate, Timothy Szlachetko, Jennifer Tang, Anna Terweil, Katharine Waggoner, Marion Werner, Cookie Woolner, and Mary

Zaborskis, as well as my colleagues at the Center for Place, Culture, and Politics seminar. I send special thanks to Marika Cifor, Rachel Corbman, Rachel Goffe, Serin Houston, Elizabeth R. Johnson, Shaka McGlotten, Cait McKinney, Diana Ojeda, Matt Watson, Elise Weaver, and Elizabeth W. Williams, who read various versions of this text over the years. I am forever thankful for the support I received from colleagues during my years in Digital and Computational Studies at Bowdoin College, American Studies at Trinity College, and my new home in Geography at the University of Kentucky. Your scholarship infuses mine wherever I may wander.

I am thankful also to my friends and colleagues who shared their support and thoughts, especially Emily, Zoë, Phoebe, and Ezra Peck-McClain; Jama, Graham, Elliot, and Ronan Lowe; Michael King, Ben Mason, Ed Weaver, and Adriana Salerno; Amy, Greg, and Sam Gordon Richane; Matt, Jenny, Arya, and Kaya Wong; Alissa and Barthe MacMillan; T. L. Cowan and Jas Rault; Van Sloan-Morgan; Kate Bergren, Carol Clark, Tamsin Jones, Beth Notar, and Lesley Farlow; Eleanor Townsley and Michelle Markley; Alanna Hoyer-Leitzel and Dan Deschaine; Sarah and Levi Williamson; Gina Mamone and Chelsea Dobert-Kehn; Jill Choder-Goldman, David Radmore, and Lily Perkins; Julie Bolcer and Sivan Schecter; Priscilla McCutcheon, Matt Zook, Matt Wilson, Betsey Beymer-Ferris, Anna Secor, Michael Samers, Tad Mutersbaugh, Alice Turkington, Patricia Ehrkamp, and Rett McGoodwin; my Norwegians and my Germans; Marlene Attardo, Gerry Grass, and Teddy Stephen; and, of course, Linda Gieseking. As Whitman wrote, "I know very well I could not" be "without a friend or lover near," and so I live my days delighted by and devoted to our friendships and our family.

Jenny Schecter would use the word "evanescence" here to tell you how lucky I was to find my cat and dog co-parent, best friend, partner in crime, partner in BBC mystery–watching, and truly favorite human, Elizabeth W. Williams. You are the brightest, funniest, and most brilliant star in my constellation. My life and this book, obviously, are so much better for my having met you and built a world with you, Miss Lady, and Gaybe. These nooks and this book are for you, my family.

I am also thankful to you, reader, for caring or being curious enough about lesbian-queer spaces and history to pick up this text. I hope that in reading this book you can recognize queer worlds you did not know existed; identify queer worlds that existed alongside yours that sound just like yours or those of friends you know or wished you knew (and will meet any day now—put down that phone when you're ready and find them!); and come to know that you, too, can imagine and enact new worlds. It is up to all of us to act on behalf of justice, and then some. And so I write. So you write, organize, sew, fix cars, volunteer, play rugby, carry a parasol, take T, don't take T, take HRT, help someone else take T or HRT, take estrogen, don't take estrogen, smile at someone as they are on estrogen, love, lead a stitch-and-bitch, run an international conglomerate, run a soup kitchen, have friends, hold hands, have children, don't have children, adopt children, foster children, help a lover or friend die, have pets, make dinner, fuck, don't fuck, play board games, cuddle, and/or watch *Watermelon Woman* or *But I'm a Cheerleader* for old times' sake or for the very first time (do it, reader, do it). So we go on. We have much more in common than we could ever imagine—in our desires for a better world if not our identities and experiences—and we have much to learn by recognizing, supporting, and acting in coalition across our beautiful differences, across generations and geographies, races and classes, abilities and ideals. Onward, together. And gayme on.

# APPENDIX I

## Identity Terms

Navigating the world of lgbtq identities, spaces, and cultures requires constant interrogation, vigilant patience, and a blended sense of hopeful wonder and frustrated cluelessness. Jess '96 shared, "I think 'queer' is not . . . an umbrella [term]. Well, . . . it functions that way also, but queer identity as a specific thing . . . that's been solidified in the last ten years— that maybe wasn't true before? Like being adamant about being queer and not gay." Jess's equivocation about the meanings of queer involves defining, undefining, questioning its construction, and then positioning it against another identity (gay) to give it its meaning.

At the same time, Ruth '90 pointed out, claiming an identity "depends on location and translation"—i.e., who you are speaking with and where. She also expressed her frustration with having to self-identify but understood it afforded recognition as well: "Our movement is about fighting stereotypes and fighting oppression—and yet here we are in these little, little boxes." As much as I too hate these boxes, I rely on the identities given by participants during our intake conversations (as many shifted over time or even during interviews) in order to express how they saw themselves. Building on the conversation around terminology offered in chapter 1, here I reflect and sometimes expand on other language and terms used in *A Queer New York*.

To *identify* or *self-identify* are ways lgbtq people commonly recognize an individual's agency in defining his/her/their own identity or identities.[1] I use the popular *lgbtq* acronym to refer to lesbian, gay, bisexual, trans, and queer people when I speak to gender and sexual minorities. My use of the "lgbtq" and "tgncp" acronyms are lowercase to signal that, while these acronyms speak to my participants' identities and those they most often referenced in our conversations, they do not fully represent Two-Spirit, intersex, questioning, and other gender and sexual identities. These acronyms do not include many others, as well, but I keep to them as they reflect the nomenclature my participants most often used and include most of the identities with which they identified.

The most often used identity among my participants, *lesbian*, describes a woman (broadly and self-defined) who loves, partners with, is attracted to, sleeps with, and/or has sex with another woman (broadly and self-defined). Those that identified—either exclusively or not—as "lesbian" in the 2000s often mentioned a connection to a historical category and series of oppressions, as well as its use as a political label that prioritized women's experiences. *Queer* is a more fluid term that encompasses a nonnormative sexual and gender identity and/or politics that emerged through late 1980s and 1990s activisms, and has grown in use since the 1990s; the concept emphasizes plurality and a refusal of categories rather than reductionism or fixity. About half of the participants who came out in the 1980s and 1990s generation found that the queer identity now afforded them the ability to more fully represent themselves. Similarly, those who did not use "lesbian" mentioned they felt an essentialized identity attached to women alone refused trans and genderqueer bodies, or that it was "old-fashioned" in a new queer world.

Other identifiers are equally essential to urban lesbian-queer life. *Dyke* was employed to indicate a more radical, political angle because of its derogatory connotations. Participants across generations argued that they were constantly "reclaiming" the dyke identity, and I include it in the subtitle of the book to participate in that reclaiming. Participants rarely used *gay*, stating they felt it referred more to men. As white, middle-class Eva '98 shared, "It's like, well how does somebody *obviously* do gay? 'Cause sometimes [when] I'm in certain circles I'm like obviously gay. I mean, it's not as if I don't feel that way, 'cause I certainly do." In the 1980s and 1990s, "lesbian" and "gay" became increasingly common terms at the expense of the medicalized *homosexual*, a term that held negative connotations for all. Throughout the period addressed in this study, there was also increasing renegotiation and refusal of the bisexual identity. *Bisexual* defines those people who love, partner with, are attracted to, sleep with, and/or have sex with people of both sexes. As my participants' stories attest, bisexuals are often disregarded or unwelcome by lesbians and queers, or anticipate that they will be. As an example, after a lifetime of dating women and trans men, multiethnic, working middle-class femme

Dana '98 no longer felt she had a voice in my research project when she began dating a cisgender man. Even when I encouraged her return, she expressed worry that other participants might not be welcoming. One participant identified as *asexual,* meaning that they had romantic but not sexual relationships.

The terms *woman* and *man* became increasingly de-essentialized during my research period and in the years since. I apply them in the broadest sense to invoke my own participants' connections to these terms. I use *transgender and gender non-conforming people (tgncp)* to encompass those who identified as genderqueer, butch, masculine-presenting, transgender, androgynous, and so on. *Trans* encompasses transgender, transsexual, and transvestite people but is most often an abbreviation for *transgender* identity, denoting those who do not conform unambiguously to conventional notions of gender. I do not use the term "trans" to identify all tgncp since some of my participants identified as "butch and transgender" or andro at one time, and now as trans; I hope the use of "tgncp" allows for a longer and more inclusive temporal pull. No participants identified as *intersex,* having biological characteristics of both sexes.

*Fags, fairies,* and *dandies* are derogatory terms reclaimed by gay men and also claimed in the 2000s by some lesbians and queers in my study. These identities help to articulate more feminine masculinities that were otherwise undefined. *Futch* developed as a crossover to unite "fag" and "butch," even though now it also stands for a butchy femme or femmey butch. Usually distinct from butch, a *boi* was a younger, masculine-presenting, genderqueer person assigned female at birth. Boi often identified young butches or trans men who were still early in their transition. Those bois journalist Ariel Levy spoke to for a well-publicized *New Yorker* story described preferring less relationship responsibility and enjoying casual sex in comparison to older butches.[2] "Bois" could also refer to sexually submissive or more effeminate butches, and/or "bois" can be used to refer solely to masculine-presenting Black and Latinx women, pointing to the ways in which masculinity has again been reinterpreted by lesbians and queers.[3]

*Cisgender* or just *cis,* a word not yet common in our 2008–2009 conversations, describes "people who do not identify with a gender diverse experience."[4] *Butch* describes lesbians and queer women with a more traditionally masculine gender presentation. *AG, ag,* or *aggressive* is a newer identity deployed in the 2000s by, for, and about more masculine-presenting Latina and Black, working-class lesbians and queers, similar to if not descendent from the *stud* identity popular among the same group in the 1980s and 1990s. *Femme* claims a more traditionally feminine-presenting identity, often queering the meanings and portrayals of femininity. To be feminine does not mean one is femme; to be masculine does not mean one is butch, stud, or aggressive/ag/AG. *Genderqueer,* coined in the mid-1990s, refuses a gender identity and/or label, and/or does not ascribe to only masculine or feminine gender identities. Since my period of study, *genderfluid, gender non-conforming,* and *gender non-binary* (a.k.a. *non-binary* or *enby*) are used more often. As Blaise '02 noticed even then: "There's been some kind of shift from binary definitions and recognizing possible limitations and oppressive . . . forces saying, 'These are the categories [*bangs table*] and you have to be in one.'" *Androgynous* and/or *andro* identities blur and often queer appearances and embodiments of that which is read as masculine or feminine.

These identity terms are described to the best of my ability and surely fall short of the rich complexity and diversity of their use in New York City over the past twenty-five years. As mentioned in the preface, I did not discuss my burgeoning trans identity with participants—I often worried I would be judged for it, not just among participants but the public in general. However, looking back, I now understand that disclosing it would have made possible different types of conversations, while limiting the possibility for some others I recorded here.

*Biographical Sketches of Participants*

Participants are listed in order of year of coming out. All participants were given the option of using their own name or changing to a pseudonym when I completed the research in 2009. However, given the anti-lgbtq sentiment and the hatred and vitriol directed at those most marginalized, erased, and exploited since the late 2010s, I have since changed all of the names to pseudonyms to protect their identities.

Participant names are followed by the year they came out (if these years varied during interviews, the year listed during our phone intake was used), and followed by their age at the time of the interviews, class, race/ethnicity, the first identifiers they gave for their sexuality and/or gender in our phone intake conversation, their occupation and, finally, their pronouns as used during our interviews. I refer to three generations to speak to my participants' experiences as they framed them, which I refer to as the 1980s, 1990s, and 2000s, and which were cleaved by two periods of intense change: 1991 to 1995, and 2001 to 2003.

THE 1980S GENERATION

Yasmin '83: age 43, middle-class, Latina, lesbian woman, social worker and activist, she/her/hers

Gloria '83: age 53, middle-class, white, butch lesbian, mother, economist, she/her/hers

Noelle '83: age 42, middle-class, white, lesbian and queer, publicist and writer, she/her/hers

Birtha '84: age 50, middle-class, white, queer dyke, artist, she/her/hers

Wanda '85: age 42, middle-class, Black/Cuban, lesbian, middle school teacher and activist, she/her/hers

Jackie '85: age 41, upper middle-class, white, queer dyke, professor, she/her/hers

Chris '86: age 54, middle-class, white, genderqueer dyke, high school teacher, she/her/hers

Esther '87: age 56, middle-class, white Jewish, lesbian woman, administrative social worker, she/her/hers

Phyllis '88: age 37, middle-class, white Jewish, dyke lesbian, editor, she/her/hers

Felicia '89: age 30, middle-class, white, queer lesbian woman, movie distributor, she/her/hers

Naomi '89: age 35, middle-class, African American, lesbian dyke, high school teacher, she/her/hers

Ruth '90: age 38, middle-class, white Jewish, lesbian woman, administrator and activist, she/her/hers

Janice '79/'91: age 47, middle-class, white, lesbian female, piano teacher, she/her/hers

Susan '92: age 31, working middle-class, white Jewish, lesbian dyke, teacher and writer, she/her/hers

### THE 1990S GENERATION

Vanessa '93: age 34, working middle-class, white, lesbian female, fundraiser, she/her/hers

Bailey '95: age 29, working middle-class, mixed-race/Black, dyke lesbian, receptionist, she/her/hers

Heather '95: age 40, working middle-class, white, qenderqueer queer, psychologist and activist, they/them/theirs

Quinn '95: age 30, working middle-class, white, lesbian woman, comedian and writer, she/her/hers

Sally '96: age 30, working middle-class, white, lesbian gay, writer and editor, she/her/hers

Eileen '96: age 27, working middle-class, white, lesbian femme, deejay and marketing consultant, she/her/hers

Jess '96: age 26, working middle-class, white, queer dyke, graduate student, she/her/hers

Linda '96: age 39, working middle-class, white, femme lesbian, social services, she/her/hers

Annabelle '97: age 33, middle-class, white, femme lesbian, communication and PR, she/her/hers

Gretch '98: age 22, working middle-class, white, queer lesbian, student, she/her/hers

Dana '98: age 25, working middle-class, multi-ethnic, queer female, dance teacher, she/her/hers

Alex '98: age 26, working middle-class, Afro-Caribbean, lesbian woman, librarian and activist, she/her/hers

Eva '98: age 32, middle-class, white, lesbian gay, actor, she/her/hers

Sudie '99: age 27, working middle-class, white, queer female, graduate student, she/her/hers

Mia '99: age 22, working middle-class, Latina, bisexual female, personal assistant, she/her/hers

Cullen '99: age 27, working middle-class, white, queer dyke, graduate student, she/her/hers

Rachel '00: age 35, middle-class, white, gay lesbian, social worker, she/her/hers

THE 2000S GENERATION

Lily '01: age 22, working middle-class, white Jewish, queer femme, sex educator and retail, she/her/hers

Blaise '02: age 25, working middle-class, white, queer genderqueer, marketing outreach, she/her/hers

Maral '02: age 21, working middle-class, white Armenian, queer female, student, she/her/hers

Tre '02: age 21, working middle-class, Afro-Caribbean, lesbian female, student, she/her/hers

Faith '03: age 24, working middle-class, white, female lesbian, medical student, she/her/hers

Kate '03: age 29, working middle-class, white, queer female, bookkeeper, she/her/hers

Olivia '03: age 19, working middle-class, mixed-race/Puerto Rican, lesbian female, student, she/her/hers

Holly '03: age 31, working middle-class, white, lesbian female, writer, she/her/hers

Magdalene '04: age 26, working middle-class, white, queer femme, social worker, she/her/hers

Victoria '04: age 19, working middle-class, white, queer, student, she/her/hers

Kristene '04: age 25, middle-class, white, queer, nonprofit employee, she/her/hers

Donna '05: age 20, working middle-class, white, queer female, bartender, she/her/hers

Lina '05: age 25, middle-class, white, lesbian female, non-profit employee, she/her/hers

Kathy '05: age 21, working middle-class, white, lesbian female, stage manager, she/her/hers

Isabelle '06: age 25, working middle-class, white, queer female, graduate student, she/her/hers

Tara '06: age 19, working middle-class, Hispanic, femme lesbian, student, she/her/hers

## APPENDIX III

*Methodological Details*

So how do you write the stories of the invisible? My approach was to record not only "lesbian" and/or "queer" spaces but my participants' everyday lives, to support participants in articulating the rich and complicated geographies of their urban worlds. As such, I drew on interviews and archival research, accompanied by mental-mapping and artifact-sharing exercises, as well as data analysis.

Beyond snowball sampling (friends of friends, acquaintances of acquaintances, and so on), sites of recruitment included posts to newyork.craigslist.org, myspace.com, and facebook.com; an email announcement to friends, interested parties, and colleagues; posts to queerstudies-l, wmst-l, gender-studies-l (at NYU), and the Center for Lesbian and Gay Studies listservs. Flyers were placed, with permission, at eighteen bars, clubs, and parties throughout New York City that I selected by surveying online ads, listings, discussion boards, and blogs to reach a socioeconomic and racially diverse population: Albatross, Starlette Sundays (Sunday nights at Starlight Lounge and then Angels and Kings), The Stonewall Inn, The Duplex, Cubbyhole, Rubyfruit Bar & Gill, Henrietta Hudson, Victoria (second Saturday of the month at the Stonewall Inn), Sunday Nights at 2A, Snapshot (Tuesdays at Bar 13), Nubian Dreams (fourth Sunday of the month at Taj Lounge), GirlNation (Saturday nights at Nation), Bum Bum Bar, Chueca Bar, Metropolitan, Choice Cunts (last Friday of the month at Sultana), Ginger's, and Cattyshack. Flyers were also placed, with permission, at the LGBT Community Center of New York City on various posting boards including Lesbians, Bisexuals, BDSM, Jobs, General, Black, Asian, Latina/o, People of Color; Bronx Community Pride Center; Hunter College LGBT Center; Queens Community Pride Center; all Babeland locations; Cowgirl Hall of Fame restaurant; and Bluestockings Bookstore.

A total of 101 potential women and tgncp participants contacted me. I conducted phone intakes with those who fit the eligibility requirements: they must have come out between 1983 and 2008 and spent most of their time since then in New York City. Due to time constraints, only 47 participants could take part. Once I realized more white women and tgncp were interested in taking part, I consistently attempted to recruit more women and tgncp of color but to no avail. The lack of Indigenous, Native, First Nations, Asian, and Asian American participants in this study may be due to any number of reasons, including my own white settler assumptions in the ways or places I recruited for this study, and/or language I used to recruit participants, such as my search for "lesbian and/or queer" participants who had "come out."[1] For example, ethnographer Michelle Tam describes how the histories of racism, migration, and colonialism led her non-heterosexual, Chinese Canadian participants to identify as "queer (and) Chinese" rather than "a singularly *queer Chinese* subject."[2]

I wanted to articulate generational experiences, so I turned to group interviews. Sociologist Karl Mannheim posited a generation as "the union of a number of individuals through naturally developed or consciously willed ties . . . [and involves what] may be described as *participation in the common destiny* of this historical and social unit."[3] My queer feminist reading of Mannheim's theorization rejects his sole dependence upon the biological rhythms of heteronormative lifespans. Struck by popular claims of a "gay generation gap," I was inspired by activist and policy leader Loree Cook-Daniels's generational map to situate my interviews attentive to both age and period of coming out.[4] I focus on each participant's self-defined moment of coming out as their claim to generational membership.

A remarkably underused methodology, multigenerational group interviews enabled participants to talk about spaces and experiences over time, and therefore mark shifts in generational knowledge while affording the collective meaning-making of group interviews. Participants were invited to take part in three types of interviews: (1) group interviews with a within-generational cohort; (2) group interviews with a cross-generational cohort; and (3) a collective follow-up, private, online conversations. Dedicated to paying women and tgncp for their undervalued time, I used fellowship funds to pay participants $25, $25, and $20 per meeting, respectively.

I use "group interviews" to speak more accurately to process, and to turn away from the marketing nomenclature of "focus groups."[5] I broke participants into five "generational cohorts" of five-year time spans (based upon when they came out) to examine shorter periods in more detail and let participants mark the catalysts that partitioned the larger generational breaks into the 1980s, 1990s, and 2000s generations. The five generational cohorts included: 1983–1987 (eight participants), 1988–1992 (six), 1993–1997 (nine), 1998–2002 (twelve), and 2003–2008 (twelve). I led a total of twenty-two within- and across-generation group interviews with mental-mapping and artifact-sharing exercises, including one women and tgncp of color group interview. I attempted to create racially and class diverse interview groups, but the composition of each group was dependent on who showed up.

Drawing upon participants' coming out years was an essential tactic to contextualize their understandings of lesbian and queer life, culture, and spaces. Coming out meant different things for participants as the social context of outness changed dramatically over the decades. At the same time, per many of my participants, coming out is usually a lifelong process negotiated through race, class, age, family dynamics, and gender, as well as the time of coming out. Participants of color and women who came out in the 1980s, as well as all working-class participants, used the phrase "in the life."[6] Femme-identified Esther '87 shared: "God knows how many times we have to come out for whatever fucking reasons." Coming out is not always easier today (whenever that may be), and all shared stressful, sometimes violent, stories involving family, friends, exes, partners, health care providers, passersby on the street or in the subway, people from out of town, police, civil-service agents, shop clerks, and so on. Coming out related to self-identifying to family, friends, other lgbtq people, strangers, or one's self; attending spaces marked lesbian or queer; dating or engaging in sexual relations; and/or finding information in books, films, music, websites, or social media that made sense of their experiences.

Before our group interviews, I asked participants to draft and/or label a mental map of those spaces and places they identified as lesbian or queer around the time of coming out. Mental mapping has been found to be particularly helpful in evoking vivid spatial memories, allowing participants to tell their stories in ways that words alone cannot articulate, keeping participants focused on the discussion of space and place, and helping to articulate injustices and inequalities.[7] I also invited participants to bring and share objects or "artifacts"—i.e., mementos that were important to them around their time of coming out—as a means of introduction, and to ground themselves in the period in which they came out. Artifacts were helpful in comparing my findings with that of other lgbtq research that uses coming out stories as a point of departure. The artifacts participants shared included buttons, photos, zines, books, jewelry, an ex-girlfriend's tie found under the bed that same day, a photo frame, a music box, hairpins, magazines, journals, postcards, and a handmade bracelet from Dyke March 2004. Participants in some across-generation group interviews made composite mental maps while others produced story sheets that compared notions of safety, access, and comfort during the coming out years and today. The dual quality of the verbal and visual conversations sparked many emotional memories that fueled vivid conversations of lesbian-queer life in New York City over the years.

I asked participants about their everyday experiences of lesbian and queer spaces and places important to them, both at the time of their coming out and at the time of our conversations. I shared ideas that groups produced in their conversations with the following groups and so on. I also introduced ideas and concepts from literature, theory, and popular culture, and ideas hatched from archival research so that participants could be in conversation with my ideas throughout. To that end, my research participants contributed to the theories and ideas in this work by commenting on my early ideas.

I am often asked if my participants knew one another before the study. When Bailey '95 said to her multigenerational co-interviewees, "You all look very familiar to me," she was likely not wrong. A few participants were dating or had dated, a few were friends or became friends, but most were acquaintances or strangers of varying degrees. For example, Chris '86 and Jackie '85 remembered each other from being arrested during an ACT UP zap; Wanda '85 recalled Lily '01 from the preceding week when Wanda had bought a vibrator from her (in her job as a sex toy salesperson) for her niece's birthday; a handful of participants mentioned having the same Callen-Lorde Community Health Center gynecologist (I never did get an appointment at that highly sought-after doctor); some worked at the same nonprofits, restaurants, and agencies decades apart; and many recognized one another from Dyke Marches, trips to the Michigan Women's Folk Festival, bars, meetings at the Center, and even local and national lesbian TV, ads, and films.

I also wanted to dig into the details of the time period through archival materials. Like literary scholar Christopher Nealon, I wanted to piece together the "history of mutually isolated individuals, dreaming similar dreams" to write a story that belongs "to the people who lived its history."[8] In 2008 and 2009, I sought those materials that explicitly focused on lesbian-queer life throughout the entire city. At that time, most lgbtq-specific collections, such as the New York Public Library (NYPL) Gay and Lesbian Collection and the LGBT Community Center Archives, offered significantly fewer resources on lesbian-queer experiences or had not fully indexed those records. In comparison, the Lesbian Herstory Archives (LHA) focused exclusively on that population and contained all of the publications held in other archives, so I decided to focus my attention there. The materials of the nascent and independently run Black Gay and Lesbian Archives in Harlem were in the process of being donated to the NYPL's Schomburg Center for Research in Black Culture. As many of the Schomburg materials were collected without dates or locations, as is common in activist archives, it will take some time for me to review these materials.

The LHA, also an activist archive, had only two collections that consistently recorded locations and dates: organizational records and publications, so I draw only on these (incredible) materials.[9] The LHA's 2,300-plus organizational records include materials regarding social, political, and cultural groups, a total of 391 of which were based in the city during my period of study. I examined one issue per year from six periodicals, relying on national or continental publications when no New York City–based publication was available (see jgieseking.org/AQNY).

TABLE A.I. Periodicals

| PUB YEAR | PUB TITLE | NYC-BASED | #/DATE |
|---|---|---|---|
| 1983–1986 | Big Apple Dyke News | yes | 3.1 Jan-Feb, 4.5 Oct-Nov, 5.2 Wint, 6.1 Spring |
| 1987–1991 | WomanNews | yes | 8.7 Jul-Aug, 9.6 Jun, 10.6 Jun, 11.2 Feb, 12.5 May |
| 1991–1995 | Deneueve | no | 1.1 May-Jun, 2.6 Dec, 3.1 Feb, 4.4 Aug, 5.3 Jun |
| 1996–1999 | HX: For Her | yes | 001 Oct, 036 Sept, 075 Jun, 111 Apr |
| 2000–2001 | Curve | no | 10.6 Oct, 11.2 Apri |
| 2002–2008 | GO NYC: A Cultural Roadmap for the City Girl | yes | 1.1 Apr-May, 2.3 Jun, 3.7 Dec-Jan, 4.6 Nov-Dec, 5.2 Jun-Aug, 6.6 Nov-Dec, 7.7 Dec-Jan |

Beyond lesbian and queer publications and other local periodicials, I drew widely on newspaper articles in the pro-lgbtq *Village Voice* and the much more mainstream *New York Times* (*NYT*). Gloria '83 summarized the queer relationship to the *NYT* perfectly: "You know, I read the *Times* if I want something straight." The *NYT*'s heteronormative and often gentrification-sympathetic approach allowed me to contextualize lesbian-queer experience in the city's "public" eye.

The data visualizations (graphs and maps) throughout this book draw from a range of datasets and fact sheets and helped me to contextualize participants' experiences, some of which can be found at the companion website to *A Queer New York* (jgieseking.org/AQNY). My jump into data visualizations of archival records (ranging from GIS maps to graphs) is a new approach that allowed me to detect patterns across generations. These multigenerational snapshots often act as common texts from which to make sense of these women's fragmented and fleeting spaces across the city. More about the methods to producing these data visualizations can be found on the site.

I primarily draw on US census data, but less so on census data regarding sexuality. Such census data regarding sexuality during my period of study (since 1990) only captured those who (1) self-identify as women, (2) identify as partners, and (3) cohabitate.[10] Single, cisgender lesbians and gays, as well as single tgncp of all sexualities, remain uncounted. Further, as queer geographers Michael Brown and Lawrence Knopp write, census tract borders do not match neighborhood boundaries, and lgbtq, gay, and lesbian neighborhood boundaries surely also vary according to individual experience and memory.[11] I often relied on NYU's Furman Center for Real Estate and Urban Policy's annual reports. However, these reports do not provide socioeconomic data by decade, so I tabulated percentages by taking the average of census tracts within a neighborhood; this method is not ideal but it is the best possible statistical glimpse of neighborhood life.

The analysis I conducted on these materials took some time as I produced over a dozen bottom-up (themes from the interviews) and top-down (themes from the literature) codes to make sense of patterns across my research, which I then had to focus even further to produce these chapters. Determined to prioritize the voices of the women and tgncp I interviewed, the extensive archival research I conducted receives less room in this book. It is my hope that future papers and, perhaps, monographs will allow me to further discuss the findings I could not fit into this text, ranging from conversations around cosmopolitanism to ones around trauma and mourning, from appearance and style to gender identity, from access to medical knowledge and health care to trends in periodicials around alcohol and travel ads, from stories of families to even more stories of friendship.

# NOTES

PREFACE

1  Elizabeth Kennedy and Madeline Davis, *Boots of Leather, Slippers of Gold: The History of a Lesbian Community* (New York: Penguin, 1994), 189.

2  I address the use of the lower-case "lgbtq" (and "tgncp") acronym in Appendix I.

3  Christopher J. Lee, "Why Queers Love Astrology," *RECAPSmagazine* (blog), 2011, http://recapsmagazine.com; see also Kevin P. Murphy, "When Gay Was Good," in Queer Twin Cities, ed. Twin Cities GLBT Oral History Project (Minneapolis: University of Minnesota Press), 305–18; David K. Seitz, *A House of Prayer for All People: Contesting Citizenship in a Queer Church* (Minneapolis: University of Minnesota Press, 2017).

4  Adrienne Rich, "Note Towards a Politics of Location," in *Blood, Bread, and Poetry: Selected Prose, 1979–1985* (New York: W.W. Norton, 1986), 210–32.

5  Cf. Ryan Conrad, ed., *Against Equality: Queer Revolution, Not Mere Inclusion* (Oakland: AK Press, 2014).

6  Samuel Stein, *Capital City: Gentrification and the Real Estate State* (London and New York: Verso, 2019).

7  George Chauncey, *Gay New York: Gender, Urban Culture, and the Making of the Gay Male World, 1890–1940* (New York: Basic Books, 1994).

8  Sarah Schulman, *My American History: Lesbian and Gay Life during the Reagan/ Bush Years* (New York: Routledge, 1994); Amber L. Hollibaugh, *My Dangerous Desires: A Queer Girl Dreaming Her Way Home* (Durham, NC: Duke University Press, 2000); Mignon R. Moore, *Invisible Families: Gay Identities, Relationships, and Motherhood among Black Women* (Berkeley: University of California Press, 2011); Christina Hanhardt, *Safe Space: Gay Neighborhood History and the Politics of Violence* (Durham, NC: Duke University Press, 2013); Hugh Ryan, *When Brooklyn Was Queer: A History* (New York: St. Martin's Press, 2019).

9  Cf. Jasbir Puar, "In the Wake of It Gets Better," *Guardian*, November 16, 2010, www.theguardian.com.

10  Madeline Davis, "The Production of Lesbian Spaces in the 1970s" panel, Lesbians in the 1970s series, CLAGS: Center for Lesbian and Gay Studies, New York, March 19, 2010.

CHAPTER 1. NAVIGATING *A QUEER NEW YORK*

1  Cubbyhole bar is at 281 W. 12th Street; until 1991, it was at its original location, 438 Hudson Street, where Henrietta Hudson bar is presently located.

2 Cf. John H. Rogers, "Origins of the Ancient Constellations: II. The Mediterranean Traditions," *Journal of the British Astronomical Association* 108, no. 2 (1998): 79–89.

3 Amin Ghaziani, *There Goes the Gayborhood?* (Princeton, NJ: Princeton University Press, 2014); Patricia Leigh Brown, "Gay Enclaves Face Prospect of Being Passé," *New York Times*, October 30, 2007, www.nytimes.com; Scott James, "There Goes the Gayborhood," *New York Times*, June 21, 2017, www.nytimes.com; Heather Dockray, "New York's Lesbian Bars Are Disappearing: Here's Why Their Survival Matters," *Brooklyn Based* (blog), April 10, 2015, http://brooklynbased.com.

4 Maggie Nelson, *The Argonauts* (Minneapolis: Graywolf Press, 2015), 141.

5 David Harvey, *Social Justice and the City* (Baltimore: John Hopkins University Press, 1973); Henri Lefebvre, *The Production of Space*, trans. Donald-Nicholson Smith (Malden, MA: Wiley-Blackwell, 1992).

6 Harvey, *Social Justice and the City*; Derek Gregory, *Geographical Imaginations* (Malden, MA: Wiley-Blackwell, 1994); Jen Jack Gieseking, "Geographical Imagination," in *International Encyclopedia of Geography*, ed. Douglas Richardson et al. (New York: Wiley-Blackwell/Association of American Geographers, 2017).

7 Hanhardt, *Safe Space*, 9.

8 David K. Seitz, "The Trouble with Flag Wars: Rethinking Sexuality in Critical Urban Theory," *International Journal of Urban and Regional Research* 39, no. 2 (2015): 251; see also Roderick A. Ferguson, *Aberrations in Black: Toward a Queer of Color Critique* (Minneapolis: University of Minnesota Press, 2003).

9 Kimberlé Crenshaw, "Mapping the Margins: Intersectionality, Identity Politics, and Violence Against Women of Color," in *Critical Race Theory: The Key Writings That Formed the Movement*, ed. Kimberlé Crenshaw, Neil Gotanda, and Garry Peller (New York: New Press, 1996), 357–83.

10 The core texts of urban political economy that fuel my work in this book include the following: David Harvey, *The New Imperialism* (New York: Oxford University Press, 2003); Harvey, *The Limits to Capital* (New York: Verso, 2007); Harvey, *Rebel Cities: From the Right to the City to the Urban Revolution* (New York: Verso, 2013); Neil Smith, *The New Urban Frontier: Gentrification and the Revanchist City* (New York: Routledge, 1996); Don Mitchell, *The Right to the City: Social Justice and the Fight for Public Space* (New York: Guilford Press, 2003); Cindi Katz, *Growing Up Global: Economic Restructuring and Children's Everyday Lives* (Minneapolis: University of Minnesota Press, 2004); Ruth Wilson Gilmore, *Golden Gulag: Prisons, Surplus, Crisis, and Opposition in Globalizing California* (Berkeley: University of California Press, 2007).

11 Cf. Cindi Katz, "Vagabond Capitalism and the Necessity of Social Reproduction," *Antipode: A Radical Journal of Geography* 33, no. 4 (2001): 711; Katz, *Growing Up Global*; Laura Briggs, *How All Politics Became Reproductive Politics* (Oakland: University of California Press, 2017).

12 Mona Domosh, "The 'Women of New York': A Fashionable Moral Geography," *Environment and Planning D: Society and Space* 19, no. 5 (2001): 573–92.

13 Jack Halberstam, *In a Queer Time and Place: Transgender Bodies, Subcultural Lives* (New York: NYU Press, 2005), 36; see also Mathias Detamore, "Queer Appalachia: Toward Geographies of Possibility" (PhD diss., University of Kentucky, 2010); Andrew Gorman-Murray, Barbara Pini, and Lia Bryant, eds., *Sexuality, Rurality, and Geography* (Lanham, MD: Lexington Books, 2012); Mary L. Gray, Colin R. Johnson, and Brian J. Gilley, eds., *Queering the Countryside: New Frontiers in Rural Queer Studies* (New York: NYU Press, 2016).

14 Karen Tongson, *Relocations: Queer Suburban Imaginaries* (New York: NYU Press, 2011), 29.

15 Herring even begins his book's first chapter with a section titled "I Hate New York." Scott Herring, *Another Country: Queer Anti-Urbanism* (New York: NYU Press, 2010).

16 Kath Weston, "Get Thee to a Big City: Sexual Imaginary and the Great Gay Migration," *GLQ: A Journal of Lesbian and Gay Studies* 2, no. 3 (1995): 253–77.

17 Sallie A. Marston, "The Social Construction of Scale," *Progress in Human Geography* 24, no. 2 (2000): 219–42; Geraldine Pratt and Victoria Rosner, "Introduction: The Global and the Intimate," in *The Global and the Intimate: Feminism in Our Time*, ed. Geraldine Pratt and Victoria Rosner (New York: Columbia University Press, 2012), 1–27.

18 Tamar Y. Rothenberg, "'And She Told Two Friends': Lesbians Creating Urban Social Space," in *Mapping Desire*, ed. David J. Bell and Gill Valentine (New York: Routledge, 1995), 169.

19 Judith Butler, *Gender Trouble: Feminism and the Subversion of Identity* (New York: Routledge, 1989); Butler, *Bodies That Matter: On the Discursive Limits of Sex* (New York: Routledge, 1993).

20 Lise Nelson, "Bodies (and Spaces) Do Matter: The Limits of Performativity," *Gender, Place & Culture: A Journal of Feminist Geography* 6, no. 4 (1999): 331–53.

21 Elizabeth Grosz, "Bodies-Cities," in *Sexuality & Space*, ed. Beatriz Colomina (Princeton, NJ: Princeton Architectural Press, 1996), 241–54.

22 Cf. Lawrence Knopp, "Sexuality and the Spatial Dynamics of Capitalism," *Society and Space* 10, no. 6 (1992): 651–69; David J. Bell et al., "All Hyped Up and No Place to Go," *Gender, Place & Culture* 1, no. 1 (1994): 31–48; Gill Valentine, "(Re)Negotiating the 'Heterosexual Street,'" in *BodySpace: Destabilizing Geographies of Gender and Sexuality*, ed. Nancy Duncan (New York: Routledge, 1996), 155–69; Liz Bondi, "Gender, Class, and Gentrification: Enriching the Debate," *Society and Space* 17, no. 3 (1999): 261–82; David J. Bell and Jon Binnie, "Geographies of Sexual Citizenship," *Political Geography* 25, no. 8 (2006): 869–73; Marlon M. Bailey and Rashad Shabazz, "Editorial: Gender and Sexual Geographies of Blackness: Anti-Black Heterotopias (Part 1)," *Gender, Place & Culture* 21, no. 3 (2014): 316–21; Bailey and Shabazz, "Gender and Sexual Geographies of Blackness: New Black Cartographies of Resistance and Survival (Part 2)," *Gender, Place & Culture* 21, no. 4 (2014): 449–52.

23 Henri Lefebvre, "The Everyday and Everydayness," trans. Christine Levich, *Yale French Studies*, no. 73 (1987): 7–11.

24 Iris Marion Young, *Justice and the Politics of Difference* (Princeton, NJ: Princeton University Press, 1990); Michelle Fine, "Bearing Witness: Methods for Researching Oppression and Resistance—A Textbook for Critical Research," *Social Justice Research* 19, no. 1 (2006): 83–108.

25 Barbara Smith, "Where Has Gay Liberation Gone? An Interview with Barbara Smith," in *Homo Economics: Capitalism, Community, and Lesbian and Gay Life*, ed. Amy Gluckman and Betsy Reed (Routledge, 1997), 206.

26 Katz, *Growing Up Global*, 251.

27 J. K. Gibson-Graham, *A Postcapitalist Politics* (Minneapolis: University of Minnesota Press, 2006); see also Amanda Huron, *Carving Out the Commons: Tenant Organizing and Housing Cooperatives in Washington, D.C.* (Minneapolis: University of Minnesota Press, 2018).

28 Amy L. Spring, "Declining Segregation of Same-Sex Partners: Evidence from Census 2000 and 2010," *Population Research and Policy Review* 32, no. 5 (2013): 694, 696, 699.

29 Cf. Kristen Day, "Embassies and Sanctuaries: Women's Experiences of Race and Fear in Public Space," *Society and Space* 17, no. 3 (1999): 307–28; Rachel Pain and Susan J. Smith, *Fear: Critical Geopolitics and Everyday Life* (Aldershot, UK: Ashgate, 2008); Leslie Kern, "Selling the 'Scary City': Gendering Freedom, Fear and Condominium Development in the Neoliberal City," *Social & Cultural Geography* 11, no. 3 (2010): 209–30.

30 Cf. Martin P. Levine, "Gay Ghetto," *Journal of Homosexuality* 4, no. 4 (1979): 363–77; Knopp, "Sexuality and Spatial Dynamics"; Stephen Vider, "'The Ultimate Extension of Gay Community': Communal Living and Gay Liberation in the 1970s," *Gender & History* 27, no. 3 (2015): 865–81.

31 Catherine J. Nash and Andrew Gorman-Murray, "LGBT Neighbourhoods and 'New Mobilities': Towards Understanding Transformations in Sexual and Gendered Urban Landscapes," *International Journal of Urban and Regional Research* 38, no. 3 (2014): 756–72; see also Dean Spade, *Normal Life: Administrative Violence, Critical Trans Politics and the Limits of Law* (Durham, NC: Duke University Press, 2015).

32 "Pride Map 2008," *Next Magazine*, June 2008.

33 It remains tempting to write an entire book on the closing of lesbian bars and dyke activism, but the mythology of queer neighborhood liberation requires its own interrogation through the lens of constellations.

34 Manuel Castells, "Cultural Identity, Sexual Liberation and Urban Structure: The Gay Community in San Francisco," in *The City and the Grassroots: A Cross-Cultural Theory of Urban Social Movements* (Berkeley: University of California Press, 1983), 139.

35 Cf. Michael Brown, "Gender and Sexuality II: There Goes the Gayborhood?," *Progress in Human Geography* 38, no. 3 (2014): 457–65.

36 Lisa Duggan, "The New Homonormativity: The Sexual Politics of Neoliberalism," in *Materializing Democracy: Toward a Revitalized Cultural Politics*, ed. Russ

Castronovo and Dana D. Nelson (Durham, NC: Duke University Press, 2002), 175–94; see also Susan Stryker, "Transgender History, Homonormativity, and Disciplinarity," *Radical History Review*, no. 100 (2008): 144–57; Gavin Brown, "Homonormativity: A Metropolitan Concept That Denigrates 'Ordinary' Gay Lives," *Journal of Homosexuality* 59, no. 7 (2012): 1065–72.

37  Jin Haritaworn, *Queer Lovers and Hateful Others: Regenerating Violent Times and Places* (London: Pluto Press, 2015), 43–44.

38  Charles I. Nero, "Why Are the Gay Ghettos White?," in *Black Queer Studies: A Critical Anthology*, ed. E. Patrick Johnson and Mae G. Henderson (Durham, NC: Duke University Press, 2005), 231; see also Haritaworn, *Queer Lovers*, 43–44.

39  Spade, *Normal Life*, 10, citing Cheryl I. Harris, "Whiteness as Property," *Harvard Law Review* 106, no. 8 (1993): 1707–91.

40  Castells, "Cultural Identity," 140.

41  Castells, 140.

42  Julie A. Podmore, "Gone 'Underground'? Lesbian Visibility and the Consolidation of Queer Space in Montréal," *Social & Cultural Geography* 7, no. 4 (2006): 595.

43  Rothenberg, "'And She Told Two Friends.'"

44  Lauren Berlant, *Cruel Optimism* (Durham, NC: Duke University Press, 2011).

45  Smith, *New Urban Frontier*; Knopp, "Sexuality and Spatial Dynamics."

46  David Rothenberg, "Can Gays Save the City?," *Christopher Street*, September 1977, 9; see also Christina Hanhardt, "Broken Windows at Blue's: A Queer History of Gentrification and Policing," in *Policing the Planet: Why the Policing Crisis Led to Black Lives Matter*, ed. Jordan T. Camp and Christina Heatherton (New York: Verso, 2016), 41–62.

47  David S. Reynolds, *Walt Whitman's America: A Cultural Biography* (New York: Vintage, 1996), 102.

48  While I do not attend to these debates herein, by the 2000s, a "stage" theory dominated popular notions of gentrification whereby different groups supplant one another, as if gentrification is an "orderly, temporal, and sequential process." Loretta Lees, Tom Slater, and Elvin Wyly, *Gentrification* (New York: Routledge, 2007), 34; see also Damaris Rose, "Rethinking Gentrification: Beyond the Uneven Development of Marxist Urban Theory," *Society and Space* 2, no. 1 (1984): 62; Peter Marcuse, "Gentrification, Abandonment, and Displacement: Connections, Causes, and Policy Responses in New York City," *Washington University Journal of Urban and Contemporary Law* 28, no. 1 (1985): 13; Smith, *New Urban Frontier*; Japonica Brown-Saracino, ed., *The Gentrification Debates: A Reader* (New York: Routledge, 2010); Loretta Lees, Tom Slater, and Elvin Wyly, eds., *The Gentrification Reader* (New York: Routledge, 2010); Leslie Kern, "Rhythms of Gentrification: Eventfulness and Slow Violence in a Happening Neighbourhood," *Cultural Geographies* 23, no. 3 (2016): 441–57; Winifred Curran, *Gender and Gentrification* (New York: Routledge, 2017).

49  Cf. Mickey Lauria and Lawrence Knopp, "Towards an Analysis of the Role of Gay Communities in the 'Urban Renaissance,'" *Urban Geography* 6, no. 2 (1985): 152–69.

50 Cf. Lance Freeman, *There Goes the 'Hood: Views of Gentrification from the Ground Up* (Philadelphia: Temple University Press, 2006).

51 Jasbir Puar, *Terrorist Assemblages: Homonationalism in Queer Times* (Durham, NC: Duke University Press, 2007); see also Susan Saegert, Desiree Fields, and Kimberly Libman, "Deflating the Dream: Radical Risk and the Neoliberalization of Homeownership," *Journal of Urban Affairs* 31, no. 3 (2009): 297–317.

52 Stein, *Capital City*.

53 For some exceptions, see L. Lees, "A Reappraisal of Gentrification: Towards a 'Geography of Gentrification,'" *Progress in Human Geography* 24, no. 3 (2000): 389–408; Leslie Kern, "Gendering Reurbanisation: Women and New-Build Gentrification in Toronto," *Population, Space and Place* 16, no. 5 (2010): 363–79; Kern, "Selling the 'Scary City'"; Curran, *Gender and Gentrification*.

54 Smith, *New Urban Frontier*, 100.

55 Rose, "Rethinking Gentrification," 67.

56 Petra L. Doan, "The Tyranny of Gendered Spaces—Reflections from Beyond the Gender Dichotomy," *Gender, Place & Culture* 17, no. 5 (2010): 635–54.

57 Rothenberg, "'And She Told Two Friends,'" 178.

58 Brown, "Gay Enclaves."

59 Ghaziani, *There Goes the Gayborhood?*

60 Cf. Richard Florida, *The Rise of the Creative Class: And How It's Transforming Work, Leisure, Community and Everyday Life* (New York: Perseus, 2002).

61 Cf. Sharif Mowlabocus, *Gaydar Culture: Gay Men, Technology and Embodiment in the Digital Age* (New York: Routledge, 2010).

62 Shaka McGlotten, *Virtual Intimacies: Media, Affect, and Queer Sociality* (Albany: State University of New York Press, 2013).

63 Nash and Gorman-Murray, "LGBT Neighbourhoods," 760.

64 Cf. Elizabeth Freeman, "Packing History, Count(er)ing Generations," *New Literary History* 31, no. 4 (2000): 727–44.

65 John D'Emilio, "Capitalism and Gay Identity," in *Powers of Desire: The Politics of Sexuality*, ed. Ann Snitow, Christine Stansell, and Sharon Thompson (New York: Monthly Review Press, 1983), 101.

66 Michael Warner, "Media Gays: A New Stone Wall," *Nation*, July 14, 1997, 15; see also Rachel Corbman, "The Scholars and the Feminists: The Barnard Sex Conference and the History of the Institutionalization of Feminism," *Feminist Formations* 27, no. 3 (2016): 49–80; Emily K. Hobson, *Lavender and Red: Liberation and Solidarity in the Gay and Lesbian Left* (Oakland: University of California Press, 2016).

67 Angela Willey, *Undoing Monogamy: The Politics of Science and the Possibilities of Biology* (Durham, NC: Duke University Press, 2016), 99, emphasis in the original.

68 Willey, 99.

69 For other examples of dyke politics over time, see Victoria Hesford, *Feeling Women's Liberation* (Durham, NC: Duke University Press, 2013); Rachel Corbman,

"A Genealogy of the Lesbian Herstory Archives, 1974–2014," *Journal of Contemporary Archival Studies* 1, no. 1 (2014), http://elischolar.library.yale.edu; Corbman, "Scholars and Feminists"; Kristen Hogan, *The Feminist Bookstore Movement: Lesbian Antiracism and Feminist Accountability* (Durham, NC: Duke University Press, 2016); Julie R. Enszer, "'How to Stop Choking to Death': Rethinking Lesbian Separatism as a Vibrant Political Theory and Feminist Practice," *Journal of Lesbian Studies* 20, no. 2 (2016): 180–96.

70 Women also volunteer at a higher rate than men—28 percent versus 22 percent, as of 2015. Bureau of Labor Statistics, "Volunteering in the United States, 2015," February 25, 2016, www.bls.gov; OECD, "Employment: Time Spent in Paid and Unpaid Work, by Sex," 2019, https://stats.oecd.org.

71 William Leap, "Language and Gendered Modernity," in *The Handbook of Language and Gender*, ed. Janet Holmes and Miriam Meyerhoff (Malden, MA: Blackwell, 2003), 401–22; cited in Charneka (Nikki) Lane, "In the Life, on the Scene: The Spatial and Discursive Production of Black Queer Women's Scene Space in Washington, D.C." (PhD diss., American University, 2015), 93.

72 Briggs, *Reproductive Politics*, 18, 72.

73 Williams Institute, "LGBT Demographic Data Interactive," UCLA School of Law (Los Angeles), January 2019.

74 M. V. Lee Badgett, *Money, Myths, and Change: The Economic Lives of Lesbians and Gay Men* (Chicago: University of Chicago Press, 2003), 258.

75 Crosby Burns, "The Gay and Transgender Wage Gap," *Center for American Progress* (blog), April 16, 2012, www.americanprogress.org.

76 I created this (unfortunately cis-normative) graph by applying the US median annual earnings by gender (adjusted to 2010 dollars) to couples of two "men," two "women," and a "man" and a "woman." Ariane Hegewisch and Claudia Williams, "The Gender Wage Gap: 2010" (fact sheet, Washington, DC: Institute for Women's Policy Research, 2011).

77 Public policy scholar Klawitter found that lesbians make 9 percent more than their straight counterparts; according to Badgett, however, this is due to lesbians in couples working "more hours and weeks than married [heterosexual] women." Strikingly, Klawitter's claim holds true only if a lesbian has never lived with a man; another study finds that lesbians who were married to men earned 9.5 percent less than heterosexual women. I do not factor in these (and other) studies because my participants did not discuss their range of dating histories, meaning it is possible that these +/- percentages would cancel one another out for some. Moore found similar trends among middle- and working-class Black lesbians in New York City; she found that upper-class Black lesbians tended to be mutually androgynous in their relationships. Some studies assert that gay men make 9 percent (Drydakis) to 11 percent (Klawitter) less than their heterosexual male counterparts due to workplace discrimination, which, given findings about the gender/sexual dimensions of lesbian earnings, would still make for at least a

$12,000 difference in average income between lesbian and gay couples. Marieka M. Klawitter, "Meta-analysis of the Effects of Sexual Orientation on Earnings," *Industrial Relations: A Journal of Economy and Society* 54, no. 1 (2015): 4–32; M. V. Lee Badgett, "Beyond Biased Samples: Challenging the Myths on the Economic Status of Lesbians and Gay Men," in *Homo Economics*, 70; Nasser Daneshvary, C. Jeffrey Waddoups, and Bradley S. Wimmer, "Previous Marriage and the Lesbian Wage Premium," *Industrial Relations: A Journal of Economy and Society* 48, no. 3 (2009): 432–53; Nick Drydakis, "Sexual Orientation and Labor Market Outcomes," *IZA World of Labor*, 2014; Mignon R. Moore, "Lipstick or Timberlands? Meanings of Gender Presentation in Black Lesbian Communities," *Signs: Journal of Women in Culture and Society* 32, no. 1 (2006): 113–39; see also Paquette, "Surprising Reason."

78  These figures for lesbian couples' income were calculated by doubling women's average annual pay. New York City income data by gender and/or race was not consistently collected over my period of study, so I relied on national data. Data for Native American women's pay is in 2015 dollars, based on the American Community Survey data, and the remainder of the data is in 2010 dollars from the same source. Ariane Hegewisch et al., "The Gender Wage Gap in New York State and Its Solutions" (report, Washington, DC, Institute for Women's Policy Research, 2011); Kayla Patrick and Jasmine Tucker, "Equal Pay for Native Women" (fact sheet, Washington, DC, National Women's Law Center, 2017), https://nwlc.org.

79  Catherine Rampell, "Before That Sex Change, Think about Your Next Paycheck," *New York Times*, September 25, 2008, www.nytimes.com; Kristen Schilt and Matthew Wiswall, "Before and After: Gender Transitions, Human Capital, and Workplace Experiences," *B.E. Journal of Economic Analysis & Policy* 8, no. 1 (2008); Hegewisch and Williams, "Gender Wage Gap: 2010"; Hegewisch et al., "Gender Wage Gap in New York"; Lars Z. Mackenzie, "The Afterlife of Data: Identity, Surveillance, and Capitalism in Trans Credit Reporting," *TSQ: Transgender Studies Quarterly* 4, no. 1 (2017): 45–60; National Center for Transgender Equality, "Housing & Homelessness," 2018, https://transequality.org.

80  A. Finn Enke, *Finding the Movement: Sexuality, Contested Space, and Feminist Activism* (Durham, NC: Duke University Press, 2007), 69.

81  Hanhardt, *Safe Space*; see also Seitz, "Trouble with Flag Wars."

82  Miranda Joseph, *Against the Romance of Community* (Minneapolis: University of Minnesota Press, 2002), 2.

83  Podmore, "Gone 'Underground'?"

84  Podmore, 618.

85  Allan Bérubé, "How Gay Stays White and What Kind of White It Stays," in *The Making and Unmaking of Whiteness*, ed. Birgit Brander Rasmussen et al. (Durham, NC: Duke University Press, 2001), 246–47.

86  Audre Lorde and Adrienne Rich, "An Interview with Audre Lorde," *Signs* 6, no. 4 (1981): 731.

87 Cf. Enszer, "'How to Stop Choking'"; Keridwen N. Luis, *Herlands: Exploring the Women's Land Movement in the United States* (Minneapolis: University of Minnesota Press, 2018).

88 The "FtM" and "MtF" terminology has largely shifted to "trans men" and "trans women." I use this term to signal the period during which my research was conducted.

89 Hobson, *Lavender and Red*, 157–58.

90 Alix Genter, "Appearances Can Be Deceiving: Butch-Femme Fashion and Queer Legibility in New York City, 1945–1969," *Feminist Studies* 42, no. 3 (2016): 604–31.

91 "About bbh," bklyn boihood, March 12, 2012, www.bklynboihood.com.

92 Dee Rees, dir., *Pariah* (Focus Features, 2011).

93 Cf. Nan Alamilla Boyd, "The Materiality of Gender," *Journal of Lesbian Studies* 3, no. 3 (1999): 73–81; Ann Cvetkovich and Selena Wahng, "Don't Stop the Music: Roundtable Discussion with Workers from the Michigan Womyn's Music Festival," *GLQ* 7, no. 1 (2001): 131–51; Kath Browne, "Womyn's Separatist Spaces: Rethinking Spaces of Difference and Exclusion," *Transactions of the Institute of British Geographers* 34, no. 4 (2009): 541–56.

94 Participants who came out in the 1980s described how there was "suddenly" a larger number of trans women. Given that the FtM trans-surge required a moment that offered access to affordable hormones and surgeries, activism, and a network driven by word-of-mouth communications and publications, it may be that similar factors supported a 1980s MtF (male-to-female) trans-surge among trans women.

95 While debates in geography often involve a split between emotional and affective geographies, queer theory often bridges this gap and I work from that tradition here. Berlant, *Cruel Optimism*, 9; see also Cindi Katz, "Towards Minor Theory," *Society and Space* 14, no. 4 (1996): 487–99.

96 Sarah Schulman, *The Gentrification of the Mind: Witness to a Lost Imagination* (Berkeley: University of California Press, 2012), 40.

97 Anderson's *Imagined Communities* is also a key theoretical text for many lgbtq studies projects but does not focus on lgbtq populations; Robinson's *Black Marxism* should be a key theoretical text for lgbtq studies research but this has less often been the case. Castells, *City and Grassroots*, 1983; John D'Emilio, *Sexual Politics, Sexual Communities* (Chicago: University of Chicago Press, 1983); D'Emilio, "Capitalism and Gay Identity"; Allan Bérubé, "Coming Out under Fire," *Mother Jones*, March 1983; Allan Bérubé, "Marching to a Different Drummer: Lesbian and Gay GIs in World War II," in *Powers of Desire*, ed. Ann Snitow, Chrstine Stansell, and Sharon Thompson, 88–99; Jonathan Ned Katz, *Gay/Lesbian Almanac: A New Documentary, in Which Is Contained, in Chronological Order, Evidence of the True and Fantastical History of Those Persons* (New York: Harper & Row, 1983); see also Benedict Anderson, *Imagined Communities: Reflections on the Origin and Spread of Nationalism* (New York: Verso, 1983); Cedric J. Robinson, *Black Marxism: The Making of the Black Radical Tradition* (London: Zed Books, 1983).

98 Cf. Lane, "In the Life," 88–89.

99 Doreen Massey, *For Space* (Thousand Oaks, CA: Sage Publications, 2005), 147.

100 Jen Jack Gieseking, "Where We Go from Here: The Mental Mapping Sketch Method and Its Analytic Components," *Qualitative Inquiry* 19, no. 9 (2013): 712–24; see also Gavin Brown, "Listening to Queer Maps of the City: Gay Men's Narratives of Pleasure and Danger in London's East End," *Oral History* 29, no. 1 (2001): 48–61.

101 My effort to not fix these generations to any specific moment but rather look for periods of change draws from Darsey. James Darsey, "From 'Gay Is Good' to the Scourge of AIDS: The Evolution of Gay Liberation Rhetoric, 1977–1990," *Communication Studies* 42, no. 1 (1991): 43–66.

102 José Esteban Muñoz, *Disidentifications: Queers of Color and the Performance of Politics* (Minneapolis: University of Minnesota Press, 1999), 5.

103 Farhang Rouhani, "Anarchism, Geography, and Queer Space-Making: Building Bridges Over Chasms We Create," *ACME: An International Journal for Critical Geographies* 11, no. 3 (2012): 371–92; Michelle Billies, "Low Income LGBTGNC (Gender Nonconforming) Struggles over Shelters as Public Space," *ACME* 14, no. 4 (2015): 989–1007.

104 As I describe in appendix I, I asked for participants' primary identifiers for the book ("If you had to define yourself in a term, which would you pick?"), as well as other identifiers they would and would not use.

105 The term "Latinx" was not yet in wide circulation in 2008 and 2009, but I use it in cases apropos of the moment of my writing. I use "Latina and/or Hispanic" as my participants used those identifiers and those terms appear in the titles of various datasets.

106 Carlos Ulises Decena, "Tacit Subjects," *GLQ* 14, no. 2–3 (2008): 339.

107 Before my period of study, Newton writes that middle-class and working-class lesbian spaces were largely distinct, but this distinction blurred in participants' stories so that I am unable to articulate those distinctions based on my data. Esther Newton, *My Butch Career: A Memoir* (Durham, NC: Duke University Press, 2018).

108 Cf. E. Patrick Johnson, *Sweet Tea: Black Gay Men of the South* (Durham, NC: University of North Carolina Press, 2011); Latoya E. Eaves, "Spatial Articulations of Race, Desire, and Belonging in Western North Carolina" (PhD diss., Florida International University, 2014), 134, 150.

109 "Statistics on US Families," GroundSpark, 2010, http://groundspark.org.

110 Ann Pellegrini, "Mind the Gap?," *GLQ* 10, no. 4 (2004): 637–39.

111 Kath Browne, "Challenging Queer Geographies," *Antipode* 38, no. 5 (2006): 885–93.

112 Martin F. Manalansan IV, "Queer Worldings: The Messy Art of Being Global in Manila and New York," *Antipode* 47, no. 3 (2015): 567.

113 Kath Browne and Catherine Jean Nash, "Lesbian Geographies," in *International Encyclopedia of Human Geographies*, ed. Rob Kitchin and Nigel Thrift (London: Elsevier, 2009), 187–92.

114 Willey, *Undoing Monogamy*, 99.

115 Cf. David Valentine, *Imagining Transgender: An Ethnography of a Category* (Durham, NC: Duke University Press, 2007).

116 Japonica Brown-Saracino, "Are Nostalgia Tours the New Dyke Bar?," *Los Angeles Review of Books* (blog), October 6, 2017, http://blog.lareviewofbooks.org; Brown-Saracino, *How Places Make Us: How Places Make Us: Novel LBQ Identities in Four Small Cities* (Chicago: University of Chicago Press, 2018).

117 Halberstam, *In a Queer Time and Place*, 5.

118 Joan Kelly-Gadol, "Did Women Have a Renaissance?," in *Becoming Visible: Women in European History*, ed. Renate Bridenthal and Claudia Koonz (Boston: Houghton Mifflin, 1977), 148–61; Adrienne Rich, "Compulsory Heterosexuality and Lesbian Existence," *Signs* 5, no. 4 (1980): 631–60.

119 Judith Schwarz, "Living Herstory: Interview with Joan Nestle," *Off Our Backs*, May 1978; Arlene Stein, *Sex and Sensibility: Stories of a Lesbian Generation* (Berkeley: University of California Press, 1997); Elizabeth Freeman, *Time Binds: Queer Temporalities, Queer Histories* (Durham, NC: Duke University Press, 2010); see also Kennedy and Davis, *Boots of Leather*; Loree Cook-Daniels, "Living Memory LGBT History Timeline: Current Elders Would Have Been This Old When These Events Happened . . ." (Transgender Aging Network/FORGE, 2007), http://forge-forward.org.

120 Cf. Chauncey, *Gay New York*; Glenda M. Russell and Janis S. Bohan, "The Gay Generation Gap: Communicating across the LGBT Generational Divide," *Angles: The Policy Journal of the Institute for Gay and Lesbian Strategic Studies* 8, no. 1 (2002): 1–7; Halberstam, *In a Queer Time and Place*; Kath Browne, "Lesbian Geographies," *Social & Cultural Geography* 8, no. 1 (2007): 1–7.

121 Carla Freccero, "Trans-Time," *GLQ* 13, no. 1 (2007): 145.

122 Russell and Bohan, "Gay Generation Gap."

123 Cf. Carolyn Dinshaw et al., "Theorizing Queer Temporalities: A Roundtable Discussion," *GLQ* 13, no. 2 (2007): 177–95.

124 Rothenberg, "'And She Told Two Friends,'" 176.

125 Sara Ahmed, "Orientations: Toward a Queer Phenomenology," *GLQ* 12, no. 4 (2006): 570.

## CHAPTER 2. BELONGING IN GREENWICH VILLAGE AND GAY MANHATTAN

1 Natalie Oswin, "Researching 'Gay Cape Town,' Finding Value-Added Queerness," *Social & Cultural Geography* 6, no. 4 (2005): 567–86.

2 The West Village is the western area of Greenwich Village, but the names West Village and Greenwich Village are often used interchangeably. The East Village was coined as a neighborhood name by Beatnik artists of the 1950s and 1960s who sought to distinguish that area from the working-class Lower East Side. All neighborhood boundaries are based on my participants' descriptions and New York City maps at the time of my research.

3  By the time of the sexual revolution of the late 1910s and 1920s in the left-leaning, already gentrifying, bohemian Greenwich Village neighborhood, gay men "converted the street into a major cruising area, and it was soon called the Auction Block." Faderman also points out that "lesbians claimed a bit of space for themselves in the clubs that catered to them and featured lesbian entertainers." Lillian Faderman, *Odd Girls and Twilight Lovers: A History of Lesbian Life in Twentieth-Century America* (New York: Penguin, 1992), 88; see also Chauncey, *Gay New York*, 240–43; Jay Shockley, "Preservation of LGBTQ Historic & Cultural Sites—A New York City Perspective," in *LGBTQ America: A Theme Study of Lesbian, Gay, Bisexual, Transgender, and Queer History*, ed. Megan Springate (Washington, DC: National Parks Service, US Department of the Interior, 2016); see also Irwin Altman and Setha M. Low, *Place Attachment* (New York: Springer, 1992).

4  Cf. Marc Stein, *City of Sisterly and Brotherly Loves: Lesbian and Gay Philadelphia, 1945–1972* (Philadelphia: Temple University Press, 2004); Susan Stryker, *Transgender History* (Berkeley: Seal Press, 2008); Erin Siodmak, "'Homosexuals Are Revolting': Stonewall, 1969," in *Revolting New York*, ed. Neil Smith et al. (Athens: University of Georgia Press, 2018).

5  Hanhardt, *Safe Space*.

6  Cf. Julie Abraham, *Metropolitan Lovers: The Homosexuality of Cities* (Minneapolis: University of Minnesota Press, 2009).

7  I averaged percentage white or white alone (depending on year) and foreign-born population from US census data for Greenwich Village census tracts (55.1, 57, 59, 61, 63, 65, 67, 69, 71, 73, 75, 77, 79). Between 1980 and 1990, the share of white residents went from 93.4 percent to 90.3 percent. Those shares were 35 percent (1980) and 42.2 percent (1990) higher than the white residential averages for New York City as a whole. See also Amy Armstrong et al., *State of New York City's Housing and Neighborhoods in 2008* (New York: Furman Center for Real Estate and Urban Policy at NYU, 2009), http://furmancenter.org.

8  Nero, "Why Are the Gay Ghettos White?," 229.

9  Mark Rifkin, *Settler Common Sense: Queerness and Everyday Colonialism in the American Renaissance* (Minneapolis: University of Minnesota Press, 2014), 4.

10  Nash and Gorman-Murray, "LGBT Neighbourhoods," 766.

11  James Polchin, "Having Something to Wear: The Landscape of Identity on Christopher Street," in *Queers in Space: Communities, Public Places, Sites of Resistance*, ed. Gordon Brent Ingram, Anne-Marie Bouthillette, and Yolanda Retter (Seattle: Bay Press, 1997), 381–90.

12  Natalie Oswin, "Towards Radical Geographies of Complicit Queer Futures," *ACME* 3, no. 2 (2005): 81, 83, citing Heidi J. Nast, "Queer Patriarchies, Queer Racisms, International," *Antipode* 34, no. 5 (2002): 874–909.

13  Gillian Rose, "A Politics of Paradoxical Space," in *Feminism and Geography: The Limits of Geographical Knowledge* (Minneapolis: University of Minnesota Press, 1993), 150.

14  Rose, 140.

15  David W. Dunlap, "Sale of Site to Homosexuals Planned," *New York Times*, December 20, 1983, www.nytimes.com.

16  LHA organizational records do not indicate where or how materials were gathered but much of this labor was thanks to archivist Maxine Wolfe. As Wolfe was a member of ACT UP and the Lesbian Avengers, the collection may be focused at the Center given her time there, per Corbman. My participants also made repeated references to the Center and the intense social, economic, and geographic homophobia lgbtq people faced in the 1980s. Rachel Corbman to Jack Gieseking, "Book: A Queer New York RC Comments," March 25, 2019.

17  Cf. Catherine J. Nash and Andrew Gorman-Murray, "Recovering the Gay Village: A Comparative Historical Geography of Urban Change and Planning in Toronto and Sydney," *Historical Geography* 43 (2015): 87.

18  Hollibaugh, *My Dangerous Desires*, 259.

19  In his research of gay immigrant Filipino men at the turn of the century, Manalansan had only one participant with a similarly affordable, rent-stabilized apartment. Martin F. Manalansan IV, *Global Divas: Filipino Gay Men in the Diaspora* (Durham, NC: Duke University Press, 2003), 96; Timothy Collins, "An Introduction to the NYC Rent Guidelines Board and the Rent Stabilization System," NYC Rent Guidelines Board, February 2016, www.nycrgb.org.

20  Cf. Andrew Gorman-Murray and Catherine J. Nash, "Mobile Places, Relational Spaces: Conceptualizing Change in Sydney's LGBTQ Neighborhoods," *Society and Space* 32, no. 4 (2014): 622–41.

21  Joseph, *Against the Romance of Community*.

22  Cf. Edith Evans Asbury, "If You're Thinking of Living in: Greenwich Village," *New York Times*, August 14, 1983, www.nytimes.com.

23  Schulman, *The Gentrification of the Mind*; Tara J. Burk, "Let the Record Show: Mapping Queer Art and Activism in New York City, 1986–1995" (PhD diss., Graduate Center, City University of New York, 2015); Corbman, "The Scholars and the Feminists."

24  Briggs, *Reproductive Politics*, 154.

25  Schulman, *Gentrification of the Mind*, 23, 38.

26  Cf. Nash and Gorman-Murray, "Recovering the Gay Village," 87.

27  Asbury, "If You're Thinking."

28  Percentage change in the gross rent in Greenwich Village was averaged across census tracts within the boundaries of the neighborhood. Average gross rent for specified owner-occupied housing units was used for 1990, 2000, and 2010; this data was unavailable for 1980, so median gross rent was used.

29  Carlos A. Ball, *From the Closet to the Courtroom: Five LGBT Rights Lawsuits That Have Changed Our Nation* (Boston: Beacon Press, 2010), 65; re Vito Joseph Titone, Miguel Braschi, Appellant, v. Stahl Associates Company, Respondent, No. 74 N.Y.2d 201 (Court of Appeals of the State of New York, July 6, 1989).

30  Andrew Sullivan, "Here Comes the Groom," *New Republic*, August 28, 1989, https://newrepublic.com.

31  Cf. Manalansan, *Global Divas*; Gayatri Gopinath, *Impossible Desires: Queer Diasporas and South Asian Public Cultures* (Durham, NC: Duke University Press, 2005); Chandan Reddy, "Asian Diasporas, Neoliberalism, and Family: Reviewing the Case for Homosexual Asylum in the Context of Family Rights," *Social Text* 23, no. 3–4 (2005): 112; Julio Capó, Jr., *Welcome to Fairyland: Queer Miami before 1940* (Chapel Hill: University of North Carolina Press, 2017).

32  As noted in chapter 1, Janice '79/'91, a staunch Catholic throughout her early life, had first come out in 1979 but was convinced by a psychiatrist that she could be "cured" of her homosexuality through electroshock. She came out again in 1991. I list Janice with both of her coming out years as she identified herself.

33  Lesbian Herstory Archives, "St. Mark's Women's Health Collective" (organizational records, 2008).

34  Katie Batza, *Before AIDS: Gay Health Politics in the 1970s* (Philadelphia: University of Pennsylvania Press, 2018).

35  Rosemary Hennessy, *Profit and Pleasure: Sexual Identities in Late Capitalism* (New York: Routledge, 2000), 6.

36  Carolyn Kizer, "Pro Femina," in Cool, Calm, and Collected: Poems 1960–2000 (Port Townsend, WA: Copper Canyon Press, 2001); cited in Hogan, *Feminist Bookstore Movement*, 15.

37  Cf. Margaret Galvan, "Archiving Wimmen: Collectives, Networks, and Comix," *Australian Feminist Studies* 32, no. 91–92 (2017): 22–40.

38  Hogan, *Feminist Bookstore Movement*, 20.

39  Lesbian Herstory Archives, "Committee of Outraged Lesbians (COOL)" (organizational records, 2008).

40  Lesbian Herstory Archives, "Dykes Against Racism Everywhere (DARE)" (organizational records, 2008).

41  Lisa Diedrich, *Indirect Action* (Minneapolis: University of Minnesota Press, 2016).

42  Day, "Embassies and Sanctuaries," 307.

43  Maralee Schwartz and Kenneth J. Cooper, "Equal Rights Initiative in Iowa Attacked," *Washington Post*, August 23, 1992, www.washingtonpost.com.

44  Tina Fetner, *How the Religious Right Shaped Lesbian and Gay Activism* (Minneapolis: University of Minnesota Press, 2008).

45  Nash and Gorman-Murray, "LGBT Neighbourhoods," 765.

46  Neil Smith, "Giuliani Time: The Revanchist 1990s," *Social Text*, no. 57 (1998): 1; see also Smith, *New Urban Frontier*.

47  Michael Warner, *The Trouble with Normal: Sex, Politics, and the Ethics of Queer Life* (Cambridge, MA: Harvard University Press, 1999), 149–94.

48  Tom Slater, "North American Gentrification? Revanchist and Emancipatory Perspectives Explored," *Environment and Planning A* 36, no. 7 (2004): 1191–213.

49  Catherine Davy, *Lady Dicks and Lesbian Brothers: Staging the Unimaginable at the WOW Cafe Theatre* (Ann Arbor: University of Michigan Press, 2011), 8.

50  Podmore, "Gone 'Underground'?," 600.

51  Podmore, 600.

52  Armistead Maupin, *Further Tales of the City* (New York: Harper Perennial, 1994).

53  Karisa Butler-Wall, "Viral Transmissions: Safer Sex Videos, Disability, and Queer Politics," *Disability Studies Quarterly* 36, no. 4 (2016), http://dsq-sds.org.

54  Cf. Christina Hanhardt, "'Dead Addicts Don't Recover': ACT UP's Needle Exchange and the Subjects of Queer Activist History," *GLQ* 24, no. 4 (2018): 421–44; Marika Cifor, *Viral Cultures: Activist Archives at the End of AIDS* (Minneapolis: University of Minnesota Press, forthcoming).

55  Lesbian Herstory Archives, "ACT UP" (organizational records, 2008).

56  Cathy J. Cohen, "Punks, Bulldaggers, and Welfare Queens: The Radical Potential of Queer Politics?," *GLQ* 3, no. 4 (1997): 437–65.

57  Reddy, "Asian Diasporas," 112; see also Debanuj DasGupta, "Queering Immigration: Perspectives on Cross-Movement Organizing," *S&F Online* 10, no. 1–2 (2012), https://sfonline.barnard.edu.

58  Laraine Sommella and Maxine Wolfe, "This Is about People Dying: The Tactics of Early ACT UP and Lesbian Avengers in New York City (An Interview with Maxine Wolfe by Laraine Sommella)," in *Queers in Space*, ed. Gordon Brent Ingram et al. (Seattle: Bay Press, 1997), 427.

59  Sommella and Wolfe, "People Dying"; Kelly J. Cogswell, *Eating Fire: My Life as a Lesbian Avenger* (Minneapolis: University of Minnesota Press, 2014); see also Claire Bond Potter, "Taking Back Times Square: Feminist Repertoires and the Transformation of Urban Space in Late Second Wave Feminism," *Radical History Review* 2012, no. 113 (2012): 67–80.

60  The curriculum included Newman and Souza's highly controversial children's book about lesbian moms. Leslea Newman and Diana Souza, *Heather Has Two Mommies* (Topeka, KS: Sagebrush Education Resources, 1991).

61  Sommella and Wolfe, "People Dying"; James Wentzy, *ACT UP Tenth Anniversary Storytellings: Maxine Wolfe (Shea Stadium)* (Judson Memorial Church, New York, 2017), www.vimeo.com/200388124.

62  Speech given by Lysander Puccio at Halloween Parade vigil, Lesbian Avenger Documentary Project, *Lesbian Avengers Eat Fire, Too* (Outcast Films, 1993), www.youtube.com/watch?v=0400tZPETAc.

63  Linda Chapman, Mary Patierno, and Ana Simo, "Letter to George Slowik, Jr. (Publisher of *OUT*) from the Executive Producers of DYKE TV," February 7, 1994, in Lesbian Herstory Archives, "DYKE TV" (organizational records, 2008).

64  Lisa Henderson, "Queer Relay," *GLQ* 14, no. 4 (2008): 579.

65  Sara Marcus, *Girls to the Front: The True Story of the Riot Grrrl Revolution* (New York: Harper Perennial, 2010).

66  Fiona Buckland, *Impossible Dance: Club Culture and Queer World-Making* (Middletown, CT: Wesleyan University Press, 2000), 133–34, cited in Lane, "In the Life," 65.

67  Lane, "In the Life," 63.

68  Lane, 65.

69 Lane, 36.

70 Cf. Marlon Riggs, dir., *Tongues Untied* (Strand Releasing, 1989); Nikki Lane, "All the Lesbians Are White, All the Villages Are Gay, but Some of Us Are Brave: Intersectionality, Belonging, and Black Queer Women's Scene Space in Washington DC," in *Lesbian Geographies: Gender, Place and Power*, ed. Kath Browne and Eduarda Ferreira (New York: Routledge, 2016).

71 Lauren Berlant and Elizabeth Freeman, "Queer Nationality," *Boundary 2* 19, no. 1 (1992): 149–80.

72 Hanhardt, *Safe Space*, 177, emphasis in the original.

73 Alexandra Chasin, *Selling Out: The Gay and Lesbian Movement Goes to Market* (New York: Palgrave Macmillan, 2001).

74 Chasin, 18.

75 David L. Eng, J. Halberstam, and José Esteban Muñoz, "What's Queer about Queer Studies Now?," *Social Text* 23, no. 3/4 (2005): 2; see also Urvashi Vaid, *Virtual Equality: The Mainstreaming of Lesbian and Gay Liberation* (New York: Anchor, 1996); Conrad, *Against Equality*.

76 Duggan, "New Homonormativity."

77 Brown, "Homonormativity."

78 Kristene incorrectly uses the original name for the youth group that, over time, was renamed to reflect the inclusion of bisexuals (BiGLYNY) and transgender people (BiGLYTNY). I provide the full, correct name used by the group in the 2000s. Bisexuals were first included around 1990, per participants, and transgender people were included later on.

79 Many participants felt the movement was dominated by the Human Rights Campaign and other groups' narrowly focused mission to end Don't Ask, Don't Tell (DADT, 1993–2011) and the Defense of Marriage Act (DOMA, 1998–2013) in the 2000s. Cf. Kath Browne, "A Party with Politics? (Re)Making LGBTQ Pride Spaces in Dublin and Brighton," *Social & Cultural Geography* 8, no. 1 (2007): 63–87; Lynda Johnston, *Queering Tourism: Paradoxical Performances of Gay Pride Parades* (New York: Routledge, 2009).

80 Cf. Tiffany K. Muller [Myrdhal], "Liberty for All? Contested Spaces of Women's Basketball," *Gender, Place & Culture* 14, no. 2 (2007): 197–213.

81 Riggs, *Tongues Untied*.

82 Ruth Wilson Gilmore, "In the Shadow of the Shadow State," in *The Revolution Will Not Be Funded: Beyond the Non-Profit Industrial Complex*, ed. INCITE! Women of Color Against Violence (Cambridge, MA: South End Press, 2009), 41–53; Dylan Rodríguez, "The Political Logic of the Non-Profit Industrial Complex," in *Revolution Will Not Be Funded*, ed. INCITE!, 21–40.

83 Lesbian Herstory Archives, "Queers for Economic Justice Network" (organizational records, 2008).

84 Welfare Warriors Research Collaborative, "A Fabulous Attitude: Low-Income LGBTGNC People Surviving & Thriving on Love, Shelter, & Knowledge" (organizational report, Queers for Economic Justice, New York, 2010).

85 Spade, *Normal Life*; see also Max J. Andrucki and Glen S. Elder, "Locating the State in Queer Space: GLBT Non-Profit Organizations in Vermont, USA," *Social & Cultural Geography* 8 (2007): 89–104; Rae Rosenberg and Natalie Oswin, "Trans Embodiment in Carceral Space: Hypermasculinity and the US Prison Industrial Complex," *Gender, Place & Culture* 22, no. 9 (2015): 1269–86.

86 Samuel R. Delany, *Times Square Red, Times Square Blue* (New York: NYU Press, 2001).

87 Cf. Smith, *New Urban Frontier*, 220.

88 Hanhardt, *Safe Space*, 194–226.

89 DasGupta, "Queering Immigration."

90 FIERCE, Paper Tiger Television, and The Neutral Zone, *Fenced Out*, August 21, 2007, www. youtube.com/watch?v=BMrohHHdXd4; FIERCE, Paper Tiger Television, and The Neutral Zone, *Fenced Out*; "Our S.P.O.T. Campaign," FIERCE, 2009, www.fiercenyc.org.

91 Chauncey, *Gay New York*, 179–205.

92 Cf. Christian Anderson, *Gay Urbanism without Guarantees: The Everyday Life of a Gentrifying West Side Neighborhood* (Minneapolis: University of Minnesota Press, 2020), 53–57.

93 Amber Hollibaugh and Margot Weiss, "Queer Precarity and the Myth of Gay Affluence," *New Labor Forum* 24, no. 3 (2015): 23.

94 Young, *Politics of Difference*.

95 Many thanks to a Bluestockings staffer who shared these titles with me, explaining they were "fluid" and "redefined constantly" by what is in stock and the present political moment. Anna Flinchbaugh, phone interview by Jen Jack Gieseking, February 25, 2017.

96 Rothenberg, "'And She Told Two Friends,'" 167, citing Lauria and Knopp, "Towards an Analysis."

97 Cf. Cohen, "Punks, Bulldaggers"; Siobhan B. Somerville, *Queering the Color Line: Race and the Invention of Homosexuality in American Culture* (Durham, NC: Duke University Press, 2000); Katherine McKittrick, *Demonic Grounds: Black Women and The Cartographies of Struggle* (Minneapolis: University of Minnesota Press, 2006).

98 Beverley Skeggs et al., "Queer as Folk: Producing the Real of Urban Space," *Urban Studies* 41, no. 9 (2004): 1839–56.

99 Dennis R. Judd and Susan S. Fainstein, "Global Forces, Local Strategies, and Urban Tourism," in *The Tourist City*, ed. Dennis R. Judd and Susan S. Fainstein (New Haven, CT: Yale University Press, 1999), 2.

100 Jasbir Puar, "A Transnational Feminist Critique of Queer Tourism," *Antipode* 34, no. 5 (2002): 935–46; Marie Cieri, "Between Being and Looking: Queer Tourism Promotion and Lesbian Social Space in Greater Philadelphia," *ACME* 2, no. 2 (2003): 147–66.

101 Cf. Delany, *Times Square Red*.

102 Stephen M. Engel, *Fragmented Citizens: The Changing Landscape of Gay and Lesbian Lives* (New York: NYU Press, 2016).

103 Rose, "Paradoxical Space," 147, 154.

104 Gill Valentine, "(Hetero)Sexing Space: Lesbian Perceptions and Experiences of Everyday Spaces," *Society and Space* 11, no. 4 (1993): 395–413.

105 Cf. Suleiman Osman, *The Invention of Brownstone Brooklyn: Gentrification and the Search for Authenticity in Postwar New York* (New York: Oxford University Press, 2012); Johan Andersson, "'Wilding' in the West Village: Queer Space, Racism and Jane Jacobs Hagiography,'" *International Journal of Urban and Regional Research* 39, no. 2 (2015): 265–83.

106 Theodore Greene, "Queer Street Families: Place-Making and Community among LGBT Youth of Color in Iconic Gay Neighborhoods," in *Queer Families and Relationships after Marriage Equality*, ed. Michael Yarbrough, Angela Jones, and Joseph DeFilippis (New York: Routledge, 2018), 170.

107 Welfare Warriors Research Collaborative, "Fabulous Attitude"; see also Billies, "LGBTGNC Struggles."

108 Joey L. Mogul, Andrea J. Ritchie, and Kay Whitlock, *Queer (In)Justice: The Criminalization of LGBT People in the United States* (Boston: Beacon Press, 2012); Blair Doroshwalther, dir., *Out in the Night* (New Day Films, 2014).

109 Susy Buchanan and David Holthouse, "Rod Wheeler Claims on The O'Reilly Factor Lesbian Gangs Are Raping Young Girls," *Southern Poverty Law Center* (blog), October 1, 2007, www.splcenter.org.

110 Lane, "In the Life," 22, 29.

111 Veronika Belenkaya et al., "Girls Gone Wilding: Lesbians Locked Up in W. Village Beating," *New York Daily News*, August 19, 2006, www.nydailynews.com.

112 Andersson, "'Wilding,'" 273; see also Estelle B. Freedman, "The Prison Lesbian: Race, Class, and the Construction of the Aggressive Female Homosexual, 1915–1965," *Feminist Studies* 22, no. 2 (1996): 397–423; Lisa Duggan, *Sapphic Slashers: Sex, Violence, and American Modernity* (Durham, NC: Duke University Press, 2001); Cookie Woolner, "'Woman Slain in Queer Love Brawl': African American Women, Same-Sex Desire, and Violence in the Urban North, 1920–1929," *Journal of African American History* 100, no. 3 (2015): 406–27.

113 Jason Lydon et al., "Coming Out of Concrete Closets: A Report on Black & Pink's National LGBTQ Survey" (report, Dorchester, MA: Black & Pink, 2015), 5.

114 Cf. Gilmore, *Golden Gulag*; Michelle Alexander, *The New Jim Crow: Mass Incarceration in the Age of Colorblindness* (New York: New Press, 2012).

115 Kevin Markwell, "Mardi Gras Tourism and the Construction of Sydney as an International Gay and Lesbian City," *GLQ* 8, no. 1 (2002): 87.

116 Theodore Greene, "Gay Neighborhoods and the Rights of the Vicarious Citizen," *City & Community* 13, no. 2 (2014): 99–118.

117 Nash and Gorman-Murray, "Recovering the Gay Village," 93.

118 Manalansan, *Global Divas*, 63.

119 Podmore, "Gone 'Underground'?," 595.

120 Cf. Andersson, "'Wilding'"; Michael Warner, *Publics and Counterpublics* (New York: Zone Books, 2002); Warner, *Trouble with Normal*; Delany, *Times Square Red*.

121 Martin F. Manalansan IV, "Race, Violence, and Neoliberal Spatial Politics in the Global City," *Social Text* 23, no. 3/4 (2005): 41–55.

122 Weston, "Get Thee to a Big City."

123 Alexandra Juhasz, "Forgetting ACT UP," *Quarterly Journal of Speech* 98, no. 1 (2012): 69–74; see also Greta Schiller and Robert Rosenberg, dirs., *Before Stonewall* (First Run Features, 1985); Barbara Hammer, dir., *Snow Job: The Media Hysteria of AIDS* (Barbara Hammer, 1986); John Scagliotti, dir., *After Stonewall* (First Run Features, 1999); Alexandra Juhasz, dir., *Video Remains* (AlexandraJuhasz.com, 2005); Jim Hubbard, dir., *United in Anger: A History of ACT UP* (United in Anger, Inc., 2012); David France, dir., *How to Survive a Plague* (IFC, 2013); Roland Emmerich, dir., *Stonewall* (Roadside Attractions, 2015); Tourmaline and Sasha Wortzel, dirs., *Happy Birthday, Marsha!* (Star People, 2018).

124 Cf. Elizabeth A. Armstrong and Suzanna M. Crage, "Movements and Memory: The Making of the Stonewall Myth," *American Sociological Review* 71, no. 5 (2006): 724–51.

125 Nash and Gorman-Murray, "Recovering the Gay Village," 90; see also Nan Alamilla Boyd, "San Francisco's Castro District: From Gay Liberation to Tourist Destination," *Journal of Tourism and Cultural Change* 9, no. 3 (2011): 237–48.

126 University of Wisconsin–Madison Libraries, "Feminist, GWS, and LGBTQ Bookstores," *Office of the Gender and Women's Studies Librarian* (blog), April 2019, www.library.wisc.edu.

127 James, "There Goes the Gayborhood."

128 The citywide median rent was $2,900, and the citywide average household income was $52,914. By 2014, the Greenwich Village median asking rent was $3,400; the Village's median household income is from 2013. Sean Capperis et al., *State of New York City's Housing and Neighborhoods in 2014* (New York: Furman Center for Real Estate and Urban Policy at NYU, 2015), 67, 111, http://furmancenter.org.

129 Maxwell Austensen et al., *State of New York City's Housing and Neighborhoods in 2015* (New York: Furman Center for Real Estate and Urban Policy at NYU, 2016), http://furmancenter.org.

130 Sewell Chan, "Stonewall Anniversary as Gay Tourism Event," *New York Times—City Room* (blog), April 7, 2009, http://cityroom.blogs.nytimes.com.

CHAPTER 3. YOU VS. US IN BED-STUY AND CROWN HEIGHTS

1 Muñoz, *Disidentifications*, 161, 5.

2 Lisa Kahaleole Chang Hall, "Bitches in Solitude: Identity Politics and Lesbian Community," in *Sisters, Sexperts, Queers: Beyond the Lesbian Nation*, ed. Arlene Stein (New York: Plume, 1993), 223, cited in Bérubé, "How Gay Stays White," 250.

3 Cf. Latoya E. Eaves, "Black Geographic Possibilities: On a Queer Black South," *Southeastern Geographer* 57, no. 1 (2017): 80–95; Eaves, "Race, Desire, and Belonging"; Lane, "In the Life"; Lane, "All the Lesbians"; Aretina Hamilton, "'I Thought

I Found Home': Locating the Hidden and Symbolic Spaces of African American Lesbian Belonging" (PhD diss., University of Kentucky, 2018).

4 Beyond my participants' stories, these trends were found to be consistent since the release of the first American Community Survey in 2008, based on 2005–2007 data. Angeliki Kastanis and Gary J. Gates, *LGBT African-Americans and African-American Same-Sex Couples* (Los Angeles: Williams Institute, UCLA School of Law, 2013), https://williamsinstitute.law.ucla.edu; Kastanis and Gates, *LGBT Latino/a Individuals and Latino/a Same-Sex Couples* (Los Angeles: Williams Institute, UCLA School of Law, 2013), https://williamsinstitute.law.ucla.edu; Kastanis and Gates, *LGBT Asian and Pacific Islander Individuals and Same-Sex Couples* (Los Angeles: Williams Institute, UCLA School of Law, 2013), https://williamsinstitute.law.ucla.edu.

5 Chandan Reddy, "Time for Rights? Loving, Gay Marriage, and the Limits of Legal Justice Symposium," *Fordham Law Review*, no. 6 (2008): 2854.

6 Bordered by Broadway and Flushing, Classon, and Atlantic Avenues, Bed-Stuy is in north-central Brooklyn. Crown Heights lies just south of Bed-Stuy, sharing the Atlantic Avenue border along with the boundaries of the Brooklyn Botanic Garden (Washington Avenue), Empire Boulevard, and East New York Avenue.

7 These numbers reflect population density. In 1977, the historical study *A Ghetto Grows in Brooklyn* focused on Bed-Stuy as the "nation's ghetto." Bed-Stuy has also long been home to a middle-class Black population. Harold X. Connolly, *A Ghetto Grows in Brooklyn* (New York: NYU Press, 1977); see also Brian Purnell, *Fighting Jim Crow in the County of Kings: The Congress of Racial Equality in Brooklyn* (Lexington: University Press of Kentucky, 2013).

8 Myra Klockenbrink, "If You're Thinking of Living in: Crown Heights," *New York Times*, January 20, 1985, www.nytimes.com.

9 Vivian Yee, "Gentrification in a Brooklyn Neighborhood Forces Residents to Move On," *New York Times*, November 27, 2015, www.nytimes.com.

10 I averaged percentage white or white alone (depending on year) from US census data for Bed-Stuy census tracts (237 and 239 / became 1237, 255, 257, 259.2, 285.1, 285.2, 235, 241, 253, 259.1, 261, 283, 281, 287, 289, 233 229, 243, 251, 263, 265, 279, 277, 291, 293, 387, 385, 375, 227, 245, 249, 267, 269, 275, 273, 295, 297, 383, 381, 377, 379, 247, 271.1 and 271.2 / became 271, 299, and 301).

11 The persecution and restriction of housing, occupations, and social life, as well as the gating, of Jews that began in the fifteenth century in Venice soon spread throughout Europe. Ghettos were deployed by the Nazis as part of their genocide of Jews and other "undesirables" during World War II. Mitchell Duneier, *Ghetto: The Invention of a Place, the History of an Idea* (New York: Farrar, Straus and Giroux, 2016).

12 Katherine McKittrick, "Plantation Futures," *Small Axe: A Caribbean Journal of Criticism* 17, no. 3 (42) (November 1, 2013): 1–15.

13 McKittrick, 7.

14  The geographies of Black women are often described as occupying what literary scholar bell hooks calls the "margin." The margin speaks to a geography of displacement, confinement, and rejection of black women, even as it is a site of radical resistance. But the margin, to McKittrick, is an imaginary that is often "emptied out, placeless, just theory, just language." In other words, the margin exists nowhere, but Black women do. McKittrick, *Demonic Grounds*, 62, 57, emphasis in the original; bell hooks, "Choosing the Margin as a Space of Radical Openness," in *The Feminist Standpoint Theory Reader: Intellectual and Political Controversies*, ed. Sandra Harding (New York: Routledge, 2004), 153–59.

15  Lane, "In the Life," 25.

16  Michelle Fine, "Working the Hyphens: Reinventing Self and Other in Qualitative Research," in *Handbook of Qualitative Research*, ed. Norman K. Denzin and Yvonna Lincoln (Thousand Oaks, CA: Sage Publications, 1994), 72, emphasis in the original.

17  McKittrick, "Plantation Futures," 2.

18  Muñoz, *Disidentifications*, 31.

19  Darsey, "'Gay Is Good,'" 47.

20  C. Riley Snorton, *Nobody Is Supposed to Know: Black Sexuality on the Down Low* (Minneapolis: University of Minnesota Press, 2014), 12.

21  Cf. Bérubé, "How Gay Stays White," 250.

22  Kirk Johnson, "Woman Charged with Biting Officer," *New York Times*, June 10, 1987, www.nytimes.com.

23  Cathy J. Cohen, *The Boundaries of Blackness: AIDS and the Breakdown of Black Politics* (Chicago: University of Chicago Press, 1999).

24  Lane, "In the Life."

25  Riggs, *Tongues Untied*, emphasis in the original.

26  Hollibaugh, *My Dangerous Desires*, 260.

27  As noted in chapter 1, Janice '79/'91 first came out in 1979 but was convinced by a psychiatrist that she could be "cured" of her homosexuality. She came out again in 1991.

28  Cf. Karen Brodkin, "How Did the Jews Become White Folks?," in *Off White: Readings on Race, Power, and Society*, 2nd ed., ed. Michelle Fine et al. (New York: Routledge, 2004), 17–34.

29  James Baldwin, "Go the Way Your Blood Beats: An Interview with James Baldwin," in *James Baldwin: The Legacy* (New York: Touchstone, 1987), 180.

30  Decena, "Tacit Subjects," 353, 345.

31  Manalansan, *Global Divas*, 99, 121.

32  Muñoz, *Disidentifications*, 28.

33  Muñoz, 11.

34  Audre Lorde, *Zami: A New Spelling of My Name—A Biomythography* (New York: Crossing Press, 1982), 179.

35  Cohen, *Boundaries of Blackness*.

36 Cf. Jewelle Gomez, "But Some of Us Are Brave Lesbians: The Absence of Black Lesbian Fiction," in *Black Queer Studies: A Critical Anthology*, ed. E. Patrick Johnson and Mae G. Henderson (Durham, NC: Duke University Press, 2005); Shawnta Smith-Cruz, "Black Lesbians in the '70s: How a Zine Marked Herstory," *Sinister Wisdom* 107 (2018): 24–31.

37 Sharon P. Holland, "(White) Lesbian Studies," in *The New Lesbian Studies: Into the Twenty-First Century*, ed. Bonnie Zimmerman and Toni A. H. McNaron (New York: Feminist Press at CUNY, 1996), 250.

38 Participants mentioned the following texts in our interviews: Radclyffe Hall, *The Well of Loneliness* (New York: Blue Ribbon Books, 1928); Rita Mae Brown, *Rubyfruit Jungle* (Plainfield, VT: Daughters, Inc., 1973); Rich, "Compulsory Heterosexuality"; Akasha (Gloria T.) Hull, Patricia Bell-Scott, and Barbara Smith, eds., *All the Women Are White, All the Blacks Are Men, but Some of Us Are Brave: Black Women's Studies* (Old Westbury, NY: Feminist Press at CUNY, 1982); Lorde, *Zami*; Combahee River Collective, "The Combahee River Collective Statement," in *Home Girls, A Black Feminist Anthology*, ed. Barbara Smith (New York: Kitchen Table/Women of Color Press, 1983), 264–74; Cherrie Moraga, *Loving in the War Years: Lo que nunca pasó por sus labios* (Boston: South End Press, 1985); Gloria Anzaldúa, *Borderlands/La Frontera: The New Mestiza* (San Francisco: Aunt Lute Books, 1987); Leslie Feinberg, *Stone Butch Blues: A Novel* (San Francisco: Firebrand Books, 1993); Sarah Waters, *Tipping the Velvet* (London: Virago, 1999); Cherríe Moraga and Gloria Anzaldúa, eds., *This Bridge Called My Back: Writings by Radical Women of Color*, 4th ed. (Albany: State University of New York Press, 2015).

39 Linda Garber, *Identity Poetics: Race, Class, and the Lesbian-Feminist Roots of Queer Theory* (New York: Columbia University Press, 2001), 30.

40 Lesbian Herstory Archives, "LHA Organizational Record Collection" (organizational records, 2008).

41 Hobson, *Lavender and Red*.

42 Scott Lauria Morgensen, *Spaces between Us: Queer Settler Colonialism and Indigenous Decolonization* (Minneapolis: University of Minnesota Press, 2011), 118.

43 Morgensen, 121.

44 Smith, "Giuliani Time."

45 McKittrick, "Plantation Futures," 9.

46 Alexis Clements, dir., *All We've Got* (Women Make Movies, 2019).

47 Moira Rachel Kenney, *Mapping Gay L.A.: The Intersection of Place and Politics* (Philadelphia: Temple University Press, 2001), 115.

48 Kennedy and Davis, *Boots of Leather*, 43, 114.

49 Enke, *Finding the Movement*, 28.

50 Lane, "In the Life," 27, citing Rochella Thorpe, "'A House Where Queers Go': African-American Lesbian Nightlife in Detroit, 1940–1975," in *Inventing Lesbian Cultures in America*, ed. Ellen Lewin (Boston: Beacon Press), 43.

51 Chandan Reddy, "Home, Houses, Nonidentity: 'Paris Is Burning,'" in *Burning Down the House: Recycling Domesticity*, ed. Rosemary Marangoly George (Boulder, CO: Westview, 1997), 356.

52 Katherine McKittrick and Clyde Woods, "No One Knows the Mysteries at the Bottom of the Ocean," in *Black Geographies and the Politics of Place*, ed. Katherine McKittrick and Clyde Woods (Cambridge, MA: South End Press, 2007), 4.

53 Lane, "In the Life," 78, 27.

54 Lane, 87.

55 McKittrick, *Demonic Grounds*, 42.

56 Muñoz, *Disidentifications*, 5.

57 Daniel Peddle, dir., *The Aggressives* (7th Art Films, 2005); Moore, "Lipstick or Timberlands?"; Rees, *Pariah*.

58 Duggan, "New Homonormativity."

59 Cohen, "Punks, Bulldaggers," 459.

60 Hanhardt, *Safe Space*, 23.

61 Hanhardt, 23–24.

62 Bérubé, "How Gay Stays White," 247.

63 E. Cram, "(Dis)Locating Queer Citizenship: Imaging Rurality in Matthew Shepard's Memory," in *Queering the Countryside: New Frontiers in Rural Queer Studies*, ed. Mary L. Gray, Colin R. Johnson, and Brian J. Gilley (New York: NYU Press, 2016), 267, 269; see also Shaka McGlotten, "Ordinary Intersections: Speculations on Difference, Justice, and Utopia in Black Queer Life," *Transforming Anthropology* 20, no. 1 (2012): 45–66.

64 C. Riley Snorton, *Black on Both Sides: A Racial History of Trans Identity* (Minneapolis: University of Minnesota Press, 2017), 182, citing Hortense J. Spillers, *Black, White, and in Color: Essays on American Literature and Culture* (Chicago: University of Chicago Press, 2003), 205.

65 Florida, *Rise of the Creative Class*; see also Lees, Slater, and Wyly, *Gentrification*; Tiffany Muller Myrdahl, "Queerying Creative Cities," in *Queerying Planning*, ed. Petra L. Doan (London: Ashgate, 2011), 157–68; Natalie Oswin, *Global City Futures: Desire and Development in Singapore* (Athens: University of Georgia Press, 2019).

66 Rose, "Rethinking Gentrification," 67; see also Curran, *Gender and Gentrification*.

67 Stein, *Capital City*.

68 Muñoz, *Disidentifications*, 31.

69 Smith, *New Urban Frontier*.

70 Jim Yardley, "Black America Made Visible; TV Show Illuminated Culture through Lens of Bed-Stuy," *New York Times*, June 25, 1998, www.nytimes.com.

71 Robin Finn, "Walking and Talking Bed-Stuy," *New York Times*, August 22, 2013, www.nytimes.com.

72 Faderman, *Odd Girls*, 68; see also Kevin Mumford, *Interzones: Black/White Sex Districts in Chicago and New York in the Early Twentieth Century* (New York: Columbia University Press, 1997); Woolner, "'Woman Slain.'"

73 Faderman, *Odd Girls*, 68.

74 Mignon R. Moore, "'Black and Gay in L.A.': The Relationships Black Lesbians and Gay Men Have with Their Racial and Religious Communities," in *Black Los Angeles: American Dreams and Racial Realities*, ed. Darnell Hunt and Ana-Christina Ramon (New York: NYU Press, 2010), 196.

75 Fine, "Working the Hyphens," 13.

76 Sasha Wortzel and Kate Kunath, dirs., *We Came to Sweat: The Legend of Starlite* (Sasha Wortzel, 2012).

77 Eaves, "Race, Desire, and Belonging," 152–53.

78 Gilmore, "In the Shadow"; Rodríguez, "Political Logic"; see also Batza, *Before AIDS*.

79 Hanhardt, "'Dead Addicts Don't Recover,'" 424.

80 Reddy, "Asian Diasporas," 111.

81 Lesbian Herstory Archives, "African Ancestral Lesbians" (organizational records, 2008); LHA, "Asian Lesbians of the East Coast" (organizational records, 2008); LHA, "G.L.O.B.E. Community Center" (organizational records, 2008); LHA, "Sista II Sista" (organizational records, 2008); LHA, "Sisters Lending Circle" (organizational records, 2008).

82 Lane, "In the Life," 56.

83 The reference here is to professionally published periodicals, and does not account for zines and other homemade materials.

84 Agatha Beins, *Liberation in Print: Feminist Periodicals and Social Movement Identity* (Athens: University of Georgia Press, 2017), 8.

85 Mary Gray, *Out in the Country: Youth, Media, and Queer Visibility in Rural America* (New York: NYU Press, 2009).

86 Cf. Michel Foucault, *Discipline & Punish: The Birth of the Prison* (New York: Vintage, 1995).

87 Mike Bostock, "Mapping the Decline of 'Stop-and-Frisk,'" *New York Times*, September 19, 2014, www.nytimes.com; see also Public Science Project and Scott Lizama, *Public Science Shorts: This Is Our Home* (New York, 2013), www.youtube .com/watch?v=qLWWa2De2b4.

88 Brett G. Stoudt, Michelle Fine, and Madeline Fox, "Growing Up Policed in the Age of Aggressive Policing Policies," *New York Law School Law Review* 56, no. 4 (2011): 1350.

89 Welfare Warriors Research Collaborative, "Fabulous Attitude."

90 Spade, *Normal Life*, xiv.

91 Caitlin Cahill, "'At Risk'? The Fed Up Honeys Re-present the Gentrification of the Lower East Side," *Women's Studies Quarterly* 34, no. 1/2 (2006): 334–63.

92 McKittrick, "Plantation Futures," 9, emphasis in the original.

93 Manalansan, *Global Divas*.

94 Reddy, "Asian Diasporas," 110.

95 Lane, "All the Lesbians," 232, emphasis in the original.

96 Kath Weston, *Families We Choose* (New York: Columbia University Press, 1997); see also Juana María Rodríguez, *Sexual Futures, Queer Gestures, and Other Latina Longings* (New York: NYU Press, 2014); Greene, "Queer Street Families."

97 Lesbian Herstory Archives, "Imperial Kings and Queens" (organizational records, 2008).

98 Cf. Marlon M. Bailey, *Butch Queens Up in Pumps: Gender, Performance, and Ballroom Culture in Detroit* (Ann Arbor: University of Michigan Press, 2013).

99 Moore, *Invisible Families.*

100 Lane, "In the Life," 42.

101 Eaves, "Race, Desire, and Belonging," 154.

102 Johnson, *Sweet Tea*, 183.

103 McKittrick, *Demonic Grounds*, 53.

104 A Google search for each year from 2009 to 2019 for "Black lesbian (or gay) neighborhood New York City" returned no mention of such places. As I likewise expected—especially as no one referred to such places—similar Google searches for "Latino (or Latina or Latinx) lesbian (or gay) neighborhood New York City," "Asian (or Asian-American) lesbian (or gay) neighborhood New York City," and "Native American (or Indigenous) lesbian (or gay) neighborhood New York City" returned no results as well.

## CHAPTER 4. DYKE SLOPE

1 In defining the neighborhood's boundaries, some rely on the edges of major thoroughfares as I have, while others use the larger area covered by the 11215 zip code, and still others simply rely on the mere assertion that their apartment is in the neighborhood.

2 Cf. Sylvia Federici, *Caliban and the Witch: Women, the Body and Primitive Accumulation* (Brooklyn, NY: Autonomedia, 2004).

3 Melissa W. Wright, "From Protests to Politics: Sex Work, Women's Worth, and Ciudad Juárez Modernity," *Annals of the Association of American Geographers* 94, no. 2 (2004): 372.

4 Lynda Johnston, "Gender and Sexuality III: Precarious Places," *Progress in Human Geography* 42, no. 6 (2018): 931.

5 Some expections include Loretta Lees and Liz Bondi, "De-gentrification and Economic Recession: The Case of New York City," *Urban Geography* 16, no. 3 (1995): 234–53; Rothenberg, "'And She Told Two Friends'"; Lees, "Reappraisal of Gentrification"; Slater, "North American Gentrification?"; Lees, Slater, and Wyly, *Gentrification*; James DeFilippis, Robert Fisher, and Eric Shragge, "What's Left in the Community? Oppositional Politics in Contemporary Practice," *Community Development* 44, no. 1 (2009): 38–52; Kathe Newman and Elvin K. Wyly, "The Right to Stay Put, Revisited: Gentrification and Resistance to Displacement in New York City," *Urban Studies* 43, no. 1 (2006): 23–57; Elvin Wyly et al., "Displacing New York," *Environment and Planning A* 42, no. 11 (2010): 2602–23.

6 Cf. Monique Wittig, *The Straight Mind and Other Essays* (Boston: Beacon Press, 1992).

7 This focus on large US cities does not take up lesbian-identified towns and small cities such as Northampton, Massachusetts, or Asheville, North Carolina. Cf. Ann Forsyth, "'Out' in the Valley," *International Journal of Urban and Regional Research* 21, no. 1 (1997): 38–62.

8 This nomenclature is consistent with that used by scholars of urban lesbian spaces since Wolf's groundbreaking study of 1970s lesbian spaces. Rothenberg, "'And She Told Two Friends,'" 173; cf. Deborah Goleman Wolf, *The Lesbian Community* (Berkeley: University of California Press, 1979); Kenney, Kenney, *Mapping Gay L.A.*; Podmore, "Gone 'Underground'?"

9 Jack Halberstam, *The Queer Art of Failure* (Durham, NC: Duke University Press, 2011), 3.

10 Halberstam, 126.

11 Stephanie Schroeder and Teresa Theophano, eds., *Headcase: LGBTQ Writers & Artists on Mental Health and Wellness* (New York: Oxford University Press, 2019).

12 Rothenberg, "'And She Told Two Friends,'" 179.

13 Johnston, "Gender and Sexuality III," 934; see also Judith Butler, *Precarious Life: The Powers of Mourning and Violence* (New York: Verso, 2004); Hollibaugh and Weiss, "Queer Precarity."

14 See also Rothenberg, "'And She Told Two Friends,'" 179.

15 Halberstam, *Queer Art of Failure*, 3.

16 Kenney, *Mapping Gay L.A.*, 120, citing Faderman, *Odd Girls*.

17 Rothenberg, "'And She Told Two Friends,'" 175.

18 Wolf, *Lesbian Community*, 98.

19 Luis's research into women's land reveals that lesbian land was sometimes distinct and sometimes overlapping with that movement. Luis, *Herlands*.

20 Joyce Cheney, *Lesbian Land* (Minneapolis: Word Weavers, 1985), 10.

21 Herring, *Another Country*.

22 Osman, *Invention of Brownstone Brooklyn*, 192.

23 Osman, 194.

24 Armstrong et al., *State of New York City 2008*, 13.

25 Ethan Schwartz, "High-Rise Plan Alarms Low-Rise Section," *New York Times*, September 8, 1985, www.nytimes.com; Osman, *Invention of Brownstone Brooklyn*, 272.

26 Scott Lauria Morgensen, "Settler Homonationalism: Theorizing Settler Colonialism within Queer Modernities," *GLQ* 16, no. 1–2 (2010): 105.

27 Hanhardt, *Safe Space*, 82.

28 Marian Meyers, "Crack Mothers in the News: A Narrative of Paternalistic Racism," *Journal of Communication Inquiry* 28, no. 3 (2004): 194; see also Eileen Boris, "On Cowboys and Welfare Queens: Independence, Dependence, and Interdependence at Home and Abroad," *Journal of American Studies* 41, no. 3 (2007): 599–621; Cohen, "Punks, Bulldaggers"; Briggs, *Reproductive Politics*.

29 Cf. Cahill, "'At Risk'?"

30 Patricia Yaeger, *Dirt and Desire: Reconstructing Southern Women's Writing, 1930–1990* (Chicago: University of Chicago Press, 2000), 104.

31 Cf. Simone Kolysh, "Neither Queer nor There: Becoming a Raging Lesbian Scholar," in *Negotiating the Emotional Challenges of Conducting Deeply Personal Research in Health*, ed. Alexandra "Xan" C. H. Nowakowski and J. E. Sumerau (New York: CRC Press, 2017), 103–16.

32 Nadine Brozan, "Rise in Anti-Gay Crimes Is Reported in New York," *New York Times*, March 7, 1991, www.nytimes.com.

33 Lesbian Herstory Archives, "Brooklyn Women's Martial Arts/The Center for Anti-Violence Education (CAE)" (organizational records, 2008).

34 Rothenberg, "'And She Told Two Friends,'" 169.

35 Lesbian Herstory Archives, "Brooklyn Lesbians and Gays Against Hate Crimes" (organizational records, 2008).

36 Rothenberg, "'And She Told Two Friends,'" 169, emphasis in the original.

37 Kern, "Selling the 'Scary City,'" 213.

38 Johnston, "Gender and Sexuality III," 932.

39 Lesbian Herstory Archives, "African Ancestral Lesbians United for Social Change"; LHA, "Asian Lesbians of the East Coast"; LHA, "Las Buenas Amigas"; LHA, "Salsa Soul Sisters" (organizational records, 2008).

40 As noted in chapter 1, Janice '79/'91 first came out in 1979 but was convinced by a psychiatrist that she could be "cured" of her homosexuality. She came out again in 1991.

41 Cf. Delany, *Times Square Red*, 123, 128–29.

42 Cf. Sarah A. Elwood, "Lesbian Living Spaces," *Journal of Lesbian Studies* 4, no. 1 (2000): 11–27; Lynda Johnston and Gill Valentine, "'Wherever I Lay My Girlfriend, That's My Home': The Performance and Surveillance of Lesbian Identities in Domestic Environments," in *Mapping Desire*, ed. David J. Bell and Gill Valentine (New York: Routledge, 1995), 66–74.

43 Lesbian Herstory Archives, "Lesbian Herstory Archives Newsletters" (organizational records, 1975–2005).

44 I came across no evidence that any other New York City lesbian organization had purchased its own building. Cf. Clements, *All We've Got*.

45 The online real estate database company Zillow estimated the LHA building to be worth $2.87 million in 2019. "484 14th St, Brooklyn, NY 11215," Zillow, June 22, 2019, www.zillow.com.

46 Cf. Rothenberg, "'And She Told Two Friends'"; Jen Jack Gieseking, "Useful In/Stability: The Dialectical Production of the Social-Spatial in the Lesbian Herstory Archives," *Radical History Review* 2015, no. 122 (2015): 25–37.

47 Faderman, *Odd Girls*, 283; see also Ray Oldenburg, *The Great Good Place: Cafés, Coffee Shops, Bookstores, Bars, Hair Salons, and Other Hangouts at the Heart of a Community* (New York: Marlowe & Company, 1999).

48 Warner, *Trouble with Normal*, 149–94; Smith, "Giuliani Time"; see also Smith, *New Urban Frontier*.

49 Kern, "Selling the 'Scary City,'" 225.

50 Danae Clark, "Commodity Lesbianism," *Camera Obscura* 9, no. 1–2 (1991): 181–201; see also Jeanie Kasindorf, "Lesbian Chic: The Bold, Brave New World of Gay Women," *New York*, May 10, 1993: 30–37.

51 Burk, "Let the Record Show," 198.

52 Kenney, *Mapping Gay L.A.*, 120, citing Faderman, *Odd Girls*.

53 Regarding the references to US census data in this chapter, I compiled these numbers by averaging percentage white or white alone (depending on year), Hispanic ethnicity (their terminology) regardless of race, and median household income data from the US census data for Park Slope census tracts (129.01, 129.02, 131, 133, 135, 137, 139, 141, 149, 151, 153, 155, 157, 159, 161, 165, 167, 169).

54 Rothenberg, "'And She Told Two Friends,'" 143.

55 Fatima El-Tayeb, Jin Haritaworn, and Paola Bacchetta, "Queer of Colour Formations and Translocal Spaces in Europe," *Society and Space* 33, no. 5 (2015): 771.

56 Arlene Dávila, *Barrio Dreams: Puerto Ricans, Latinos, and the Neoliberal City* (Berkeley: University of California Press, 2004).

57 Lesbian Herstory Archives, "Queers for Economic Justice Network."

58 Lorena Muñoz, "Entangled Sidewalks: Queer Street Vendors in Los Angeles," *Professional Geographer* 68, no. 2 (2016): 302.

59 Muñoz, 307.

60 Drawing on the tabulated census data and Furman Center data, the neighborhood's population was 64 percent white in 1980 and 72 percent white in 2010, compared to the citywide 61 and 44 percent. Capperis et al., *State of New York City 2014*.

61 Tess Taylor, "Park Slope; Unlikely Anchors along 'Hot Fifth Avenue,'" *New York Times*, January 18, 2004, www.nytimes.com.

62 Slater, "North American Gentrification?," 1205.

63 Capperis et al., *State of New York City 2014*, 93.

64 Austensen et al., *State of New York City 2015*, 29, 42.

65 Brian Lehrer Show, *Brooklyn Elevated to Lesbian Mecca* (New York: WYNC, 2013), www.wnyc.org.

66 This average rent increase was behind that of Greenwich Village, which ranked third at 61 percent; the citywide average was 22 percent. Austensen et al., *State of New York City 2015*, 6; see also Capperis et al., *State of New York City 2014*.

67 Jennifer Fermino, "Sex-Toy Shop Has Bad Vibes in Park Slope," *New York Post* (blog), March 3, 2008, https://nypost.com.

68 Andrew Keh, "Stroller Recall Stirs Unease in Park Slope," *New York Times—City Room* (blog), November 11, 2009, http://cityroom.blogs.nytimes.com.

69 Chauncey, *Gay New York*; see also Lisa Brundage, "War Baby: Race, Nation and Cultural Conceptions of Lesbian Motherhood" (PhD diss., Graduate Center, City University of New York, 2012).

70 Briggs, *Reproductive Politics*, 161.

71 Podmore, "Gone 'Underground'?," 618.

72  Cf. Andrea Lawlor, *Paul Takes the Form of a Mortal Girl* (Iowa City: Rescue Press, 2017), 200.

73  Dannielle Owens-Reid, "Lesbians Who Look Like Justin Bieber," Tumblr, 2012, http://lesbianswholooklikejustinbieber.tumblr.com.

74  Halberstam, *Queer Art of Failure*, 5.

75  The proprietor and I encourage you to search for and find this party and others like it, and call their phone number for their address as have thousands of women and tgncp before you. However, I have decided to keep their privacy. (It is a testimony to the lesbian-queer production of space that no one has mapped it or publicly listed its address or others like it for at least four decades.)

76  Puar, "Queer Tourism," 936.

77  Halberstam, *Queer Art of Failure*, 171.

78  Audre Lorde, "The Master's Tools Will Never Dismantle the Master's House," in *This Bridge Called Me Back*, 4th ed., ed. Moraga and Anzaldúa (Albany: State University of New York Press, 2015), 94–103.

79  Halberstam, 3.

80  Cf. Nate Silver, "The Most Livable Neighborhoods in New York," *New York* (blog), April 11, 2010, nymag.com.

81  Gilmore, *Golden Gulag*, 247.

82  Rose, "Paradoxical Space," 140.

83  Joan Nestle, "Restrictions and Reclamation: Lesbian Bars and Beaches on the 1950," in *Queers in Space*, ed. Gordon Brent Ingram et al. (Seattle: Bay Press, 1997), 67.

84  Compton's Transgender Cultural District (CTDC) in San Francisco's Tenderloin neighborhood launched in 2017.

85  Deborah G. Martin, "Enacting Neighborhood," *Urban Geography* 24, no. 5 (2003): 380.

86  Tavia Nyong'o, "Let's Pretend That Everyone Is Dead," *Bullybloggers* (blog), 2012, http://bullybloggers.wordpress.com.

## CHAPTER 5. CONSTELLATING A QUEER MAP OF THE LESBIAN CITY

1  Cf. Halberstam, *In a Queer Time and Place*; Warner, *Publics and Counterpublics*.

2  Halberstam, *In a Queer Time and Place*; Lee Edelman, *No Future: Queer Theory and the Death Drive* (Durham, NC: Duke University Press, 2004); José Esteban Muñoz, *Cruising Utopia: The Then and There of Queer Futurity* (New York: NYU Press, 2009); Heather Love, *Feeling Backward: Loss and the Politics of Queer History* (Cambridge, MA: Harvard University Press, 2009); Freeman, *Time Binds*; Kara Keeling, *Queer Times, Black Futures* (New York: NYU Press, 2019); see also Mary Zaborskis, "Eve Sedgwick's Queer Children," *GLQ* 25, no. 1 (2019): 29–32.

3  Halberstam, *In a Queer Time and Place*, 5.

4 As Oswin writes, "I am tired of translating the insights of queer theory for a broader critical urban studies audience." Natalie Oswin, "Planetary Urbanization: A View from Outside," *Society and Space* 36, no. 1 (2016): 5.

5 Massey, *For Space*, 9, 11, 13.

6 Massey, 11.

7 Halberstam, *Queer Art of Failure*, 6.

8 Warner, *Publics and Counterpublics*.

9 Cf. Browne, "Challenging Queer Geographies"; Brown, "Mutinous Eruptions"; Natalie Oswin, "Critical Geographies and the Uses of Sexuality: Deconstructing Queer Space," *Progress in Human Geography* 32, no. 1 (2008): 89–103; Catherine J. Nash and Andrew Gorman-Murray, "Sexualities, Subjectivities and Urban Spaces: A Case for Assemblage Thinking," *Gender, Place & Culture* 24, no. 11 (2017): 1521–29; Johnston, "Gender and Sexuality III."

10 Oswin, "Critical Geographies," 91.

11 Oswin, 89.

12 Oswin, 96.

13 Oswin, 91.

14 Cf. M. K. Czerwiec, *Taking Turns: Stories from HIV/AIDS Care Unit 371* (University Park: Penn State University Press, 2017), 179, 180.

15 Ahmed, "Orientations," 556.

16 Cf. Greene, "Gay Neighborhoods"; Greggor Mattson, "Bar Districts as Subcultural Amenities," *City, Culture and Society* 6, no. 1 (2015): 1–8; Brown-Saracino, *How Places Make Us*.

17 Ahmed, "Orientations," 545.

18 AbdouMaliq Simone, "People as Infrastructure: Intersecting Fragments in Johannesburg," *Public Culture* 16, no. 3 (2004): 407–29.

19 Jen Jack Gieseking, "Messing with the Attractiveness Algorithm: A Response to Queering Code/Space," *Gender, Place & Culture* 24, no. 11 (2017): 1659–65; Dan Cockayne and Jen Jack Gieseking, "The Politics of (Queer Online) Visibility and the Challenge of Recognizing," in *Locating Critical Sexuality: Forecasting the Trends of "Glocal" Sexual Literacy*, ed. Michelle Marzullo, Gilbert Herdt, and Nicole Polen-Petit (New York: Anthem Press, 2020).

20 Ahmed, "Orientations," 565.

21 Ahmed, 566.

22 Ahmed, 565.

23 Ahmed, 565.

24 Cf. Tom Boellstorff, *The Gay Archipelago: Sexuality and Nation in Indonesia* (Princeton, NJ: Princeton University Press, 2005); Amin Ghaziani, "Cultural Archipelagos: New Directions in the Study of Sexuality and Space," *City & Community* 18, no. 1 (2019): 4–22.

25 Gill Valentine, "Toward a Geography of the Lesbian Community," *Women & Environments* 14, no. 1 (1994): 9.

26 Felix Endara and Sasha Wortzel, dirs., *Grit and Grind* (Felix Endara and Sasha Wortzel, 2014); Julie Tolentino et al., "The Sum of All Questions: Returning to the Clit Club," *GLQ* 24, no. 4 (2018): 467–88.

27 Warner, *Trouble with Normal*, 150, 169, 152.

28 Warner, 152.

29 Hollibaugh, *My Dangerous Desires*, 267.

30 Julie Bolcer, "Lesbian Settles Discrimination Lawsuit against Caliente Cab Co.," *Village Voice*, May 13, 2008, http://blogs.villagevoice.com.

31 Rose, "Paradoxical Space," 148.

32 Lawrence Knopp, "Ontologies of Place, Placelessness, and Movement: Queer Quests for Identity and Their Impacts on Contemporary Geographic Thought," *Gender, Place & Culture* 11, no. 1 (2004): 121–34.

33 Ahmed, "Orientations," 565.

34 Lauren Berlant and Michael Warner, "Sex in Public," *Critical Inquiry* 24, no. 2 (1998): 565.

35 Enke, *Finding the Movement*, 15, citing Michel de Certeau, *The Practice of Everyday Life* (Berkeley: University of California Press, 2002).

36 Ahmed, "Orientations," 569.

37 Gilles Deleuze and Felix Guattari, *Thousand Plateaus* (London: Athlone Press, 2000).

38 Tim Ingold, *Lines: A Brief History* (New York: Routledge, 2007), 153, 155, emphasis in the original.

39 Podmore, "Gone 'Underground'?," 596; see also Rothenberg, "'And She Told Two Friends.'"

40 Lane, "In the Life," 25.

41 Sara Ahmed, *Queer Phenomenology: Orientations, Objects, Others* (Durham, NC: Duke University Press, 2006), 553.

42 Ahmed, "Orientations," 564.

43 Ruth L. Hall and Michelle Fine, "The Stories We Tell: The Lives and Friendship of Two Older Black Lesbians," *Psychology of Women Quarterly* 29, no. 2 (2005): 181.

44 Anzaldúa, *Borderlands/La Frontera*, 99.

45 Jen Jack Gieseking, "Crossing Over into Neighbourhoods of the Body: Urban Territories, Borders and Lesbian-Queer Bodies in New York City," *Area* 48, no. 3 (2016): 262–70.

46 Ahmed, "Orientations," 561.

47 Manalansan, "Race, Violence," 152.

48 Cf. Cynthia L. Konrad, "This Is Where We Live: Queering Poor Urban Spaces in Literature of Black Gay Men," *Gender, Place & Culture* 21, no. 3 (2014): 337–52; see also Joseph Beam, ed., *In the Life: A Black Gay Anthology* (Boston: Alyson Books, 1986); Riggs, *Tongues Untied*; Essex Hemphill, ed., *Brother to Brother: New Writing by Black Gay Men* (New York: Alyson Books, 1991).

49 Manalansan, *Global Divas*, 61.

50 Muñoz, *Cruising Utopia*, 1.

51 Sally R. Munt, "The Lesbian Flâneur," in *Mapping Desire: Geographies of Sexualities*, ed. David J. Bell and Gill Valentine (New York: Routledge, 1995), 104–15.

52 Nash and Gorman-Murray, "Sexualities, Subjectivities," 1523, citing Doreen Massey, *Space, Place, and Gender* (Minneapolis: University of Minnesota Press, 1994).

53 Nash and Gorman-Murray, "Sexualities, Subjectivities," 1521.

54 El-Tayeb, Haritaworn, and Bacchetta, "Queer of Colour Formations," 774.

55 Fredric Jameson, *Late Marxism: Adorno, Or, The Persistence of the Dialectic* (London: Verso, 2007), 244, citing Walter Benjamin, *The Origin of German Tragic Drama* (New York: Verso, 1998). Dianne Chisholm extends Benjamin with the concept of "queer constellations" as the fortuitous coming together of spaces of consumption and technology that "assemble and forge dialectical images" of contemporary urbanization to confront "images of revolutionary sexuality suspended in commodity space." Dianne Chisholm, *Queer Constellations: Subcultural Space in the Wake of the City* (Minneapolis: University of Minnesota Press, 2005), x.

56 Ahmed, "Orientations," 569.

57 Cf. Berlant and Warner, "Sex in Public"; Warner, *Trouble with Normal*; Warner, *Publics and Counterpublics*; Delany, *Times Square Red*; Chisholm, *Queer Constellations*.

58 Cf. Chauncey, *Gay New York*; Warner, *Publics and Counterpublics*; John Paul Catungal and Eugene J. McCann, "Governing Sexuality and Park Space: Acts of Regulation in Vancouver, BC," *Social & Cultural Geography* 11, no. 1 (2010): 75–94; Phil Hubbard, "Kissing Is Not a Universal Right: Sexuality, Law and the Scales of Citizenship," *Geoforum* 49 (2013): 224–32.

59 Delany, *Times Square Red*.

60 "Whatever Color Is Your Hankie . . . ," *On Our Backs* 1, no. 1 (1984).

61 Cf. Pat Califia, *Sapphistry: The Book of Lesbian Sexuality* (Tallahassee, FL: Naiad Press, 1988); Pat Califia, *Public Sex: The Culture of Radical Sex* (Berkeley: Cleis Press, 1994); Carol Queen, *The Leather Daddy & The Femme* (Berkeley: Cleis Press, 1998); Cherie Seise, "Fucking Utopia: Queer Porn and Queer Liberation," *Sprinkle: A Journal of Sexual Diversity Studies* 3 (2010): 19–29.

62 Chauncey, *Gay New York*.

63 Hogan, *Feminist Bookstore Movement*, 41.

64 Alex's anecdote adds another dimension to the working-class butch praised for her ring of keys in *Fun Home*. Alison Bechdel, *Fun Home: A Family Tragicomic* (New York: Mariner Books, 2007); Sydney Lucas and Beth Malone, vocalists, "Ring of Keys," track 18 on Jeanine Tesori, comp., *Fun Home: A New Broadway Musical* (Fort Lauderdale, FL: P.S. Classics, 2014).

65 Petra L. Doan and Harrison Higgins, "The Demise of Queer Space? Resurgent Gentrification and the Assimilation of LGBT Neighborhoods," *Journal of Planning Education and Research* 31, no. 1 (2011): 17–18.

66 Jameson, *Late Marxism*, 244, citing Benjamin, *German Tragic Drama*.

67 Hollibaugh, *My Dangerous Desires*, 260.

68 On heteronormative zoning, see A. C. Micklow, "Not Your Mother's Suburb: Remaking Communities for a More Diverse Population," *Urban Lawyer* 46, no. 4 (2014): 729–51.

69 Crenshaw, "Critical Race Theory."

70 Halberstam, *Queer Art of Failure*, 171.

71 Halberstam, 6.

72 Gavin Brown, "Mutinous Eruptions: Autonomous Spaces of Radical Queer Activism," *Environment and Planning A* 39, no. 11 (2007): 2685–98; Nadja Millner-Larsen and Gavin Butt, "Introduction: The Queer Commons," *GLQ* 24, no. 4 (2018): 401; see also Huron, *Carving Out the Commons*.

73 Millner-Larsen and Butt, "Introduction: The Queer Commons," 400, citing Lauren Berlant, "The Commons: Infrastructures for Troubling Times*," *Society and Space* 34, no. 3 (2016): 393–419.

74 Leanne Betasamosake Simpson, *As We Have Always Done: Indigenous Freedom through Radical Resistance*, 3rd ed. (Minneapolis: University of Minnesota Press, 2017), 212, 213.

75 McKittrick, *Demonic Grounds*, xv.

76 Alan S. Yang, "From Wrongs to Rights, 1973–1999: Public Opinion on Gay and Lesbian Americans Moves towards Equality" (report, Washington, DC: National Gay and Lesbian Task Force, 1999).

77 Michelle Fine, "Bearing Witness," 98.

78 Fine, 100.

79 Simpson, *As We Have Always Done*, 217.

80 Cf. Simpson, 218–28.

81 Muñoz, *Cruising Utopia*, 121.

82 Chani Nicholas, "Chani Nicholas (@chaninicholas)," Instagram, May 24, 2017, www.instagram.com/p/BUPRowTFuSU.

83 Ahmed, "Orientations," 570.

84 Cohen, "Punks, Bulldaggers," 438.

85 Cohen, 450.

EPILOGUE

1 Cait McKinney, "'Finding the Lines to My People': Media History and Queer Bibliographic Encounter," *GLQ* 24, no. 1 (2018): 55–83; McKinney, *The Other Network: Lesbian Feminism's Digital Past* (Durham, NC: Duke University Press, 2020).

2 Oswin, "Critical Geographies," 100.

3 And perhaps finally find Nemo and Dory; see Halberstam, *Queer Art of Failure*, 53–86.

4 "Healthy People 2020 Lesbian Health Fact Sheet" (fact sheet, Washington, DC, US Department of Health and Human Services, November 2010).

5 Cf. Shaka McGlotten, "Black Data," in *No Tea, No Shade: New Queer of Color Critique*, ed. E. Patrick Johnson (Durham, NC: Duke University Press, 2016), 262–86; Gieseking, "Attractiveness Algorithm."

6  Zach Blas, "The Jubilee of 2033," *GLQ* 24, no. 4 (2018): 540.

7  Lesbian History Group, *Not a Passing Phase: Reclaiming Lesbians in History 1840–1985* (London: Women's Press, 1989), 2.

8  Ani DiFranco, "Both Hands," *Ani DiFranco*, track 1 (Buffalo, NY: Righteous Babe, 1990).

9  Simpson, *As We Have Always Done*, 221.

10  Eve Tuck and K. Wayne Yang, "Decolonization Is Not a Metaphor," *Decolonization: Indigeneity, Education & Society* 1, no. 1 (2012): 1–40.

11  Muñoz, *Cruising Utopia*, 27.

## APPENDIX I

1  See also Clare Farquhar, "'Lesbian' in a Post-Lesbian World? Policing Identity, Sex and Image," *Sexualities* 3 (2000): 220.

2  Ariel Levy, "Where the Bois Are," *New York*, January 12, 2004, http://nymag.com.

3  Cf. Gayle Rubin, "Of Catamites and Kings: Reflections on Butch, Gender, and Boundaries," in *The Persistent Desire: A Femme-Butch Reader*, ed. Joan Nestle (Boston: Alyson Books, 1992), 466–82; Jack Halberstam, *Female Masculinity* (Durham, NC: Duke University Press, 1998); Esther Newton, *Margaret Mead Made Me Gay: Personal Essays, Public Ideas* (Durham, NC: Duke University Press, 2000); "About bbh," bklyn boihood.

4  Eli R. Green, "Debating Trans Inclusion in the Feminist Movement: A Trans-Positive Analysis," *Journal of Lesbian Studies* 10, no. 1–2 (2006): 231–48.

## APPENDIX III

1  Cf. Sarah Hunt, "Embodying Self-Determination: Beyond the Gender Binary," in *Determinants of Indigenous Peoples' Health in Canada*, ed. Margo Greenwood, Sarah de Leeuw, Nicole Marie Lindsay (Toronto: Canadian Scholars, 2015), 24–25; May Farrales, "Gendered Sexualities in Migration: Play, Pageantry, and the Politics of Performing Filipino-Ness in Settler Colonial Canada" (PhD diss., University of British Columbia, 2017); Derek Ruez, "'I Never Felt Targeted as an Asian . . . until I Went to a Gay Pub': Sexual Racism and the Aesthetic Geographies of the Bad Encounter," *Environment & Planning A* 49, no. 4 (2017): 893–910; Dai Kojima, John Paul Catungal, and Robert Diaz, "Introduction: Feeling Queer, Feeling Asian, Feeling Canadian," *TOPIA*, March 12, 2018, https://utpjournals.press.

2  Michelle Tam, "Queer (and) Chinese: On Be(Long)Ing in Diaspora and Coming Out of Queer Liberalism" (MA thesis, Queen's University, ON, 2018), 12, emphasis in the original.

3  My theorization here especially draws upon and broadens Mannheim's notion of "political generations." Karl Mannheim, "The Problem of Generations," in *The New Pilgrims: Youth Protest in Transition* (orig. pub. 1928), ed. Philip G. Altbach and Robert S. Laufer (New York: David McKay, 1972), 103, 118, emphasis in the original; see also Lauren E. Duncan and Abigail J. Stewart, "A Generational

Analysis of Women's Rights Activists," *Psychology of Women Quarterly* 24, no. 4 (2000): 297–308; Jen Gieseking, "(Re)Constructing Women: Scaled Portrayals of Privilege and Gender Norms on Campus," *Area* 39, no. 3 (2007): 278–86.

4 Russell and Bohan, "Gay Generation Gap"; Cook-Daniels, "LGBT History Timeline."

5 For more on this method, see Sue Wilkinson, "Focus Groups: A Feminist Method," *Psychology of Women Quarterly* 23, no. 2 (1999): 221–44; Christopher Hajek and Howard Giles, "The Old Man Out: An Intergroup Analysis of Intergenerational Communication Among Gay Men," *Journal of Communication* 52, no. 4 (2002): 698–714.

6 Cf. Beam, *In the Life.*

7 Gieseking, "Where We Go from Here."

8 Dinshaw et al., "Theorizing Queer Temporalities," 179.

9 Gieseking, "Useful In/Stability."

10 In 2013, the annual American Community Survey began to identify unmarried and married same-sex couples.

11 Michael Brown and Lawrence Knopp, "Places or Polygons? Governmentality, Scale, and the Census in the Gay and Lesbian Atlas," *Population, Space and Place* 12, no. 4 (2006): 223–42; Brown and Knopp, "Queering the Map: The Productive Tensions of Colliding Epistemologies," *Annals of the Association of American Geographers* 98, no. 1 (2008): 40–58; see also Gary Gates, Jason Ost, and Elizabeth Birch, *The Gay & Lesbian Atlas* (Washington, DC: Urban Institute Press, 2004).

# INDEX

## ABOUT THE AUTHOR

Jen Jack Gieseking is an urban and digital cultural geographer and environmental psychologist. They are Assistant Professor of Geography at the University of Kentucky, where she teaches courses on digital studies and queer geographies. Jack can be found at jgieseking.org, @jgieseking, or in Lexington with his partner, dog, and cat.

A companion website to this book can be found online (jgieseking .org/AQNY). The site includes maps and graphs, and the lists of the organizations and periodicals used to visualize everyday lesbian-queer life in New York City from 1983 to 2008. While not all of these data visualizations and their implications could be fit into this book, they were created and co-created in order to visualize the invisible everyday lives and spaces of lesbians and queers—not only to researchers and teachers, but also to lesbians, bisexuals, queers, and trans and gender non-conforming people who want to know and write their own histories and geographies.

Printed and bound by CPI Group (UK) Ltd, Croydon, CR0 4YY

09/06/2025